THE RUSSIAN ARMY IN A TIME OF TROUBLES

🗳 PRIO

International Peace Research Institute, Oslo
Fuglehauggata 11, N-0260 Oslo, Norway
Telephone: (47) 22 55 71 50
Telefax: (47) 22 55 84 22
Cable address: PEACERESEARCH OSLO
E-mail: info@prio.no

The International Peace Research Institute, Oslo (PRIO) is an independent international institute of peace and conflict research, founded in 1959. It is governed by an international Governing Board of seven individuals, and is financed mainly by the Norwegian Ministry for Education, Research, and Church Affairs. The results of all PRIO research are available to the public.

PRIO's publications include the quarterlies *Journal of Peace Research* (1964–) and *Security Dialogue* (formerly *Bulletin of Peace Proposals*) (1969–) and a series of books. Recent titles include:

Robert Bathurst: *Intelligence and the Mirror: On Creating an Enemy* (1993)

Nils Petter Gleditsch, Ådne Cappelen and Olav Bjerkholt: *The Wages of Peace: Disarmament in a Small Industrialized Economy* (1994)

Kumar Rupesinghe & Khawar Mumtaz, eds: *Internal Conflicts in South Asia* (1996)

Jørn Gjelstad and Olav Njølstad, eds: *Nuclear Rivalry and International Order* (1996)

Johan Galtung: *Peace by Peaceful Means: Peace and Conflict, Development and Civilization* (1996)

THE RUSSIAN ARMY IN A TIME OF TROUBLES

PAVEL K. BAEV

PRIO
International Peace Research Institute, Oslo

SAGE Publications
London • Thousand Oaks • New Delhi

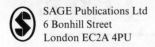 SAGE Publications Ltd
6 Bonhill Street
London EC2A 4PU

SAGE Publications Inc
2455 Teller Road
Thousand Oaks, California 91320

SAGE Publications India Pvt Ltd
32, M-Block Market
Greater Kailash – I
New Delhi 110 048

British Library Cataloguing in Publication data

A catalogue record for this book is available from the British
Library.

ISBN 0 7619 5186-5
ISBN 0 7619 5187-3 (pbk)

Library of Congress catalog record available

Typeset by M Rules
Printed in Great Britain by Redwood Books,
Trowbridge, Wiltshire

To my grandfathers,
who both were colonels in the Soviet Army,
To my father,
Captain of the First Rank (Ret.),
To my brother,
Captain in the Russian Army,
And to my son,
who will – I hope – choose a different career.

Contents

List of Maps and Tables

Preface

In December 1991 Russia established its independence – and immediately entered a period of convulsive transformations that brought dramatic changes to the domestic posture of the Armed Forces. The wide-ranging deterioration of the military machine – due to severe cuts in the national share of human and economic resources – was accompanied by a manifold increase in tasks and missions. Gone was the Cold War's habitual strategic threat, though the Army's leadership and a growing part of Russia's political elite would admit only to some reduction – and perhaps only temporarily. In fact, a new and very real threat has now arrived, in the form of numerous local wars – yet both the military leaders and the policy-makers have been slow to recognize the seriousness of this security challenge and the difficulties involved in tackling it. Moreover, internal instability and a fierce struggle for power have made the Army one of the key actors in the domestic political arena. October 1993 saw how the tanks on the streets of Moscow could determine the outcome of a constitutional crisis.

The cumulative effect of these developments has been a shrinking and degeneration of a unique social niche, that separate professional universe which the Soviet military had grown accustomed to inhabiting. Its return to the political world has given the Army a strong say in top-level decision-making and even a certain independence of action, but it has also resulted in the increasing instrumentalization of the Army for all sorts of political purposes. This intensive engagement in politics has proven utterly counter-productive in two key dimensions. Firstly, for all its increased political weight, the top brass has remained unable to secure the level of financing necessary for support of existing military structures – there is simply no money. Secondly, the political leaders have lacked sufficient power to enforce guidelines for the necessary military reform – and the Army, like any other super-bureaucracy, has proved unable to reform itself.

After three years of doing various and mostly dirty political jobs and temporizing with self-restructuring and modernization, the Russian Army found itself overstretched, undermanned and internally divided. The threshold that revealed this was the war in Chechnya: the Army had been sent to clean up a mess that had run out of control and had acquired such a scale that the chances of finding any solution had become negligible. Facing the risk of humiliating defeat, the military commanders retreated to the sole option that seemed to promise some success on the battlefield – total war. And, in turn, they duly took the blame for the ensuing massive destruction and devastating losses of human life.

Chechnya served as a forceful catalyst for all the degradation processes that had been developing in the military. It became increasingly clear that politicization goes hand in hand with de-professionalization. The best evidence of the latter was the dismissal in February–March 1995 of the three Deputy Defence Ministers who had maintained a certain professional dignity – Generals Gromov, Kondratyev and Mironov – followed by the resignation of such an arch-soldier as General Lebed. By early 1996, the frustrated Russian Army had come to a cross-roads from which it had too little energy to proceed, and no dynamic leaders to take the decision about which way to choose.

This book seeks to examine the road that preceded this watershed, in order to prepare the ground for understanding new developments – quite possibly of revolutionary character. It focuses primarily on the interaction between the Army and politics, as this has become the decisive force in reforming the former, as well as an important factor in framing the latter. Some significant 'black holes' in the analysis should perhaps be mentioned here. The nuclear dimension falls essentially beyond the scope of this book, except for certain aspects touched upon in Chapter 2.4. The whole area of military economics, including the unresolved problem of conversion, is left uncovered except for some specific questions of the military budget analysed in Chapter 3.5. The sociological aspects of civil–military relations are noted in various chapters but not examined in depth. And the specific issues of reforming and restructuring the Navy (except for some regional aspects highlighted in Chapter 4.4) and the Air Force are not dealt with here, so in some cases I have followed the tradition of using the term 'Army' for the Ground Forces only. The Interior Troops and the Border Troops are brought into the analysis only when their interaction with the Army is important for crisis developments in particular 'hot spots'. All these lacunae are intended to keep the 'red thread' as straight and tied as closely as possible to what is really central for this book: the impact of the Army on Russia's political evolution.

We start off with a historical perspective on Russia's security agenda, with a particular focus on the issue of territoriality. Then the Russian/Soviet Army's tradition of involvement in politics is examined. One subject of particular relevance for the whole book is the interaction between politics and war in Soviet military thinking. Chapter 2 deals with Russia's current security interests and the role of the Army in protecting them. The general geopolitical perspective is linked to the more burning security issues of the Near Abroad. The nuclear dimension of security is briefly touched upon here.

Chapter 3 raises the fundamental question about feasibility of political control over the Russian Army in the present-day disorganization that affects all state structures. The problem of politicization of the Army is introduced in the context of the conflictual political processes and then detailed at the level of relations between the military and political elites. The interlinked issues of stalled military reform and drastically reduced military budget are also examined here. Then several questions about external contacts of the Russian Army are elaborated in Chapter 4, which carries in its title the ambitious and ambiguous notion of 'Europeanization'. The linkages developed through various arms control agreements and the uncertain ties with NATO framed by the Partnership for Peace programme are analysed here. Particular attention is given to regional developments with the recent Barents Initiative and its implications for the Northern Fleet.

Chapter 5 takes up the issue of conflict management in the former Soviet Union. It first raises the question whether Russia's pro-active course focusing on 'hot spots' in the Near Abroad could be defined as neo-imperialist. Then the functions and functioning of the Commonwealth of Independent States are examined. The focus on conflict management in the Caucasus provides substantiation for the analysis. In Chapter 6, we take a closer look at the Russian Army's performance in a peace-keeping role. The posture of the Mobile Forces is assessed, and the operational concepts related to conflict management are scrutinized. The Chechen War provides a separate topic for this subject. The final chapter places Russia's peace-keeping activities in a broader European context. It first discusses the current and possible future roles for various European security institutions, before moving on to the issue of interaction between Russia and its main Western partners in the Balkans. Finally, some lessons are drawn from the experience of managing the political controversies between Russia and the three Baltic states.

The reader will find a great many descriptions of negative trends, dangerous developments and missed opportunities in the book. All the same, I have tried to avoid the trap of nihilism – for which Russians are so famous – forbidding myself any catastrophic scenarios. Indeed, it is too late to be pessimistic in writing about Russia. Early 1996 provides a depressingly low point of departure for any reforms compared with early 1992, but the risk of giving up is also prohibitively high. Nor should we underestimate the Russian Army's ability to recover from the worst defeats and humiliations – today, as so often in the past.

Pavel K. Baev
Oslo, February 1996

Acknowledgements

This work was made possible by a grant from the Norwegian Defence Ministry for a one-year Research Project conducted at PRIO in 1994–95. A new grant for follow-up research in 1995–97 allows me to continue the work, which I hope will result in a new book.

Research on the nuclear dimension of Russia's security and on developments in the Barents Region (as presented in Chapter 2.4 and Chapter 4.4 respectively) was supported by grants from the Norwegian Foreign Ministry. Research on Russia's peace-keeping activities, as presented in Part III of the book, was conducted under the auspices of a NATO Democratic Institutions Fellowship for 1994–96. I am extremely grateful to all of these institutions but, naturally, none of them bears responsibility for my conclusions.

My first word of gratitude is still to PRIO – an institution which enjoys a warm and friendly atmosphere while also providing a stimulating and demanding environment. I am happy to acknowledge my intellectual debt to Dan Smith, PRIO Director, who encouraged me to take up the challenge of writing this book and was its first reader. I am indebted to Margot Light, Neil Malcolm, Wolfgang Pfeiler, Christoph Royen, Richard Sakwa and David Scrivener, who spent many hours reading my manuscript and offered most valuable comments. Roy Allison and Robert Bathurst helped me with comments on separate chapters. My particular gratitude is to Susan Høivik, who not only accomplished the Herculean task of language editing but indeed was a most attentive and careful reader of this book. The responsibility for any remaining mistakes is mine.

I am grateful to Sergei Karaganov, who granted me a long sabbatical from the Institute of Europe, Moscow – which enabled me to undertake this three-year-long research project at PRIO.

My final words of gratitude go to my wife Olga – for all her patience and encouragement.

PART I

GENERALLY SPEAKING

Sometimes he thought sadly to himself, 'Why?' and sometimes he thought, 'Wherefore?' and sometimes he thought, 'Inasmuch as which?' – and sometimes he didn't quite know what he *was* thinking about.

A.A.Milne, *Winnie-The-Pooh*, Chapter 4

1
The Russian Army and Politics in Historical Perspective

1.1 Introduction

The relevance of historical perspective for a study that focuses on the contemporary transformation of the Russian Army is not immediately obvious. While commonly considered a must for all 'serious' research, a historical chapter often simply provides an illustration of the 'genuine uniqueness' of the Russian case. What turns a banality into a vulgarism are the reiterated claims from all sorts of leaders about the revitalizing of 'glorious' traditions – not that there are none, but the persistent attempts to borrow legitimacy from the past result only in their profanation. For the vast majority of officers the nearest historical analogy for the current rapid deterioration of the Army's infrastructure is perhaps the catastrophe of 1917–18. Nor does raising the traditional white–blue St Andrew's flags on former Soviet combat vessels make them into proud warriors, as long as they are simply unable to sail the blue seas.

All the same, it is mainly in tradition that the Russian Army has found support to withstand the hardships, neglect and temptations of recent years. History provides no guide out of today's transitional crisis, but if the Russian Army – as well as Russia itself – manages to survive, it would indeed become the proud successor of the first two *poteshny* (token) regiments created three centuries ago by Peter the Great.

One issue from the domain of history with a direct bearing on today's situation concerns the Army's role in defining and extending the frontiers of Russia. The self-identification of a state with certain territory, while so natural for many countries, is for Russia an acute and disturbing problem, and the Army has a big say in solving it – as the war in Chechnya is proving all too clearly. The political role of the Army – both in the last two centuries of the Russian Empire and in the more recent Soviet past – also deserves special attention due to many political functions the Army is expected to perform. And the issue of legitimacy of the use of military force, of relations between Politics and War, had become crucial even before the Chechen war gave it an existential dimension.

1.2 Security, Territory and Borders

The breakup of the Soviet Union was indeed a multidimensional catastrophe; one clear dimension certainly was the collapse of the age-old empire, but this did not mean that Russia regressed into some 'hard-core' nation-state. The present territory has no historical analogies, and that is one of the reasons why Russia feels so uncomfortable in it. Today's geopolitical muddle (which could be summarized as Russia being in some political and strategic aspects more than its territory, and in others – less) makes a peculiar combination with the perception of state borders. When some parts of the state start to drift away, borders are declared sacred and inviolable, but when there is a chance to add a piece to the state – then borders are taken as conveniently expandable. In this flexible spatial perception the Communist and imperial ideologies are inextricably mixed.[1]

It is often taken for granted that the existential pattern of the Russian Empire was expansion – with the direct political conclusion that present-day Russia invariably poses a threat to all newly independent states and potentially to the whole of East Central Europe (Brzezinski, 1995). This assumption deserves more careful examination than many of those currently circulating on the market, and first of all from the perspective of expansion as a military project.

The most convincing historical evidence is found in the pre-imperial period: the territory controlled by Moscow increased from 20,000 km^2 at the beginning of the 14th century to 430,000 km^2 in 1462 and to about 2,800,000 km^2 by 1533.[2] What is often overlooked here is that until 1480 the process actually was more about re-uniting semi-independent Russian principalities under the 'Tatar yoke' with the aim of what could be called, in modern language, national liberation. The forceful subjugation of Novgorod (1471–77), which made it possible to incorporate vast colonies in the North, was aimed more at preventing it from falling under Polish control and thus sharing the fate of such Russian cities as Polotsk, Smolensk and Kiev.[3] The real expansion – i.e. the conquest of lands populated by non-Slavic peoples and controlled by other states – started only during the reign of Ivan IV (the Terrible) (1533–84), who moved decisively against the remnants of the Golden Horde: Kazan was captured in 1552 and Astrakhan in 1554. This campaign was intended to secure the vulnerable southern border against nomadic invasions, thus allowing Moscow to re-orient its military efforts westwards; still the Crimea Tatars captured and burned down Moscow in 1571. The main strategic goal of Ivan IV was to regain the western Russian cities from Poland and re-open the trade routes in the Baltic; but he was defeated in the long Livonian War (1558–82). This failure to expand proved disastrous: the victorious Poles invaded Russia, which then descended into the 'Times of Troubles'.

---

1 Much of analysis in this section draws on my contribution to the research project conducted at the Finnish Institute of International Relations and headed by Tuomas Forsberg. (See Baev, 1995d.)

2 The year 1462 marks the accession to the throne of Ivan III (the Great), the first to assume the title of *Tsar*; the year 1533 marks the end of the reign of his son Vasily III and the accession to the throne of Ivan IV (the Terrible).

3 Many Russian historians are inclined to hold Lithuania responsible for Moscow's isolation from Europe. Lithuania, easily taking under control western and southern Russian principalities in the early 14th century, was on the path of cultural rapprochement with Russia; but at the very end of that century it opted for dynastic and later state union with Poland and came under Catholic influence. See, for example, Myakotin (1968, pp. 160–165).

Therefore, it is hardly possible to make a convincing case by a simple calculation that for 150 consecutive years Russia annexed annually approximately 35,000 km^2 of new territory (Iivonen, 1995, p. 64, fn 9). Aside from Kazan and Astrakhan, none of the territorial gains in the 16th century merits the label of conquest. And certainly the vast space by no means made Russia a 'giant', since it had a population of roughly 8 million – about the same as Poland and less than a half of France. One consequence of the turbulent events in the late 16th to early 17th centuries was Russia's retreat eastward, and its increasing isolation from Europe. Not until 1654 was Smolensk recaptured from Poland – and it lies only 350 km west of Moscow (Map 1.1).[4]

As for the expansion in Siberia which started in the final years of the reign of Ivan IV, this was more of a nongovernmental enterprise financed by merchants such as Grigory Stroganov and accomplished by a handful of Cossack adventurers. This uncontrolled and remarkably rapid colonization of the eastern frontier continued through the 'Times of Troubles' – when Cossacks certainly were the worst trouble-makers. Only to a minor degree did Siberia become a matter of state policy in 1689, when the borders with China were delimited; the Jesuits who were charged with drafting the treaty made its provisions most favourable to China (thus securing their position at the Chinese court), but the young Tsar Peter I could not care less. Before this settlement in the East, however, an event of fundamental importance for the development of the Russian state occurred: re-unification with Ukraine.

Though certainly 'the most important single feature of Russia's territorial expansion in the seventeenth century' (Florinsky, 1969, p. 133), it could hardly be described as a result of a consistent policy on the part of Moscow. The Cossacks, after half a century of uprisings and mutinies against Poland, decided in 1654 to turn to Moscow for support and took an oath of allegiance to the Tsar. Russia's control over the southern lands was mainly symbolic and the Cossacks several times expelled Russian garrisons, making alliances with Turks and Crimea Tatars. It was only after Russia settled the 'perpetual peace' with a weakened Poland in 1681 that Kiev and the lands to the east of the River Dnieper were really incorporated.[5]

When Peter I ascended the throne in 1682, his vast state was landlocked (except for Arkhangelsk in the North, which he visited in 1694) and essentially isolated; expansion – westwards toward the Baltic Sea and southwards toward the Black Sea – was recognized as a crucial precondition for survival of the state. This had to be a military enterprise since it no longer was a matter of re-uniting Slavic lands; moreover, powerful European states were inevitably

---

4 A US historian concludes: 'Poland, momentarily within grasp of uniting the Slavic world, had bungled the task; if Poland had succeeded, Siberian and eastern interests would certainly have been sacrificed to European schemes. As it was, Russia entered a new and definitely separate stage of her history, a period of enormous outward expansion and painful inner tension' (Kirchner, 1950, p. 57).

5 Michael Florinsky (1969, p. 136) makes the point: 'The Ukrainians who cherished the ideal of national independence or autonomy had good reasons to regret the decision of 1654. The subsequent history of Russo-Ukrainian relations is the disheartening record of relentless infringements of Ukrainian liberties by the Moscow–St Petersburg government, culminating in the abolition of Ukrainian national institutions in the second half of the eighteenth century.'

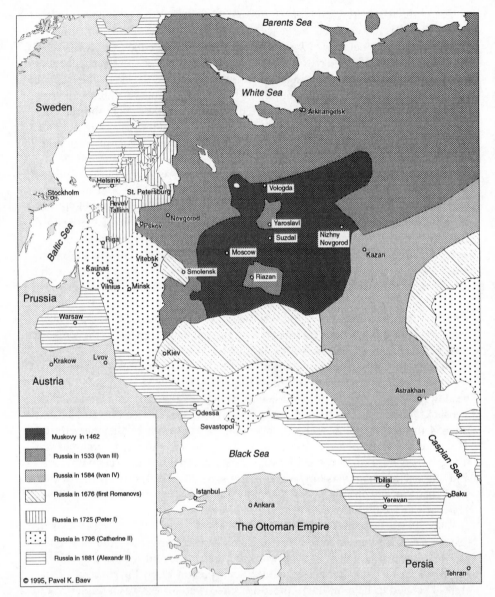

Map 1.1　*Russia's Territorial Expansion in Europe in the 15th to 19th Centuries*

involved. Despite spending long years at war and building a regular army of some 200,000 men, Peter I succeeded only in conquering Livonia (with Riga), Estonia (with Revel/Tallinn), Ingria (where St Petersburg was founded) and Southern Karelia (with Viborg) – altogether not more than 120,000 km². But he left to his successors an ambitious European project which essentially involved reducing Poland, which became a victim of its own inability to develop efficient state structures, and pushing Turkey out of Europe.

Implementation of this project took what could be called 'Russia's long 18th century'.[6] It started in 1695 (Peter's first Azov campaign) continued through three partitions of Poland (1772, 1793, 1795) to which Prussia and Austria were accomplices, and ended in 1815 at the Congress of Vienna which finalized the elimination of Poland and made Russia a status quo power. It left the struggle with Turkey undecided; while the conquest of Crimea was relatively easy, the incorporation of Moldavia marked the limit of Russia's achievements to the south-west. Taking its military superiority for granted, Russia went for the Balkans in 1854, but was defeated by the Anglo-French-Turkish coalition in Crimea. The period of European expansion was over: Moscow had to accept that none of the participants in the 'Concert of Europe' was enthusiastic about the prospect of Russian control over the Straits.[7] The fruits of yet another attempt to 'liberate' the Balkans were more peacefully stolen by the European powers at the Berlin Congress of 1878.[8] All Russia could do was to compensate by steady advances in the Caucasus, which remained the theatre of almost relentless wars from the early 18th century up to the 1920s.

As for expansion in Asia, it remained largely a nongovernmental enterprise almost until the late 19th century. Nikolai Muravyev, Governor-General of East Siberia, took the initiative in exploiting the dislocation of China shattered by Western interventions, to annex the lower Amur and Primorye regions (Vladivostok was founded in 1860). Perhaps Moscow would have as easily sold off these lands as it sold Alaska in 1867 – if only anyone were interested in such a deal. It was not until the 1890s with the construction of the Trans-Siberian railway that the government became seriously involved in Far Eastern matters – only to suffer a humiliating defeat by Japan in 1905. Central Asia saw more or less the same pattern. By the 1850s Russian settlers gradually moving southward reached the borders of the densely settled Muslim khanates of Bokhara, Kokand and Khiva. As Michael Florinsky (1969, p. 324) has argued: 'The conquest of these and adjacent regions was due largely to the endeavour (and insubordination) of three generals – Cherniaev, von Kaufmann and Skobelev'. Their advances were taken much more seriously in London than in Moscow, so the former insisted on drawing up the Afghan border in 1887; but Russian control over the regions to the north of that line remained a superficial formality (Map 1.2).

From this brief description we might perhaps conclude that territorial expansion was much less of an existential pattern of the Russian state than commonly perceived. The incorporation of new provinces was driven not so much by

---

6 As Adam Ulam (1974, p. 4) has pointed out: 'Many elements of Russia's great historic fortune in the eighteenth century were to weigh heavily on her destiny well into our days.'

7 Paul Kennedy (1989, pp. 170–177) has made a convincing analysis of how this ambitious attempt 'to break up the Russian Empire' resulted in heavy strains in France and particularly Britain. As Richard Rosecrance (1995, p. 148) has pointed out in a recent article: 'To be sure, after the fall of Sebastopol in the Crimea, the British Cabinet did not succumb to Palmerstone's grandiose schemes to defeat Russia in the Baltic as well, and in this sense British "overexpansion" was controlled.'

8 What distinguished this attempt (and made the failure of diplomacy more bitter) was the nationalistic pan-Slavic slogans; wide popular support was mobilized for liberation of the Bulgarians and the Serbs. This manifestation of Slavophile ideas ignored the desperate struggle of Poles for independence; the 1863 revolt was suppressed as brutally as the previous one in 1830–1831, neo-nationalism notwithstanding.

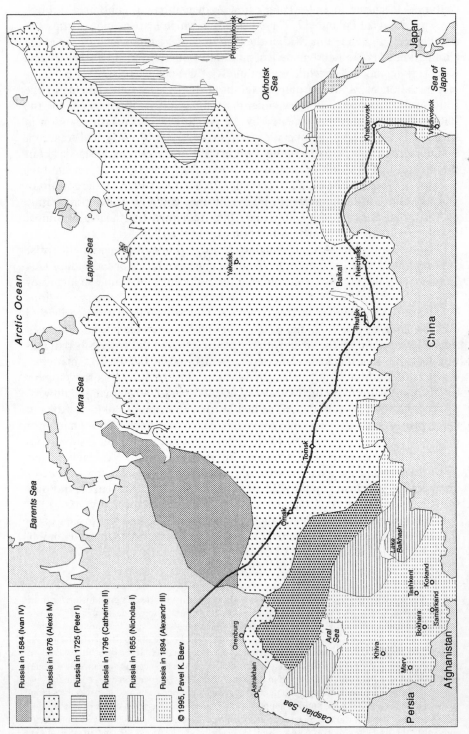

Map 1.2 *Russia's Territorial Expansion in Asia in the 16th to 19th Centuries*

Russia in 1584 (Ivan IV)
Russia in 1676 (Alexis M)
Russia in 1725 (Peter I)
Russia in 1796 (Catherine II)
Russia in 1855 (Nicholas I)
Russia in 1894 (Alexandr III)

© 1995, Pavel K. Baev

messianic ideas or economic greed as by the fear of penetrating invasions and concern about being isolated from Europe.[9] What Russia did was primarily to pick up the bits and pieces of neighbour-states debilitated by internal unrest (Poland, Turkey, Persia) or exhausted by other wars (Sweden). Many of these acquisitions were considered fortuitous and subject to bargaining;[10] vast territories in the East and South were barely explored. Perhaps Russia's accelerated growth in the first decade of the present century had many unhealthy features (Kennedy, 1989, pp. 232–241), but the costs of maintaining the Empire (so-called 'imperial overstretch') hardly made a considerable impact on its survivability.[11]

Characteristically, Russia entered World War I without ambitious territorial claims, except for eastern Galicia, as confirmed by Emperor Nicholas II during his visit to the captured city of Lvov (Lemberg) in April 1915. Seeking to boost the sagging morale of their crucial ally, Britain and France swallowed their 'Crimean' geopolitical reservations and agreed to reward Russia's efforts with the long-desired trophy – the Straits. But when this agreement was announced in the Duma in December 1916, the news, according to the British ambassador, 'fell perfectly flat' (Florinsky, 1969, p. 400). No expatiations on Russia's 'historical mission in the Bosphorus' were able to generate any enthusiasm; it was Lenin's slogan about 'immediate peace without annexations and indemnities' that commanded growing public support.

The Bolshevik Revolution of 1917 pushed the country, already bled white by the war effort, into complete disintegration fostered by foreign interventions. And yet, the empire in its main features was restored in the course of only a few years. The spatial perceptions and the policy of border-building were to experience a remarkable evolution during the 75 years of the resulting Soviet state.

In *the initial phase*, territory was seen as a variable in the global battle, and borders moved as fast as the frontlines of the 'permanent revolution' proclaimed by Trotsky and expanded by the Red Army's bayonets. Ideologically motivated Bolsheviks were eager to accept seemingly humiliating territorial compromises and to create buffer-states (such as the Far Eastern Republic) in order to concentrate their forces for the next breakthrough.[12] To some extent – as far as

---

9 Attempts to present Russia's expansion as a pre-planned process which includes the stages of conquest, assimilation and new conquest (Iivonen, 1995, pp. 73–75) are historically untenable and would seem to be ideologically motivated.

10 Thus, for example, Sevastopol was recaptured at the negotiating table after the Crimean War in exchange for Kars, which was duly returned to Turkey – to be taken back in the next war.

11 Geir Lundestad (1993, pp. 7–14) has developed an important argument on Kennedy's point about 'imperial overstretch', arguing first, that the military spendings were only one part of the imperial expense; and secondly, that the direct benefits gained by the imperial state tended to diminish while the overall expenses tended to increase. See also his introduction in Lundestad (1994, pp. xii–xiii). In Russia's case in the early 1900s, the military efforts were obviously concentrated on the Western direction and not on Russia's own provinces; as for the cost-effectiveness, the empire still paid substantial dividends, particularly in terms of raw cotton for the booming textile industry in Central Russia.

12 Even if formally recognized by Moscow, the independence of the newborn states was not taken seriously. Note Stalin's (1953 [1920], p. 365) words written in October 1920: 'The so-called independence of so-called independent Georgia, Armenia, Poland, Finland etc. is only an illusion, and conceals the utter dependence of these apologies for states on one or another group of imperialists.'

Ukraine and Crimea, Far East and Caucasus were concerned – this approach proved successful (the re-conquest of Central Asia took some ten years more). But the Polish campaign of 1920 convincingly showed that Russia had exhausted its revolutionary energy. The obvious ebb of revolutionary movements in Europe (Hungary in 1919 appeared to be a non-starter) brought Lenin to his theoretical conclusion on the possibility of the victory of socialism in one particular country.[13] It actually justified the beginning of real state-building, which also meant territorial settlement with capitalist neighbours.

This opened *the first stage* in the evolution (which could be called 'recognition'), which was forced by a sheer lack of power. One necessary step in establishing relations with the reluctant West was to delineate the boundaries – hence to recognize formally the priority of traditional borders over the 'revolutionary frontiers'. At this stage ideology still played a key role and provided the idea of the border as a gap between two historical epochs: the imperialist past and the communist future – as materialized in the first state of 'workers and farmers'. In this sense it is quite possible to say that the borders of the USSR only formally ran across space: in essence they went across time (Strada, 1991). Thus the territorial expansion of the 'state of the future' was presented as a linear function of time, and the 'frontier' remained open for new adventures. The operational planning became a task for the *Comintern*, organized to transcend the formal borders and, as Lenin (1974 [1918], p. 331) put it, 'to strengthen the connection between one temporarily isolated section of international socialism and other sections'.

The second stage of this evolution (which could be called 'consolidation') began approximately 12 years after the October coup. This watershed, named by Stalin as the Year of Great Breakthrough, was marked by a striking reversal in state-building, from Europe-oriented 'proletarian' internationalism'[14] to self-centred nationalism, and the subsequent transformation of the state as such from ideological to bureaucratic. The role of ideology while remaining pivotal became primarily functional: to justify the hyper-centralization of state structures. Accordingly the content of the ideology began shifting towards traditional empire-building/saving concepts enriched with a new image of 'Besieged Fortress'. Romanticism yielded to a new pragmatism: while the goal of conquering the world was moved to the indefinite future, a more practical task was set for the near term – to regain the lost territories.

The third stage – 'expansion' – started in the late 1930s, when Stalin abruptly contracted a political alliance with Hitler. The lack of ideological justification for this alliance was striking, and painful for many in the USSR, but the empire ideology already dominant in the Kremlin (though perhaps less so on

---

13 Trotsky insisted on a different conclusion – to shift the direction of the offensive to the East: 'The road to India may prove at the given moment to be more readily passable and shorter for us than the road to Soviet Hungary' (as quoted in Ulam, 1974, p. 121).

14 The Soviet involvement in China, while seemingly a deviation from Euro-centrism, was actually to a substantial degree subordinated to the main goal of the first stage – to win a breathing spell and not to alienate major European powers. The crushing defeat of the Chinese Communists in 1928 added to the introvert trend in the USSR.

the grassroots level) required no justification for territorial enlargement. The legitimacy of the westward expansion to pre-1914 borders was taken for granted; the severe repression and resettlement of the indigenous populations was intended to preclude any further border revisions. Only Finland succeeded in defending its independence in the Winter War (1939–40) – at the expense of Karelia, which was completely evacuated. The expansion continued through Russia's victory over the treacherous Nazi ally, but got a new quality that influenced the character of borders. While the pre-War acquisitions and two new trophies – East Prussia and Sakhalin/Kurils (both 'ethnically cleansed') – were fully integrated in the state, after 1945 priority was given to the creation of an external 'security belt' as legitimized by the Yalta/Potsdam agreements.[15] Even the most rigid control from Moscow provided the 'peoples' democracies' in Eastern Europe with a status essentially different from that of the Soviet republics.

The role of ideology in state-building became purely formal as the cult of Stalin turned the 'world revolution' into an abstract idea. The new borders were fortified to make them impenetrable and to minimize contacts with 'outsiders'; even the *Comintern* – which in the previous stage was transformed into an intelligence-propaganda structure – was dissolved. The Future was finally captured within state borders, and the unpopular slogan 'The Frontier is under Lock!' confirmed that there was no escape.

The fourth stage of evolution, from the mid-1950s to the mid-1980s, involved the crystallization and erosion of 'Communist' borders. During this long period the Soviet leadership sought to preserve Stalin's heritage while avoiding extremes. Some attempts to revitalize the role of ideology were considered of crucial importance, but the diminishing persuasiveness of quasi-Marxist dictums made it necessary to maintain the 'information border'. A new and important factor came with the deep traumas in the national (and particularly in the military) mentality caused by the shock of the German invasion in 1941. No further proof of the inherent aggressiveness of 'Imperialism' was needed, and the obsessive idea of Defence made any claims to a monopoly on the future seem ritual indeed.[16] The two epochs were engaged in a sort of trench warfare; for 40 years Defence remained the best justification for the efforts to encircle the 'Socialist camp' with a bastion-border – the Wall.[17]

The character of borders inside this Socialist camp was determined by the

---

15 One example confirming this priority is the return of the Belostok area to Poland, while Lvov (which had never been a part of the Russian empire) was retained in order to have direct access to Hungary and Czechoslovakia. The special Commission in the Soviet Foreign Ministry for the peace treaties headed by Maxim Litvinov took security as the main guideline. The papers of the Commission (634 files) are now available from the Foreign Policy Archives. I am indebted to Vlad Zubok, Senior Researcher at the Nobel Institute, Oslo, for sharing this information.

16 The prevailing of security over ideology was most evident on the border with China, which after the armed incidents in 1969 was fortified beyond rationale, despite the unquestionably 'communist' nature of the neighbour.

17 Original and thoughtful analysis of the concept of the Wall as an element of European political philosophy has come from a project conducted under the aegis of the Nordic Summer University. (See Tunander, 1995.)

recognition in the Kremlin that homogeneity was beyond reach. The social gap between the USSR and its 'brother-countries' in real terms was becoming less and less bridgeable, despite successful military interventions and heavy economic dependence. Dangerous heterogeneity made it necessary to erect interstitial borders between the 'Socialist Citadel' and the outer strongholds, and so a multi-layer hierarchy of borders emerged, with the territory of the allies actually serving as 'military buffer' and 'cordon sanitaire' for the USSR. A certain amount of discriminate expansion beyond the external perimeter of the Fortress was considered as being both of strategic and ideological importance – to deliver proof that the Future was indeed on its way. The successful Soviet enterprises in Cuba and Vietnam paved the way for adventures in Africa and then – the disaster in Afghanistan.[18] By the mid-1980s strategic overextension and ideological impotence had become self-evident. The heretical idea of a gradual retreat to 'defendable borders', implicitly influenced by Alexandr Solzhenitsyn, began gaining new supporters.[19]

Still, few in the political class were able to foresee that the retreat could go further than Soviet withdrawal from Afghanistan and 'Finlandization' of Eastern Europe. The internal borders of the USSR remained by and large as Stalin had made them. Indeed, on closer examination, his cartographic exercises are far from capricious: borders were drawn deliberately to generate ethnic tensions, to make each republic a sort of *Matreshka*-doll with minorities inside minorities – all dependent on Moscow.[20] When Gorbachev finally realized the fragility of the whole construction in 1990, this only made him reluctant to grasp the sole remaining option – to treat the Baltic republics as a special case, and perhaps let them go in order to save the rest.[21] Soon afterwards, the astonishingly peaceful collapse of the Soviet Union left the newborn states with unnatural territories and historically unjustifiable borders – and with ample opportunities to undo the old injustices by force.

---

18 The Soviet invasion in Afghanistan makes a meaningful illustration of Charles Kupchan's (1994, p. 16) argument that 'under conditions of high vulnerability – when one would expect elites to go to greater lengths to bolster the security of the metropole than under low vulnerability – decision-makers do just the opposite. They engage in behavior that only exacerbates the metropole's security predicament'. On the surface of it, the USSR's strategic situation in the late 1970s did not meet Kupchan's criteria of 'high vulnerability', but taking into consideration – with the wisdom of hindsight – the deep erosion of internal structures, we still can make the case. For a precise review of Kupchan's argument see Rosecrance (1995).

19 Solzhenitsyn (1990) made an emotional point in his later celebrated brochure: 'We do not have the power for the Empire – and we don't need it, and let it fall from our shoulders: now it is smashing and sucking us, and fostering our downfall.'

20 Paul Goble (1993, p. 80) has argued: 'By converting the ethnic identity of all groups into official nationalities with a clearly defined territorial dimension, Stalin institutionalized ethnic tensions, justifying his authoritarian regime and guaranteeing that the collapse of the Soviet Union would follow ethnic lines.'

21 On holiday in Crimea on the very eve of the coup, Gorbachev (1991, p. 115) argued in an article: 'Today a genuinely voluntary community of peoples is being put together and that will give unprecedented stability to our Union . . . In the course of 1,000 years in one case, of 200 to 300 years in another and of 50 in the third case [i.e. the Baltic republics – P.B.] such realities had taken shape for the healthy growth of which was required a vital, real federation and not some loose community or association.'

1.3   An Army for the Russian Empire and for the Soviet *Derzhava*[22]

It is often taken as an indisputable historical fact that the Russian Army has no tradition of direct interference in politics, and particularly in staging coups. While perhaps worth cultivating, this assumption ignores too much contradictory historical evidence. But before reviewing the annals of the Russian Army's involvement in domestic affairs and mutinies against inattentive Tsars, it is tempting to indicate the cultural roots of this widespread misperception.

The numerous military campaigns had all the intrigue and drama that history could possibly provide – yet they still occupy only a tiny corner in the classical Russian literature. The triumph in 1709 over Sweden was rewarded by one fragment in Pushkin's 'Poltava'; the Napoleonic Wars inspired only a few poems (Lermontov's 'Borodino' tops the list), and Tolstoy's early 'Sevastopol Tales' remain the most noticeable reflection of the Crimean War. The conquest of the Caucasus received more attention, but it was probably the romantic nature and the freedom-loving character of the highlanders that attracted writers. Certainly, Tolstoy's *War and Peace* alone could compensate for the general lack of interest, but – as far as the 'War' side is concerned – its message is so strongly anti-military that it rather complements than contradicts the overall tradition.

All those glorious generals and admirals who claimed so many victories for the Russian crown in the 'long 18th century' left no distinguished memoirs, Russians in this respect being no different from the foreigners who were so amply represented in the high command. Historians – starting from Karamzin, and including Klyuchevski and Solovyev – were more interested in social processes than in military manoeuvres. Moreover, during the period of cultural late-Renaissance from the mid-19th to the early 20th centuries, Russian scientists and authors made a significant impact in such different fields as sociology (Pitirim Sorokin) and macro-economics (Wassily Leontief), philosophy (Nikolai Berdyaev) and psychology (Nikolai Bekhterev) – but not a single prominent military theorist could be named.[23] And even in the area of revolutionary and socialist thinking, where Bakunin and Kropotkin were succeeded by Lenin and Trotsky, nothing close to Friedrich Engels' works on military strategy was produced.

Indeed, the Russian Army traditionally existed in a sort of 'cultural vacuum'. One reason for this was perhaps the harsh atmosphere inside the military, created by dehumanizing drill and discipline.[24] Another plausible reason was the

---

22 The Russian word *derzhava*, meaning a proud state (but not exactly 'great power' since the equivalent is *velikaya derzhava*), has become the central notion for the self-assertive and national-patriotic course. Its advocates are duly called *derzhavniki*.

23 Andrei Kokoshin (1988) in several articles has argued that the works of Alexander Svechin made a significant contribution to military theory. It should be noted that Svechin, although a *tsarist* general, wrote his most important works while teaching in the Red Army Military Academy in the 1920s; after Mikhail Tukhachevsky took him as a target for criticism, he was duly forgotten, to be 're-discovered' only in the late 1980s when defensive operations came into vogue.

24 Fedor Dostoevsky, found guilty of conspiracy in 1849, was condemned to death; at the last moment the sentence was commuted to four years of hard labour in Siberia, to be followed by four years serving as a soldier – the latter being a telling indication of the prestige and conditions of military service at the time.

widespread opposition in the Russian *intelligentsia* to the absolutism of which the Army was part and parcel. When Peter the Great created the regular Army, he immediately started to put it to use for various domestic purposes – whether the eradication of *raskol* (the split in the Orthodox Church originating in the reform of the 17th century), the construction of St Petersburg, or 'pacifying' Cossack revolts. His successors duly followed his example, never hesitating to use troops in order to protect serfdom; and it was Catherine II who dispersed the most serious peasant uprising in 1772–74 by sending her best Field Marshal Alexandr Suvorov against the rebels. As for the non-Russian provinces of the empire, it was only Poland that caused much trouble, raising arms for independence in 1794, 1830–31 and 1863. Each time the Tsar's Army was used not only to defeat the rebels but also to implement massive repression. Emperor Nicholas I, eager to help any and every European monarch with similar problems, was invited to do so only once – in 1849, a Russian expeditionary corps was called in to disperse the national liberation movement in Hungary.

Only after the military reform of 1874, which introduced compulsory service of limited duration, did attitudes in the officer corps towards taking on the gendarme role start to change. By then, the main internal threat was political terrorism, and the Army by and large was saved from being involved in this struggle. And it was not until the early 20th century that the Army itself was to become a threat to the regime – but this problem also had its roots in history.

In his early years, Peter I saw the violence of several mutinies of the *streltsi* elite regiments based in Moscow. Hence his determination to create a new Army – and the first two regiments actually saved the throne against a new mutiny during his journey through Europe in 1698. The Tsar replied with severe repression. He disbanded the *streltsi* troops and then concentrated extraordinary efforts on building a regular European-style Army, which remained his first state-building priority up to the battle of Poltava (1709). It soon became obvious that in seeking to make the Guard with its privileged status the guarantor of the regime, Peter I secured for the latter a dominant political role. Moreover, by making the Army the framing structure of the state, the great Russian emperor actually laid the foundation for the crucial dependence of the regime upon the efficiency of its military machine.

After the sudden death of Peter the Great in 1725, the Guards regiments (their ranks filled mostly by noblemen) became more Praetorian than the *streltsi* ever had been, determining the order of succession to the throne.[25] After the period of German domination (Empress Anna, trying to secure her rule, even created a new Izmailovsky Guards, a regiment where officers were mostly Baltic Germans), the Guard brought to power Peter's daughter Elizabeth in 1741. Her successor Peter III was dethroned by a Guards coup in 1762 in

---

25 As Paul Miliukov (1968, p. 334) argued: 'A new era began, the era of the supremacy of the Guard. This newly born social force was employed for the first time at the emperor's bier. The fate of Peter's reform was bound up with the question of the succession to the throne, which was still open and which was to be settled by force.'

favour of his wife Catherine II, and the brief reign of her son Pavel I was cut short by another coup in 1801. In this perspective, the Decembrist military revolt of 1825 was merely a continuation of the coup tradition, though the goals of its 'Westernized' and liberal-minded leaders (among them many Guards officers) included restricting the monarchy by a Constitution and abolishing the institution of serfdom.

After that time, the pattern of the Guards' political dominance was clearly discontinued. It could be argued that, paradoxically, the gradual increase of Russia's military power resulted in a much diminished internal political role for the Army. Indeed, the triumphs during the 'long 18th century' over Swedes and Poles, Turks and finally over the broad European coalition led by Napoleon not only made Russia the dominant military power of continental Europe but also contributed much to consolidation of the state and the Romanov dynasty. By the mid-19th century, the whole situation looked static and unchangeable, when suddenly the disastrous Crimean War revealed the backwardness of the Russian Army and the paralysis of the whole social structure of the state.[26] The consequences of this military defeat for regime stability were so severe that the ensuing major internal reforms (abolition of serfdom in 1861) and the victory over Turkey in the 'liberating' war of 1877–79 only partly alleviated them. And the humiliating defeat by Japan in 1905 multiplied the factors of instability and gave rise to the first revolutionary situation.

This revealed once again the direct link between the survivability of an authoritarian regime and the efficiency and reliability of its military tools. The Army for the last time saved the regime against a major social unrest: and for the first time it showed its own revolutionary potential.[27] The far-reaching reforms that followed were denied sufficient time to consolidate new social structures, and Russia found itself entering World War I in a highly unstable phase of transition. As far as the military organization was concerned, the first battles demonstrated that the recent reforms had significantly increased combat-worthiness on the levels of regiments, divisions and corps, but the operational and strategic command was dominated by dogma and palace intrigue.[28]

---

26 As Richard Pipes (1994, p. 23) argues: 'The defeat in the Crimea dealt a severe blow to the prestige of the monarchy, in part because Russia under Nicholas I had devoted so much money and effort to building up what was to have been the world's mightiest army, and in part because she was beaten on her own soil by the allegedly decadent democracies.' On the latter point it could perhaps be questioned, whether Turkey, or Sardinia or France of Napoleon III could qualify as 'democracies'. But Platonov (1928, p. 360) made a somewhat similar point: 'It was not a mere accidental conflict of interests in the East but a fundamental difference in political principles which divided Russia from the West.'

27 It was symptomatic that a chain of mutinies went through the Navy, which had suffered the most severe defeat in the war with Japan.

28 One main priority of the prewar military buildup had been to re-create the Baltic Fleet which had been destroyed in the war with Japan. While this extensive programme proved useless in terms of operations in World War I, it greatly increased the concentration of 'revolutionary forces' near St Petersburg. It was mostly educated and skilled men who were drafted into the Navy, and this made the Kronstadt barracks a natural target for Bolshevik propaganda; detachments of sailors were in the vanguard of those few thousand strong 'masses' that conducted both the February and the October Revolutions in 1917.

Logistics proved the weakest link, so the war of attrition inevitably brought the Army to the brink of collapse.[29]

In the final analysis, it was the increasing uncontrollability of the Army that determined the outcome of the political turmoil in the centre. The Tsar's disastrous incompetence as commander-in-chief turned the majority of the officer corps against the monarchy, so a mutiny of several 'rear' regiments in the capital was sufficient to deliver the fatal blow.[30] And it was the unfolding military crisis that prevented the unstable coalition of several centrist and liberal political parties from consolidating its power in the period between February and October 1917.[31] The Provisional Government did not have enough authority to rescind the suicidal Order no. 1 issued by the Petrograd Executive Committee, according to which the soldiers' committees were to organize elections of officers.[32] It is indeed striking how in the course of only a few months, an army with some 5,000,000 men under arms and engaged in permanent fighting, simply ceased to exist. Up to 2,000,000 soldiers deserted from the trenches by September, and when the desperate generals led by Lavr Kornilov attempted to take political control, they found no reliable troops to carry out orders. The failure of the first Russian 'parliamentarian democracy' was sealed by its inability to check the disintegration of the Army; in much the same way the attempt to enforce Communist rule inevitably faced massive armed resistance. So the collapse of the military structure doomed Russia to civil war.

The Bolshevik leaders demonstrated their unbelievable statesmanship and determination struggling against heavy odds. They came to power with no concept of military organization except that the Tsarist Army had to be disbanded,

---

29 Over 15 million men were drafted into military service during the first two years of war; by 1917, up to 37% of the male population of working age were under arms (Florinsky, 1969, p. 401). Disorganization of the economy by the end of 1916 led to a supply crisis in the main industrial centres; accordingly the public attitude changed from irritation at the conduct of war to protest against the war as such. The leaders of the main political parties in the Duma remained blind to this shift, discarding the idea of a separate peace as 'shameful and incompatible with the honor and dignity of Russia' (Miliukov, 1967, p. 429).

30 The Socialists were quick to accommodate to these aspirations, changing in the night of mutiny the name of their main framework political structure from 'Soviet of Workers' Deputies' to 'Soviet of Workers' and Soldiers' Deputies'. An eyewitness described the arrival of this new force at the Tavrida Palace which was the February epicentre: 'The soldiers were the last ones to appear, but they were the real masters of the situation. It is true that they themselves did not admit this; they rushed into the palace, not as conquerors, but as people afraid of taking responsibility for committing a breach of discipline, for the murder of commanders and officers. They were even less sure than we were that the revolution had won' (Miliukov, 1967, p. 393).

31 As Miliukov, Foreign Minister in the Provisional Government, testifies in his memoirs (1967, p. 428): 'It was thought that the liberation of Russia from the tsarist yoke would, by itself, evoke enthusiasm in the country and would be expressed in an increase in the fighting capabilities of the army.' As the uncertain offensive in Galicia in June turned into a disorganized retreat, the support for the Provisional Government in the ranks just disappeared.

32 As Robert Bathurst (1993, p. 80) argues: 'Suddenly a society which had been hierarchically organized for all of the centuries of its existence, and which at the front in World War I was operating collectively, fighting for its survival under the most adverse material and organizational circumstances, was to adopt an alien, democratic, system of choosing leaders and making decisions . . . The military culture could not adapt to the proposed structural changes: it collapsed to be reborn in the traditional Russian forms as the Red Army and Navy.'

yet in a matter of months the romantic ideas about a 'workers' militia' had been dropped and the regular army was built anew on the basis of compulsory mobilization and 'iron revolutionary' discipline.[33] Thousands of experienced field and staff officers were brought back to command it.[34] The German invasion of Ukraine, as well as Allied interventions in Arkhangelsk, Odessa and Vladivostok stimulated the mobilization of patriotic feelings, and every victory gave new credibility to a regime which at first had seemed quite unviable.

By the end of 1920 the only functioning structure of the state was the 5,500,000–strong Red Army. Continuing battles in the Far East and Central Asia as well as uprisings inside the country called for sustained military efforts. But Lenin, with undeniable foresight, recognized that the Army could not be the main pillar of the new Socialist state – indeed, it could even become a threat. So the military reform was launched in 1921 simultaneously with the New Economic Policy – and it envisaged an unprecedented tenfold reduction in the Army's strength as the point of departure.[35] Within the Party leadership there may well have been serious concerns that the Army could become the decisive factor in the heated debates which in fact were a struggle for leadership, since the only Bolshevik leader who commanded wide support in the military hierarchy (and who actually built it) was Trotsky. Demobilization and cautious 'purges' of potential Trotskyists conducted by Mikhail Frunze (more reshuffling followed his mysterious death in 1925) helped to reduce the political role of the Army to a minimum during the turbulent period of 1924–29.

When the early successes of industrialization in the mid-1930s made it possible to increase the strength of the Red Army to 1,500,000 men, Stalin – in anticipation of its possible consolidation as a political force – unleashed severe repression against the military leadership. Not only was the cohort of 'Red Marshals' (Bliykher, Egorov, Tukhachevsky, Uborevich, Yakir) eliminated, but the whole officer corps was decimated.[36] A direct consequence of this self-destruction was appallingly poor command on all levels, which can in turn explain the spectacular initial success of the German invasion in June 1941. And immediately after

---

33 Two weeks after the coup, Lenin authorized warrant officer Krylenko to take control over the Supreme Headquarters (Stavka) in Mogilev; in addition a telegram was sent to all units ordering them to start negotiations with the Germans, effectively ending centralized control over the Army. On 23 February 1918, several rallies were organized in order to attract volunteers to defend the 'Socialist Fatherland' – this day is still celebrated as the birthday of the Russian Army.

34 Arguing that professionals were indispensable for the Army, Lenin (1974 [1919], p. 448) wrote in a proclamation in mid-1919: 'The guerilla spirit, its vestiges, remnants and survivals have been the cause of immeasurably greater misfortune, disintegration, defeats, disaster and losses in men and military equipment in our army and in the Ukrainian army than all the betrayals of the military experts.'

35 This massive demobilization stretched defence capacities so thin that delegates of the X Party Congress in 1921 were commissioned to lead the assault on mutinous Kronstadt, and cadets of the Military Academy were sent against the rebellion in the Tambov region in 1921–22.

36 According to estimates made during Khrushchev's anti-Stalin campaign, about 20% of the officers were condemned in 1937–38. What was particularly striking, all commanders of military districts, all corps commanders, nearly all division and brigade commanders and about half the regimental commanders were either executed or imprisoned. In the first months of the war with Germany, about 25% of imprisoned officers were rehabilitated. (See Scott & Scott, 1981, p. 19.)

the great victory in 1945, Stalin again took preventive measures against his overly self-confident generals, sending hundreds to the GULAG and having those who seemed too popular (like Rokossovsky or Zhukov) transferred to obscure posts.[37]

Still, it was the handguns of Marshal Zhukov, General Moskalenko and several other generals that decided the outcome of Khrushchev's plot against Beria, who had all chances to grasp power after Stalin's death in 1953.[38] But when the confident voices of the military leadership persuaded the CPSU Central Committee to back Khrushchev against the 'anti-Party group' in 1957, the leader recognized that the dependence had grown out of bounds. Several months later Zhukov was accused of harbouring 'Bonapartist ambitions' and stripped of his responsibilities as Defence Minister, then Marshal Sokolovskiy was replaced as Chief of the General Staff and Marshal Konev as the Commander-in-Chief of the Warsaw Pact. After getting rid of these authoritative 'war heroes', Khrushchev felt free to proceed with deep cuts in the Army; but the alienated military leadership gave their heartfelt support to the plotters who overthrew him in 1964. Thus, even if none of the three post-Stalin 'palace coups' went so far as to bring the tanks to Moscow's streets, the outcome in each case was determined by the attitude and direct participation of the military leadership.

The 20-year period that followed Khrushchev's fall – now commonly called *zastoi* (stagnation) – saw the consolidation of a pattern of relations between the Party leadership and the military hierarchy in which the latter often preferred – and also were expected – to stay 'outside politics' so as to conduct politics of their own. Thus, the blame for increasing hyper-militarization of the state could hardly be placed entirely on the top brass. In a peculiar way, the Army was less than an integral part of the Soviet military–industrial complex, which was more a union between the 'super-elite' (about 50 general directors and general designers) of the military enterprises and the top bureaucrats from nine ministries of the Military–Industrial Commission (VPK) and the Defence Department of the Central Committee of the CPSU (Kokoshin, 1994, pp. 45–47). The promotion of Dmitry Ustinov, the authoritative leader of this alliance, to the position of Minister of Defence in 1976 gave the captains of industry a decisive voice in setting the ambitious Soviet armaments programmes in the late 1970s and early 1980s.[39]

While strategic arms control had been elevated to a central foreign policy issue since the early 1970s, this did not give the military any bigger say in politics. It

---

37 Massive demobilization was again used to reduce the internal 'weight' of the Army; Khrushchev later gave figures on the scale of reductions from 11.4 million men in 1945 to 2.9 million in 1948. They are taken now as generally accurate, though US estimates from the late 1940s took 4.0 million as the minimum and 4.5 million as the most probable level which justified the scenarios of Soviet *blitzkrieg* in Europe. (See Evangelista, 1982/1983.)

38 According to some sources (see, for example, Burlatski, 1990, pp. 47–49), Marshal Zhukov – hero of many battles – in his retirement insisted that the most perilous moment of his life had been the arrest of Beria.

39 The prevailing of the industrial interests as formulated by the VPK over the Army's requirements was coined in the phrase: 'We will give the military not the arms they want but the arms they need.' (See Shlykov, 1995, p. 23.)

was primarily the dynamics of production that drove the international intrigues around the Tu-22 'Backfire' bombers and the SS-20 missiles (Garthoff, 1983). The General Staff was generally kept off these exciting events but it had been granted carte blanche to develop the concept of 'deep operations' and to design the 'operational manoeuvre groups' (OMG) – and there was scant pressure to coordinate those with the guidelines of European policy.[40] But when the military leadership presented its war plans as a foundation for the direct claim on a greater share of economic resources, the 'elders' of the Politburo became alerted to the lack of political control – so the leader of the 'military professionals', Marshal Ogarkov, was quietly removed from his position as Chief of the General Staff in September 1984. His disciples (Akhromeev, Gareev, Petrov, Varennikov) had learned their lesson and did not press their objections against the 'supreme' decision to invade Afghanistan, which from the military point of view was nothing but a senseless waste of resources (Gromov, 1994).

By the mid-1980s the Soviet Army, although considered to be the most solid and reliable structure of the state, actually had very little influence on political decision-making, which was concentrated in the increasingly narrowing circle of the Party elite.[41] The military machine accumulated a disproportionate share of the national wealth but these self-destructive efforts were essentially purposeless, except for the conviction that the 'invincible' Army was in itself the final proof of 'greatness' of the Socialist *Derzhava*. The political function of the Army had become reduced simply to consumption of human and material resources: hence so little understanding in the military leadership of the scale of economic and social crisis. The Army was expected to symbolize rather than to ensure the 'inde-structible unity' of the conglomerate Soviet state which was rapidly becoming unsustainable. But the military culture remained pro-active, and as the new generation of Afghan-hardened warriors moved to the top of the military hierarchy, a new period opened up in the Army's involvement and interference in politics.

1.4   War, Politics and Neo-Clausewitzianism

The eternal question of the interplay between Politics and War – despite the answer which Carl von Clausewitz hammered out some 150 years ago – has continued to bedevil security relationships on various levels across the former Soviet Union. The dominant perception during the long Brezhnev era was that the 'internal function' of the military in a 'ripe' socialist society was negligible; the turmoil in Poland came as a reminder that the 'brother' countries were not so advanced, and that tanks could be called to protect the regime. Still, it was reassuring that the level of violence was clearly receding from those of Hungary (1956) and Czechoslovakia (1968). While the military were ready (albeit far

---

40 Making plans for the OMGs' breakthrough was a sort of cottage industry in Western security studies in the early 1980s, but only a few analysts pointed out the counter-productiveness of Soviet conventional buildup for the promotion of the USSR's political goals in Europe. (See Lebow, 1985.)

41 That Marshal Ustinov indeed was one of the 'king-makers' during the uncertain transition of power from Brezhnev to Gorbachev, does not contradict this conclusion. Ustinov's personal rank in the Party hierarchy had little to do with his control over the Army to which he never really belonged.

from enthusiastic) to perform their ill-famed 'international duty' in Poland, they felt sure that Novocherkassk would never be repeated and every notion of this 1962 workers' uprising and the Army's hesitation in quelling it was eradicated. A chain of violent crises during perestroika shattered this comforting perception, and the breakup of the USSR effectively made every Army unit a participant in political battles.

As new political elites started to discover that sovereignty was very much a question of force, the Russian military leadership came to realize that it had under its control a prevailing force and hence a highly valuable political instrument. The immediate concerns were about the reliability of direct control, and the doubts were that this was an instrument too valuable to be entrusted to politicians. The gradual erosion of democratic values and institutions in Russia paved the way for a renaissance of Clausewitzianism in political thinking, while military views on the use of force devoid of any ideology became unabashedly pragmatic.

The divergence between political and military perceptions of usability of force can be traced to the middle of the Gorbachev epoch. When in May 1987 the Military Doctrine of the Warsaw Pact was released, with a claim that its defensive character 'proceeds from the fact that in today's circumstances the use of the military way of resolving any disputed question is inadmissible' ('On the Military Doctrine . . .', 1987), this was generally taken by the Soviet military as an international public relations exercise.[42] But Gorbachev was indeed serious in his belief that in the nuclear age war as such could no longer be a continuation of policy, and – unlike in many other fields – he succeeded in translating words into deeds, as with the unilateral cuts announced in December 1988 and the CFE Treaty signed in November 1990. The military were forced to include in the Draft Doctrine published in December 1990 statements that 'war has become totally outdated, unacceptable and impermissible as a means of achieving political objectives', and that force should be 'unreservedly renounced' as an instrument of policy.

This Draft precisely reflected the 'mix of belligerence and insecurity' (quoting from Stephen Foye, 1993g, p. 46) which characterized Soviet military thinking at that time and which brought the top Army leaders to the coup of August 1991. But the failure of this attempt to bring tanks to the streets as the compelling political argument revealed that even the top brass of the Soviet Army – to say nothing about the officer corps en masse – was not at all convinced as to the acceptability and real value of such a role.[43] Nor was Gorbachev's anti-Clausewitzian appeal particularly convincing: what was intended to be a message of non-violence

---

42 One contradictory piece of evidence is Marshal Akhromeev's posthumous memoir (see Akhromeev & Kornienko, 1992, pp. 121–126). Akhromeev claims that as Chief of the General Staff he personally set forth the main guidelines of the new doctrine in autumn 1986; they were properly discussed in the General Staff Academy and by the end of the year approved by the Defence Council. The major innovation was the shift of the strategic objective from victory as such to preventing the enemy's success, and terminating the conflict. Raymond Garthoff (1994, pp. 529–530) tends to take this claim as a real point of departure of the new military thinking.

43 As far as the testimonies can be trusted, it was the agreement between General Gromov, Deputy Minister of the Interior, and General Grachev, Commander of the Airborne Troops, not to take any actions that aborted the coup. Both indicated the inevitable bloodshed as the main reason for cancelling the assault. (See 'Why the "Thunder" Did Not Crash', 1994.)

became – after the tragic events in Tbilisi, Baku and Vilnius, with the blame for all put on the Army – a message of hypocrisy. But the deep resentment against political games and especially domestic gendarming was in a way 'genetically encoded' in every Soviet officer. It was not only the lack of a coup d'etat tradition or the 'Tbilisi syndrome' that were the factors here, but rather the intrinsic feeling of belonging to a caste of professionals with a special duty and restrictive rules. John Lepingwell (1992, p. 566) put it succinctly: 'The professional focus on external security threats and the reluctance to engage in internal security missions played a significant role in the decision to withdraw support from the coup.'

The event that eventually broke this 'genetic code' was the dissolution of the Soviet Union – spontaneous and voluntaristic as it was. Hopes for excluding the military structures from the enthusiastic 'nationalization' and preserving the 'integrated military-strategic space' proved short-lived.[44] And it was the military who first discovered that the violent ethnic conflicts were a natural continuation of the policy of national self-determination.[45] It was no longer possible for the Army to restrict the applicability of the Clausewitz dictum to the 'outer' world as the behaviour of every political fragment of the USSR started to follow the logic of the 'breathtaking' (after Bernard Brodie, 1984, p.706) Chapter 6 of Book Eight of Clausewitz's *Vom Kriege* ('On War').

Perhaps Mikhail Gorbachev would have eagerly subscribed to such conclusions as 'Clausewitz, in short, was not a modern man', calling his theory 'short-sighted, a recipe for immediate success, but in the longer term destructive to all parties concerned, even nihilistic' (Keegan, 1992, p.4). But for Gorbachev's many successors in the suddenly independent states, the direct access to military instruments was an exciting initiation into the real power. As for the main heir in the Kremlin, he felt no immediate need to put the military instruments in use; at least for the first year the democratic process granted President Yeltsin all the power he wanted. But all too soon the military leaders in Moscow were to feel the pressure from the enthusiastic experiments in the Near Abroad.

It is possible to argue that this pressure was anticipated and maybe even welcomed, since the graduates of the Soviet General Staff Academy could be described as 'natural Clausewitzians' for whom the instrumental formula was almost an article of faith. It would be a gross exaggeration to say that the Prussian theorist supplied the Russian military mind with much of its furniture, despite the excellent testimonial that Lenin provided him in *Socialism and War* (1974 [1915], p. 304).[46] In

---

44 Ukraine's uncompromising drive for building its own armed forces took the August coup as the point of departure. For Ukrainian leader Leonid Kravchuk it was the ultimate lesson in Clausewitzianism when General Varennikov burst into his office and announced that the commander of Kiev military district would supervise how the orders from Moscow were followed. (See Litvin, 1994, pp. 271–272.)

45 According to a survey conducted at the All-Army Officers Meeting on 17 January 1992, 57% of the 5,000 participants considered armed conflicts between Russia and other CIS member-states possible in the near future. (See Putko, 1992.)

46 Lenin in 1915 added a point of clarification to the dictum 'of one of the profoundest writers on the problem of war', naming violence by its name among 'other means'. In the judgement of some Soviet theoreticians, this contribution 'radically changed the statement of the problem' (Sokolovskiy, 1975, p. 430).

the volumes of *Voennaya Misl* ('Military Thought') one can hardly find anything close to such attempts of contemporary interpretation as, for example,
Beyerchen (1992/93). Actually, the two-volume Russian translation of *Vom Kriege*
from 1937 in the Officer's Library series was never reprinted, so generations of
scholars had to rely on Lenin's quotations. But the legitimacy of the military
instruments of politics was made indeed axiomatic; pacifist propaganda, anti-war
campaigns and peace-loving committees were phenomena existing in a kind of
parallel universe far away.

Afghanistan made it clear that ideology played only a secondary role in providing this legitimacy. The Communist Party's failure to formulate sound
guidelines for pushing the Army into this quagmire compromised its monopoly on
identifying the 'just' causes of war.[47] It is noteworthy in this context that the concept of *bellum justum* – Just War – which in the Western debates often serves as
complementary to the Clausewitzian approach (Smith, 1994) – in Soviet/Russian
military-political thinking is simply non-existent. When the ideological justification finally collapsed, the military turned to pragmatism – which actually came in
two different blends, depending on the specific 'Afghan' experience.

On the one side were the 'warriors' who blamed the politicians for failing to
convert their battle successes into victory. Their reading of Clausewitz was that
in a war the military should take control of policy (or at least have a major say)
in order to steer it properly. On the other side were the 'peaceniks' who paid the
price for the conclusion that the 'Afghanistans' of this world had no military
solutions.[48] The latter perhaps came closer to the 'genuine' Clausewitz in recognizing that in each phase a war had to be guided by rational political goals, and
accordingly insisted on adjusting the military instruments to the non-violent
means of conflict management. Coming to personalities, we can name General
Pavel Grachev as the chief of the first tribe and General Boris Gromov as the
most prominent representative of the second group; and they took turns leading
the Army on the road from Kabul to Grozny.

But for a while it was the corporate interest of preserving the integrity of the
Army that brought all Afghan-hardened generals together and hid the differences. The split within the Soviet military machine allowed for a psychological
compromise that recognized military force as a useful and legitimate instrument
in the Near Abroad but kept it out of internal Russian politics. But this compromise appeared to be shaky on both premises. In the Near Abroad even carefully
measured use of force to protect directly threatened military interests paved the
way for ambitious neo-imperialistic policies aimed implicitly or explicitly at
re-establishing dominance over all former Soviet republics. And in the internal

47 Odd Arne Westad (1993) discovered in the Soviet archives plentiful evidence of minimal military involvement in the planning of the invasion. Thus the mission of Deputy Defence Minister
General Pavlovsky in August–October 1979 was primarily about assistance for reforming the Afghan
Army. Much later, General Varennikov confirmed the strong reluctance in the military leadership to
send troops (see Borovik, 1989).

48 First Deputy Defence Minister Kokoshin (1993) tried to formulate a theoretical basis for this
approach: 'The idea of total defeat of the enemy in the very physical sense dominated in the previous epoch. But today we should keep in mind that every armed conflict is a very peculiar
combination of military measures and also political, propagandistic and other steps.'

arena and more specifically in Moscow it became increasingly difficult for the military leadership to resist the political pressure for throwing its weight (and thereby its tanks) into the battle.[49]

The gradual change of the political discourse that eventually made military force a useful instrument and violence an acceptable means could be attributed to several factors. Certainly, developments in the Near Abroad made an impact – perhaps not so much the Russian peace-making interventions, as the violent coups and seizure of power in Dushanbe, Tbilisi and Baku. The political process in Russia was rapidly losing its superficially democratic nature and mutating into a direct clash between factions in the leadership, none of which had vested interest in resolving the conflict by truly democratic means. And the 'wild capitalism' which emerged as a natural (albeit perhaps unexpected) product of Gajdar's economic experiments brought with it such an astonishing corruption and swift degradation of moral standards that the 'law of the jungle' triumphantly wiped out many regulators that had prevented major societal cataclysms during perestroika.

That Yeltsin had arrived at the final decision to use force and if necessary massive violence against his rivals became clear by late summer 1993 when he personally sent up a series of trial balloons.[50] But it was not at all clear whether the Army was ready to take responsibility for this violence. A really powerful push was needed to persuade the military (except, maybe, the long-since-persuaded Defence Minister) to cross the threshold that had stopped them in August 1991.[51] The street violence in Moscow created the necessary cause; it is the job of future historians to find out what were the spontaneous reactions and what was cold-headed planning in Yeltsin's entourage.[52]

Many in the Army may have hoped that this dramatic appearance on the political arena would be duly rewarded and followed by a swift retreat to their professional niche. Neither hope was fulfilled. Yeltsin, knowing that the October events deprived him of support from the 'thinking class',[53] that the regions were

---

49 According to a survey conducted in October 1993, 67% of the officers considered that the main threat to Russia's security came from inside and not from outside. (See Zhilin, 1994a.)

50 At that time, many political analysts predicted continuation of the slack confrontation. Thus, Lilia Shevtsova (1993) argued that 'an army in a fit state to fight, ready to end its neutrality' was needed for any forcible breakthrough. Later, Yury Boldirev (1993), spelling doubts about the President's statement 'We were not preparing for a war', asked: 'What did the President mean by promising a heated autumn with preliminary preparation fire? Was it not clear that there would be people ready to defend the law, that conditions had been created for the activity of various extremist and bandit groups that subsequently became an additional reason for the authorities to use force? Or was this what was required?'

51 Deputy Defence Minister General Mironov confirmed later that the Army had maintained its neutrality in the internal struggle until 'the events rushed over the edge and started to threaten the security of the state, i.e. until we had armed violence'. (See *Moskva. Osen-93*, 1994, p. 591.)

52 The leading article in *Moscow News* with the telling headline 'A President's Trap? A Trap for the President?' (see Gevorkyan & Zhilin, 1993) pointed to many suspicious circumstances of the crisis. On the other hand, Otto Latsis (1993b), recalling the 'Occam's razor' principle, argued that looking for a plot is redundant where slovenliness provides a sufficient explanation.

53 Ilya Milstein (1994) offers a good description of impossible choices for the intelligentsia: 'At that time democracy, armed with tanks, crushed legality, armed with only grenade launchers. Intellectuals were humiliated by this victory because it was achieved through murder and lawlessness.'

only temporarily subdued, and that the social pressure would grow – needed the Army as a permanent political instrument. The new Military Doctrine approved in November 1993 fixed a sort of compromise: a greatly increased internal role for the armed forces was identified but the commitment for allocation of all necessary resources was included. The President's men wasted no time in exploiting the first part of the compromise: the Army was engaged in the fight against organized crime (more for show than for real) and even in tax collection (remarkably ineffective).[54] But nothing was delivered on the second part of the deal.

The cumulative impact of the deep dissatisfaction within the ranks on the instrumental political role and the desperate situation concerning the sustainability of the military structures threatened to transform the Army into a dangerous and unpredictable force. Yeltsin had to take this seriously, 'especially since October had already abolished the taboo on bloodshed, as it also abolished other deterring mechanisms' (Shevtsova, 1994a). His answer to this potential challenge was to create an alternative force – by beefing up the Interior Ministry Troops based in and outside Moscow to the level of some 50,000 and also empowering the Presidential Security Service, which became as much of a Praetorian as the Guard had been at the twilight of the Peter the Great's reign (Galeotti, 1994a). The chiefs of the new Praetorians had few scruples against employing their forces in financial rackets and political blackmail (Parkhomenko, 1995): thus, President Yeltsin, instead of taking precautions against possible military coup, had actually made himself hostage to his own bodyguards.

Looking at the prevailing thinking, we can characterize the situation in Moscow by late 1994 as ripe for another violent breakthrough. Perhaps the unashamedly neo-Clausewitzian political mentality went a few steps ahead of the military views that harboured residual reservations. Mark Galeotti (1994c, p. 482), noting the 'self-congratulatory matter of factness' with which the politicians met the first anniversary of the October events, adds that 'as far as the regime is concerned, emergency measures and the forcible imposition of the power of the centre are perfectly acceptable tactics'. On the military side, there were growing doubts and suspicions that military force was becoming a substitute rather than an instrument of politics. Hence the increasing reluctance to take on new political assignments; but when the direct order was given to move into Chechnya, the military leadership failed to stand on its objections – much the same way as with Afghanistan some 15 years before.

The war in Chechnya marked a crucial watershed in the development of democratic processes in Russia, particularly in military–civilian relations. This war was by no means a continuation of a consistent state-building policy: it was more the continuation of political squabbles and intrigues in Moscow. The disastrous Chechen campaign had a tremendous societal impact, and with it came a new readiness in military circles to take control of politics from the increasingly isolated President Yeltsin and his entourage. The main obstacle here was

---

54 Ignored were the recommendations of many Western experts such as Michael Desch (1993, p. 474): 'The Yeltsin government needs to ensure that the Russian military not only modernizes but also professionalizes: the Russian military ought to be kept out of domestic politics.'

the acute institutional crisis in the Army, so the most serious question mark in the reiterated references to General Pinochet concerned the obvious lack of cohesion in the military leadership. But in the final analysis, as Michael Desch (1993, p. 473) puts it, 'all the military needs . . . is to be less divided than Russian society in general to be a force in domestic politics'.

1.5   Conclusion

It would certainly be naive to believe that a history-oriented analysis of the Russian military culture could provide firm guidelines to the behaviour of the Russian Army in the near future. Still, several clues might be found in the preceding pages.

One of them is the crucial importance of territory in the Russian military perceptions. If there is any one issue capable of mobilizing the Army for decisive action, it is a threat to the territorial integrity of the Russian Federation – and Chechnya, with all reservations about the real political aims of this war, may serve as a case in point. The strong historical tradition of military expansion and 'winning back' territories lost in previous misfortunes also gives grounds for concern. If it seems implausible that the Russian Army could ever be used in order to restore the USSR – and Chechnya has yielded the final evidence that there is neither the desire nor the power for such a crusade – there remains another option: that the Army could march under the banner of reunification of all 'eternal' Russian lands, particularly those now populated by ethnic Russians. The current flabbiness of the Russian state (despite the hypertrophied state apparatus), with its vague identity and uncertain borders, adds plausibility to such a scenario.

The centre-oriented and strictly hierarchical military mentality has up to now effectively prevented any 'regionalization' of the Russian Armed Forces, but permanent and severe lack of resources in the centre could eventually overcome this. As control over economic resources is increasingly coming into the hands of regional political bosses, the military commanders are finding themselves increasingly dependent on their generosity. Transdniestria in 1992 and Abkhazia in 1993 provided some examples of Russian military units 'going native', and the Chechen war has provided more evidence. This phenomenon should not be interpreted as only war-related; thus, the governors of Khabarovsk and Maritime *krai* paying less and less attention to orders and directives from Moscow and making their own foreign policy vis-a-vis China, are increasingly able to rely on support of the command of the Far Eastern Military District.[55] One consequence of such a 'regionalization' could be a series of local military enterprises reminiscent of the Cossack adventures in the Far East in the 18th century or General Skobelev's campaigns in Central Asia in the mid-19th century.

Another issue that could prompt direct military interference in politics would

---

55 For a penetrating analysis of this trend see Fadin (1995). More positive regional developments in the North West with a unique international dimension related to the Barents Region are addressed in Chapter 4.4.

be the collapse or complete disorganization of central state control (Brusstar & Jones, 1995, pp. 40–42). One development of this sort could arrive in connection with the results of the parliamentary elections in December 1995. The Communist Party claimed a victory, but not a very convincing one: it now controls only about one-third of the seats in the State Duma, the lower house of the Russian Parliament. The Communists will hardly be able to capture the most desired prize – the Presidency, in June 1996. Whatever 'coexistence' may emerge, it could degenerate into another confrontation between the executive and legislative powers. In such a situation, the military leadership would be faced with not just a choice between the two sides as in autumn 1993: at stake would be the sustainability of the whole political system that reproduces the deadlocks and violent confrontations. In general, as the Yeltsin regime in its decline increasingly resembles the long autumn of Brezhnev – with the growing concentration of power in the hands of advisers and bodyguards, uncontrollability and unaccountability of bureaucrats, flourishing corruption, etc. – the greater are the incentives for the military leadership to remove it, before a wide-ranging social explosion tears the country apart.

2
Russia's Security Interests and the Army

2.1 Introduction

The collapse of the Soviet Union raised such wrenching questions about the identity of Russia that many in Moscow tried to hide behind a comforting illusion of continuity. The whole fundamental transformation was perceptionally reduced to dismantling a redundant superstructure as well as getting rid of a few troubled provinces and allowing some others to go their way. This pitiful psychological self-defence could not of course alleviate the consequences of the unprecedented and lasting geopolitical disorientation. On the one hand, the status of the principal heir contributed to the perception that Russia was in fact the USSR writ small. On the other hand, there was a strong desire to escape from the Communist past and open new horizons.

It was perhaps the Russian Army that suffered most from the breakup of the all-Union structures. Rehabilitation required leadership and time, but due to political turmoil the military bureaucracy was left to set its own guidelines, under the enormous pressure of urgent problems. The year 1992 saw a yawning gap between political and military views on the character of Russia's security interests and the means of providing for their protection. Each suffered from its own inconsistencies and lack of realism, which led to discrepancies between general guidelines and practical policies. Three years of further evolution hardly added any harmony to this distorted picture.

The analysis in this chapter will divide – perhaps artificially – global security perceptions from policies in the Near Abroad in order to identify differences in the trajectories of political and military thinking. The nuclear dimension of security comprises a separate topic with its own unique mix of political and military guidelines.

2.2 Russia and the World: Geopolitical and Geostrategic Perspectives

Up to the very last day of the USSR, foreign relations in general and fundamental geopolitical issues in particular remained the domain of Gorbachev. Yeltsin's staff was certainly no match for this first-class team of experts elaborating the New Political Thinking. Only a few mid-ranking officials in search of career opportunities joined the Russian Foreign Ministry (like Andrei Kozyrev) or the presidential structures (like Dmitri Rurikov and Andrei Fedorov, who became close advisers for Yeltsin and Rutskoi, respectively). Thus, the abrupt dissolution of the Soviet Union in December 1991 had the side-effect of interrupting Moscow's geopolitical thinking as such.

As the victorious Russian bureaucrats moved into the offices that symbolized imperial power (Yeltsin to the Kremlin, his entourage to the Party Headquarters at Staraya Ploshad, and Foreign Minister Kozyrev to the Stalinist skyscraper in Smolenskaya Square), they started to discover how unprepared they actually were for the job. Kozyrev was pressed to produce new guidelines for Russia's foreign policy, but remained reluctant to invest serious efforts in conceptualizing, which was unfamiliar ground for him. The first attempt to define the required list of guidelines was undertaken by a narrow circle of Kozyrev's close associates in spring 1992, but the resulting draft document was distinguished mainly by its lack of vision and complete inability to formulate priorities.[1] Small wonder that it was rejected out of hand by the Parliament.

A new and substantially revised version of the document entitled 'The Concept of the Foreign Policy of the Russian Federation' (1993) was presented to the Parliament in January 1993 and found a more favourable attitude – due mostly to the promise to put into the foundation the national interests and not some amorphous 'universal values' inherited from the now all but officially condemned New Political Thinking. (For a useful analysis see Sergounin, 1993.) But despite the claim of defining 'key directions' and providing a 'flexible system of coordinates' (Kozyrev's cover letter as quoted in Aron, 1994, p. 17), this paper was aimed more at answering the criticisms directed at the Foreign Ministry from all sides of the political spectrum, than at introducing a true policy focus.

Russian military thinking during 1992–93 followed a remarkably different trajectory compared to the political debates on security. While foreign policy in early 1992 attempted a clear break with the Soviet past, the initial military efforts to rethink new realities were not particularly impressive. The draft Military Doctrine released in May 1992 was clearly a sample of the old mentality prevailing among the 'armchair' generals. While not naming the USA and NATO as the enemy, it unambiguously pointed to them in referring to 'some states and coalitions' which wished to dominate the world and continued to regard force as a means of resolving disputes (see Draft Military Doctrine . . ., 1992). The main focus of the document was on the requirements for the Russian military posture coming from the necessity of coping with this threat. (For a detailed analysis see Dick, 1992.) One illustration of this could be the discovery made by the newly appointed Russian Defence Minister Grachev that Moscow had now become a border military district; he even proposed creating a new 'first strategic echelon' with headquarters in Smolensk in order to rectify this 'mind-boggling' situation.[2]

---

1 Alexei Arbatov (1993b, p. 19) has made the point: 'It failed to formulate or even to identify in general terms the new Russian national interests and priorities abroad, which differed from either a scaled-down neo-imperialistic version of traditional hard-nosed Soviet ambitions, or from a repetition of the sweet utopian slogans of Gorbachev's "new political thinking".'

2 See *Izvestia*, 1 June 1992. Among strategic planners the relevance of the concept of 'Defence of the Western Perimeter' was by then seriously questioned. Head of the Main Operational Department General Barynkin went much further in assessing new threats than the draft Doctrine at the hearings on the Law on Defence in May 1992. (Personal records.)

Besides the universal military conservatism, there were institutional reasons for this continuity which bordered on irrelevance. The obvious structural disproportions and imbalances of the Russian Army in the new strategic environment provided an opportunity for radical reformers, and newly appointed Defence Minister General Grachev could become 'Gajdar in uniform'. Building conceptual defence, the chiefs of the General Staff tried to block the destructive radicalism and convince Grachev to accept a go-slow approach.[3] These concerns found full understanding in the newly formed Security Council headed by Yuri Skokov. He incorporated the key geostrategic postulates into the draft of the first fundamental document entitled 'Programme for National Security of Russia', which argued that 'Russia should act as a force countering the USA' since the latter was aspiring for global dominance.[4]

Debate on the draft Doctrine was rather shallow and remained within a narrow circle of military elites with very little participation of politicians or the 'civil strategists' who had acquired a position of influence during the Gorbachev epoch.[5] Few attempts to propose a future-oriented geostrategic vision were recorded.[6] But gradually there came a recognition of the urgency of the new challenges, and with it – a devaluation of traditional threat perceptions.[7] The old fear of invasion from the West and NATO's *blitzkrieg* began to give way to concerns that the mighty Alliance could seize the opportunity provided by some local conflicts to push the disintegration of the Russian Federation. General Mikhail Kolesnikov (then the first deputy chief of the General Staff) went public, blaming NATO for planning an intervention aimed at taking control over the Russian nuclear arsenal.[8] In this context the breathtaking statement made by CIS Commander-in-Chief Air Marshal Shaposhnikov, that any intervention from Turkey in Transcaucasus could lead to a Third World War, becomes easier to comprehend.[9]

Therefore, by autumn 1992 the political and military perspectives were concentrated heavily on the West and had one thing in common: insufficient

---

3 Attending a major conference on the draft Doctrine in the General Staff Academy in May 1992, Grachev was particularly impressed by General Rodionov's keynote speech in which the threat to Russia's vital interests from the USA and NATO was described in detail. (See FitzGerald, 1992.)

4 The document was never formally endorsed and not even released. For details see Parkhomenko (1992a); useful comments are in Lough (1993a).

5 Interestingly enough, it was Vice President Rutskoi of all politicians who took an active part in these debates, subscribing wholeheartedly to the General Staff position. See his articles in *Krasnaya Zvezda* (1992) and *Voennaya Misl* (1993).

6 A rare example of perspective thinking is Sinaisky (1992). But his opinions carried little weight against the firm orthodox views of Gareev (1992). For an example of more recent and far more sophisticated geopolitical analysis see Pirumov (1994).

7 Already in spring 1992, the Main Intelligence Directorate (GRU) admitted – to the amazement of many parliamentarians – that it was unable to name the most likely adversary or to identify the most threatened strategic direction. For the report on parliamentary hearings see *Krasnaya Zvezda*, 14 May 1992.

8 At the session of the Council on Foreign and Defence Policy in July 1992. (Personal records.)

9 The statement was intended to be an answer to the sharp warning from Ankara, that according to the Kars Treaty (1922), Turkey was the guarantor of security of Azerbaijan's Nakhichevan enclave. (See *Izvestia*, 8 May 1992.)

attention to the immediate neighbourhood. The most serious attempt to bridge the gap and at the same time to provide a new focus was probably the report 'Strategy for Russia' (1992) prepared by the newly formed Council on Foreign and Defence Policy, which included a score of influential politicians, civil strategists and military experts. This remarkably consistent and comprehensive Report placed heavy emphasis on two assumptions: (a) that Russia's interests were not symmetrical to those of the West and the divergence between the two would increase; (b) that the main priority was not the West, but the Near Abroad, since the crucial external challenges to Russia's security would come from the newly independent states. Sergei Karaganov, who initiated the creation of the Council and became its Director, advocated an 'enlightened post-imperial course' which should moderate the competition with the West and provide for conflict management in the Near Abroad.[10]

As for the political leaders, they continued to operate on the basis of an essentially different assumption – that the external challenges to Russia's security had decreased drastically and would reach a record low level in the near future. The Foreign Ministry tried to channel the debate into the course of the traditional and by definition fruitless argument between 'Westernizers' and 'Eurasianists', where the most interesting contributions for the latter case were made by Lukin (1992), Pozdnyakov (1993) and Stankevich (1992).[11] Kozyrev convincingly advocated his pro-Western line and even tried to ridicule his opponents in his famous caricature speech to the CSCE Conference in Stockholm in December 1992.[12]

One area where 'Eurasian' ideas appeared to complement strategic perspectives was the Pacific, and summer 1992 saw a frontal clash between those two and Kozyrev's course. The case in point concerned relations with Japan deadlocked over the Kuril Islands issue. The Foreign Ministry prepared President Yeltsin's visit with a remarkably commercialized 'islands-for-cash-and-credits' agenda, while the conservative opposition raised hell about 'irreversible retreat' from the Far East and the military supplied it with ammunition regarding the strategic importance of the Kuril passages for the Pacific Fleet. The abrupt cancellation of Yeltsin's visit at the very last moment was taken by many experts as the turning point in Russian diplomacy (Arbatov, 1993b, p. 24; Desch, 1993, p. 468).

When President Yeltsin berated the Foreign Ministry in late 1992 for lack of a comprehensible concept, hasty attempts were made to modify the position which Sergei Karaganov (1994c, p. 17) characterized as 'liberal internationalism or mondialism'. Then, for some time, Kozyrev lost the main responsibility for designing the foreign policy, which duly went to the Security Council and its

---

10 For an insightful analysis of the competition between the Council and the Foreign Ministry see Crow (1992c).

11 The latter in particular launched a fierce attack on the democrats for betraying the imperial heritage. For an extensive analysis see Neumann (1993a).

12 His best effort in conceptualizing the course was the article 'Transfiguration or Kafkaesque Metamorphosis' (Kozyrev, 1992b). For a complimentary comment on the Stockholm speech see Safire (1992).

ambitious Secretary, Yuri Skokov. He introduced and at times enforced inter-departmental coordination, marrying different approaches in the document entitled 'The Basic Provisions of the Foreign Policy Concept' which was endorsed by Yeltsin in April 1993.[13]

This Concept envisaged a new tough approach to protecting Russia's national interests, with the main aim of breaking the pattern of general retreat vis-a-vis the West. This involved restoration of Russia's 'Great Power' status, with its legitimate sphere of interests covering the former Soviet Union. This was not elaborated further since Skokov was sacked (on grounds of his questionable loyalty), and the subsequent bureaucratic squabble paved the way for Kozyrev to seize back the initiative (Orlov, 1993a). But it would scarcely be an exaggeration to say that starting from this document, geopolitics has successfully replaced Communist ideology as the conceptual basis for Russia's foreign policy. As Christoph Royen (1995, p. 41) has observed, geopolitics filled a certain vacuum in thinking which led to the reappearance of 'black-and-white perceptions in the foreign policy analyses'. But the majority of the political elite eagerly subscribed to the recently-condemned *Realpolitik* logic, placing it within a broad geo-graphical context and leaving the remnants of the New Political Thinking for the experts in the Gorbachev Foundation and a handful of liberal columnists. Accordingly, a precondition for Kozyrev's rehabilitation was that he underwent a complete change of spots and subscribed to that geopolitical perception which he had used to characterize as 'besieged-fortress mentality'.

A chance for Kozyrev to bring closer the new geopolitical and evolving geostrategic perspectives and to confirm his new credentials arrived in August–September 1993, when the issue of NATO enlargement suddenly esca-lated into a real relationship crisis. The Foreign Ministry used all available means to deliver the message that any fixed schedule for admission of the four East Central European countries to the Alliance was unacceptable to Moscow, and that even a symbolic NATO military presence in Poland would be viewed as a major security challenge. Amidst loud speculations on the risks of NATO and Russian troops facing one another, Sergei Karaganov (1993) issued a warning that the Atlanticization of Poland would be 'bound to trigger a negative reac-tion among a considerable part of the Russian military elite'. While this probably was true, it is also noteworthy that by that time the residual threat from NATO had been substantially reassessed in the General Staff. For that rea-son the Russian top brass were not particularly eager to join the anti-NATO campaign, and refrained from producing any calculations on the potential imbalance of forces.[14] (For a good review of the debates see Crow, 1993b.) Actually, the generals took a much more active stance only a few months later, demanding for Russia the most privileged status in NATO's Partnership for

---

13 The document was never published. Leon Aron (1994) argued that Skokov's paper was just a 'leaner version' of Kozyrev's concept, but the extensive quotations provided in his chapter actually testify to a serious input from the military. The origin of such goals as to counter attempts from 'third parties' to increase tensions in the CIS or to exploit the instability in their own interests could easily be traced to the General Staff.

14 Alexei Arbatov (1994b, part 2) had to refer to the calculations made by US experts.

Peace programme. This in itself was testimony to a drastic devaluation of the threat from the West, fostered by the competition for 'being first at the doors of NATO' (Karaganov, 1994a).

The 'enlargement issue' indeed brought the first evidence that Russia's foreign policy-makers were ready to go an extra mile in order to meet the military.[15] Further evidence was the twice-postponed presidential visit to Japan in October 1993 which made it clear that territorial concessions were not possible. This made irrelevant the 'package' proposal drafted by moderate liberals (see Arbatov & Makeev, 1992) which was based on the concept of a 'bridge between the West and the East' – while the gap certainly existed, but only in the 'Eurasian' view. Interestingly enough, the general devaluation of the strategic threat from the Pacific direction opened the way for a massive increase in economic relations with China, including exports of arms and military technologies (Miasnikov, 1994). Both the military and the politicians remained blind to the potential of conflict with China.[16]

The real watershed in the evolution of Russia's foreign policy came with the parliamentary elections in December 1993. Kozyrev joined the list 'Russia's Choice' which was formed around a modest democratic platform and was expected to be a clear winner. But the results came as a huge disappointment for Yeltsin's entourage. The stunning success of the statist-nationalistic platform of Zhirinovsky was taken by the Kremlin as testimony to the urgent necessity of shifting foreign policy priorities much further toward Russo-centrism. From early 1994, Russian foreign policy rhetoric became increasingly demanding and offensive, with Kozyrev occasionally trying to be more nationalistic than Zhirinovsky himself.[17] This hard-nosed line heard some criticism from the liberal press, but found remarkably broad support among the political elite, and few objections in the Parliament.[18]

The yardstick for Kozyrev's manoeuvres was the new Military Doctrine approved by the Decree No. 1833, signed by President Yeltsin on 2 November 1993. The military leadership had lobbied for this document for a long time, though the expectations of using it to cut the Gordian knot of unsoluble problems were perhaps, as Stephen Foye (1993g, p. 45) has put it, 'a direct throwback to the Soviet period'. Perhaps it was also a desire to compensate for the old sins

---

15 At that time *The Economist* (30 October 1993) discovered somewhat belatedly that Russia had at least two foreign policies: one run by civilians, another by the Army, and asked rhetorically: 'Your policy or mine?'

16 Renée de Nevers (1994, p. 69) has argued convincingly: 'Given both Russia's own weakness and the vulnerability of its far east to a country with territorial claims on it, both arming China and providing it with the means to arm itself may not be in Russia's interests, despite the advantages of hard-currency sales in the short term.'

17 A natural step in this evolution was Kozyrev's decision to leave the Russia's Choice parliamentary faction when it opposed the President in December 1994 on the issue of the Chechen war. Alexei Pushkov (1994b) commented: 'As should be expected, in choosing between liberalism and the ideology of power, Kozyrev opted for the latter. This not only irrevocably characterizes the minister himself, but generates genuine concerns about the future of Russian foreign policy.'

18 Suzanne Crow (1993c) was one of the first analysts to identify this emerging consensus and predict its lasting character. The Foreign Ministry showed some surprise about finding itself in the political mainstream half a year later.

of omission: Soviet military doctrine, while expected to provide answers to all questions, had never existed as a single document (Glantz, 1994). It was widely considered that the military leaders had won official approval for the doctrine as a part of the price for the pivotal support they had given to Yeltsin against the Parliament one month earlier.[19] Indeed, the contribution of civilian experts to this document is barely visible but still it hardly can be taken as a genuine reflection of the military view of the world.

What is immediately obvious and marks the most serious departure from the Draft 92 is the cardinal re-evaluation of the sources of military threat (Dick, 1994). Local wars are identified as the main threat, with a special warning: 'Of particular danger are the armed conflicts engendered by aggressive nationalism and religious intolerance' (see 'Basic Provisions . . .', 1994). The sections on the tasks of the Armed Forces and on the principles of their development concentrate on countering this main threat. Certainly, this new emphasis is but a realistic recognition that the arrival of a clear and present danger makes the old mythical threat redundant indeed. But the doctrine does not stop here; it extends to the commitment to use military force against internal sources of military threat, of which a long list is provided. It is no secret that the General Staff was not at all happy about this expansion of the Army's internal responsibilities; but the Security Council persuaded the Defence Minister that, without such a provision, it would hardly be possible to legitimize his own 4 October battle order for the Army, which decided the outcome of the tragic confrontation in Moscow.[20]

As for the erstwhile adversaries, they were warned not to undermine strategic stability 'by violations of international agreements in the sphere of arms control and reductions and the qualitative and quantitative arms buildup'. While this reads like a ritual claim to moderate the arms race, perhaps a more serious signal directly addressed to NATO was including in the list of sources of military threat the 'expansion of military blocs and alliances to the detriment of the interests of the military security of the Russian Federation'. These harsh words were somewhat softened during spring 1994 when Grachev and Kozyrev with a new accord tried together to strike a bargain, asking for a special programme to complement the Partnership for Peace agreement. The ambitious Russian draft for this programme eventually became a one-page protocol to the framework agreement signed on 22 June with a vague promise 'to pursue a broad, enhanced dialogue and cooperation in areas where Russia has unique and important contributions to make, commensurate with its weight and responsibility as a major European, international and nuclear power' (Kozyrev, 1994a, p. 5). This face-saving formula failed to defuse the mine, instead allowing controversies to accumulate. This in turn led to the second 'enlargement crisis' which started to unfold in late 1994.

---

19 According to some sources, the Security Council decided to abandon its own draft doctrine in favour of the document prepared by the Defence Ministry. See Foye (1993f).

20 According to Karaganov (1994b, p. 45), it was only after a long fight and 'allegedly under pressure from democratic politicians, that the military elite agreed to state in the new military doctrine that regular troops can be used to contain the destabilizing activities of extreme nationalists and secessionists, and to counter violent attempts to overthrow the constitutional order'.

By then it had become clear that the polarized views within the Russian political and military elite on whether the West was the key partner or the main threat, had clearly drawn nearer. At the one end of the spectrum, there was bitter disillusionment with the perspectives of building a meaningful partnership; at the other end was a devaluation of the scale and intensity of the threat coming from NATO. The middle ground could be described as a perception that currently there is no conflict between the main interests of Russia and major powers of the West and that any controversies – though sometimes sharp – are related to secondary interests.[21] Accordingly, neither a real and committed Western involvement in the CIS area, nor full-fledged partnership were taken as plausible options.

A corollary to this was that Russia should rely basically on itself in facing the new security challenges. No efficient collective security system was envisaged for Europe at large in the foreseeable future (Karaganov, 1994d). Demands for strengthening the CSCE structures, renewed since early 1994, were primarily instrumental in preventing NATO enlargement, which for many Russian politicians had become a matter of principle.[22] While the 'architectural' objections from Moscow were not so convincing on their own merits (Nikonov, 1994), they struck at the heart of the logical inconsistency of the Western rationale for enlargement since the elementary question of 'Why?' remained unanswered (as clearly pointed out by Asmus, Kugler & Larrabee, 1995). Nor was Russian foreign policy able to exploit this conceptual muddle. The CSCE summit in Budapest in December 1994 saw Moscow in complete isolation, arguing that priority should be given to all-European institutions – which actually implied an informal 'concert' of major powers perhaps modelled after the 'Contact Group'.[23]

A further corollary was that in this unstructured security system Russia could secure its interests only by regaining its 'Great Power' status. This notion has never failed to touch a sensitive chord in the Russian political mentality, so both President Yeltsin and Foreign Minister Kozyrev (who coined the phrase 'Russia is doomed to be a Great Power') occasionally played with it in the course of the struggle with the Parliament in 1993. But it was in 1994 that *derzhavnost* became an *idée fixe*.[24] Not a single public address went without a pledge to remind forgetful partners and particularly neighbours that Russia was a special case and had special rights.[25] In the heat of this rhetoric, speakers tended to

---

21 This assessment was elaborated in the report 'Strategy for Russia – 2' (1994) which also called for preservation of 'a belt of semi-demilitarized states' in Central Europe, thereby making the question of NATO enlargement irrelevant.

22 It was hardly coincidental that in early July 1994 Russia made a formal proposal for enhancing the CSCE and turning it into the main coordinating body to oversee the activities of other European institutions. This came only two weeks after signing the Partnership for Peace agreement with NATO. For a useful analysis see Mihalka (1994b).

23 Sergei Stankevich argued in March 1995 that the most promising scheme for Russia's policy was that of a 'Europe of states' (Personal records from NUPI seminar). This 'innovation' could seem ridiculous if one could forget about the trend toward re-nationalization of security which is growing in the shadow of the agonizing Common Foreign and Security Policy (see Bertram, 1995a).

24 See note 22 in Chapter 1.

25 Among the few dissenting voices mention should be made of Pavel Kandel (1993), who pointed to exclusion from Europe as a consequence of 'great-powerness', and Yakov Krotov (1993), who saw 'greatness' as the Emperor's new clothes. For my own reflections see Baev (1994f).

forget that the USSR had been known as an 'incomplete superpower' since its rank had been achieved only by dint of enormous military efforts. Today, in the mid-1990s, Russia lacks even this, and actually could qualify as 'great' only by the scale of its internal problems.[26]

The military leadership, while occasionally paying lip service to the 'Great Power' issue, was probably more aware that the forces under its control were no match for the Soviet Army. Certainly, the military doctrine has its own 'Alice in Wonderland' perspective, especially in its economic and technological aspects (Dick, 1994), but its geostrategic setting looks more moderate and realistic compared both to the Draft 1992 and to the current political guidelines. While the General Staff still takes NATO for something more potent and hideous than the sum of its member-states, there is hardly any desire to prove Russia's 'greatness' by entering into open competition with the Alliance.

In general, the 'geo'-perspective is rapidly becoming less and less relevant for both political and strategic thinking in Russia. The importance of the 'outer world' is objectively diminishing as the financial support for reforms grows shallow and strategic threats are evaporating, but perceptional disengagement goes much further. If in the political arena there are at least some attempts to instrumentalize certain 'external' issues for internal and particularly electoral purposes, for the military the influence of the former adversaries has fallen dramatically. And the rather abstract perspectives of building a multidimensional partnership with the West are becoming determined by – and one could even say, hostage to – Russia's actions and intentions in its immediate neighbourhood.

2.3   Russia's Foreign and Military Policies in the Near Abroad

The discrepancies between the policies conducted by the Foreign and Defence Ministries were more than merely a question of differences in geopolitical and geostrategic perspectives. From late 1991 to early 1994 both sets of policies underwent a complicated and uneven evolution that at times narrowed the gap, but never were any meaningful steps taken to bridge it.

Muddle and disorganization – these characteristics were common in analyses of Russia's semi-foreign policy towards the former sister-republics in 1992 (Migranyan, 1994a/b; Rogov, 1994b). It was not only the scale of the societal transformation and the intensity of the internal political struggle that resulted in this discord. First attempts to set basic political guidelines were remarkably counter-productive and put foreign policy at odds with military policy. The lack of integration was recognized as a fundamental flaw, so the year 1993 saw consistent efforts from the Kremlin to adjust its course according to the military realities – or rather, to the realities created by the military. Due to these efforts, an impressively broad consensus started to emerge among the political elite; the forceful change of institutional framework in October–December 1993 actually

---

26 Victor Kalashnikov (1993), insisting that its economic performance is downgrading Russia to 'the second echelon', sent an early warning that 'the relics of superpowerness could hide from the politicians the real capabilities and the new status of Russia'.

helped to consolidate it. Hence the surprising consistency in Russia's behaviour in the Near Abroad and the low-profile debates on the security priorities through most of 1994. But gradually a new gap emerged between *derzhavny* aspirations and military realities. The frail consensus was eventually shattered by the intervention in Chechnya in December 1994. In order to assess the inevitable further readjustments, we need to come back to the starting point in early 1991.

The outcome of competition between eroding Soviet and fledgling Russian power structures, personified in a clash between the two leaders, was decided not only in Moscow (with the August coup attempt) but not least in relations among and between the various republics. Gorbachev – carried away by the excitement of international events – had failed to pay them proper attention during the crucial years of 1989–90. He had also taken for granted the support of the military for his empire-saving course, overlooking the growing resentment among the ranks at the 'gendarme' role which also implied being held as a scapegoat. And when Gorbachev rushed to settle a new Union Treaty in mid-1991, the republican leaders entertained serious suspicions as to his real intentions and to the role of the Army. In fact, the Novo-Ogarevo process, which was expected to produce this Treaty, from the very beginning provided a convenient stage for Yeltsin, who managed to make his best showing exactly when Gorbachev revealed his fatal weakness – in Lithuania in January 1991. While the man who was to be the last Soviet President was unable either to back the Army and take responsibility for the bloodshed in Vilnius or to condemn it, Russia's leader immediately rushed to the Baltic republics, declaring support for their independence. The course of further events confirmed that for Yeltsin no price was too high for seizing real power: if on the way the fragile new federation designed by Gorbachev should have to be dismembered – so be it.[27]

The event that decided the fate of the Soviet Union in early December 1991 was also related to inter-republican relations. A meeting of Russian, Ukrainian and Belorussian leaders in a secluded *dacha* in Belovezhskaya Puscha (a unique forest preserve in Belorussia) was intended to accommodate the Ukrainian drive for independence which had been boosted by a recent referendum. What actually emerged from that meeting – the declaration on dissolution of the USSR – came like a bolt out of the blue. No protocols or records of the meeting exist and the reflections of the participants are so blurred that the circumstances of this brainstorming session look more than suspicious.[28] But for Yeltsin it was certainly a nurtured improvisation: Gorbachev, as Yeltsin's personal Carthage, was finally destroyed.

Arriving at real power, Yeltsin's advisers and assistants continued to congratulate themselves on the brilliant *fait accompli* since it seemed much easier both

---

27 Tatyana Tolstaya (1994) gives a good insight in her highly charged review of Yeltsin's memoirs: 'He didn't feel like thinking about what would follow this "freedom": collapse, poverty, the explosion of nationalistic hostilities, a sea of blood, millions of refugees.'

28 Yegor Gajdar, speaking at a seminar in Oslo in April 1995, admitted that in Autumn 1991 Gennady Burbulis, Andrei Kozyrev and himself had written a memo to President Yeltsin with a conclusion that the dissolution of the USSR would give Russia the best starting point for accelerating the process of economic reforms. (Personal records.)

to launch economic reforms and to build partnership with the West, cutting off structurally backward and inefficient areas of what had been the Soviet Union. Rapprochement with 'civilized nations' – that was the priority goal of the Russian Foreign Ministry, and Kozyrev considered it perfectly possible to talk his way out of relations with former republics by promising to build a 'belt of good-neighbourliness'. A direct implication of this Westward orientation was that insufficient heed was paid to the most urgent problems with new neighbours and potential seats of conflicts close to Russia's borders. Even the paramount issue of dividing the Soviet military heritage received rather offhand treatment, except for nuclear weapons (see Chapter 2.4). Gennady Burbulis, who was made responsible for general coordination in external relations and who cherished ambitions of creating a 'super-ministry', failed to produce any statesmanship.[29] Deputy Foreign Minister Fedor Shelov-Kovedyaev alone tried to make Russia's Near Abroad a priority issue, but his resignation in October 1992 showed that the chance to establish a normal democratic pattern of relations was missed.[30]

The empty space in this area left by a disorganized Foreign Ministry was quickly filled by the military – not that the latter were particularly eager to do it. It could rather be said that the military leaders, while slow to recognize that the habitual 'fixed' confrontation was gone, were quick to react to the new threats to Russia's security interests. While the Foreign Ministry was trying to pretend that conflicts in the new independent states were none of Russia's business, the Defence Ministry discovered that troops subordinate to it were directly involved in many of them. In Tadzhikistan, provocative attacks on Russian officers intensified; in Azerbaijan and Georgia, garrisons were besieged by local paramilitary forces demanding weapons; in Moldova, the 14th Army found itself in the line of fire; and in the Baltic states, the Russian forces became the cause of a sharp political conflict. The Defence Ministry in Moscow faced the fact that if it were to continue its temporizing, the troops in the hot spots would start to act on the initiative of the regional commanders turning warlords.

Under these circumstances, the decision to begin giving battle-orders – even if they were not in full correspondence with the doctrinal provisions and in complete disagreement with the political line – was only natural. Otherwise, disintegration would have become the pattern, as Grachev himself admitted

---

29 Alexei Arbatov (1994b, part I, p. 11) reacts with devastating criticism: 'The performance of the Ministry of Foreign Affairs was marked by inefficiency and numerous errors, there was a total lack of interest in independent analysis. In contrast to the Shevardnadze period, there was almost no contact with the academic community. This disorganization was characteristic, of course, of the whole decision-making mechanism . . . Paradoxically, the role of the Foreign Ministry in the whole system was weaker than ever before, and this was accompanied by serious intradepartmental deterioration, which had to be the result of subjective factors.'

30 His desperate attempts to mobilize intellectual and bureaucratic resources are illustrated in a bitter article (Shelov-Kovedyaev, 1992a). After resignation, he released a revised version of his report to the President entitled 'Strategy and Tactics of Russian Foreign Policy in the Near Abroad'. In it he argued that Russia pursuing the chosen course of reforms should become a 'recognized leader' in the former USSR and that the West was ready to recognize its 'special interests' providing that the unilateral use of force would be excluded. See Shelov-Kovedyaev (1992b); a good review is in Lough (1993b, pp. 55–56).

half a year later: 'Any right-thinking person – particularly a military man – real-
izes that we took over an army that was practically unmanageable.'[31] Moldova
became the decisive place for a new activist military policy; the nomination of
General Lebed as the 14th Army Commander (against President Yeltsin's pref-
erence) was, perhaps, the decisive moment.[32] The quick success of this
intervention, followed by another one in South Ossetia, paved the way for far-
reaching changes in strategic planning, which now started to earmark the
regions of the Near Abroad as potential theatres of military operations.

For some time, the Westernizers in Russia's political leadership continued to
insist on their assessment of the external situation as 'exceptionally favourable'
and stuck to the naive perception that the military force had no relevance as an
instrument of policy. As a result the Foreign Ministry, which was at the forefront
of this campaign, became marginalized in policy-making in the Near Abroad
and excluded from conflict management.[33] Kozyrev (1992a) went public several
times, blaming the military or the 'war party' (pointing specifically at General
Lebed) for war-mongering, with predictably little practical effect.

The above-mentioned report 'Strategy for Russia' (1992) was perhaps the first
signal that the changes to come would be more on the political side; indeed,
already in early 1993 they were announced in several increasingly self-assertive
speeches by President Yeltsin. (This early phase of evolution is best analysed in
Lough, 1993a, 1993b.) The new line in the Near Abroad was formally drawn up
in the 'Foreign Policy Concept' produced by the National Security Council in
April. Russia was declared the guarantor of stability in the former Soviet Union;
accordingly, any conflicts in the neighbourhood and or actions that could undermine the integration process in the CIS framework were branded threats to
Russia's security interests.

From this point on, the priority attention to the Near Abroad was properly
fixed. Every major political address now contained references to Russia's 'legitimate sphere of influence' which should be protected against encroachments
from other powers. What is peculiar about this *Vogelflug* geopolitical vision is
lack of details and regional priorities. As John Lough (1993a, p. 23) has put it:
'Policy is framed in heavy generalities to the point where only generalities are visible.' Most often, the whole post-Soviet space is presented as Russia's sphere of
vital interests, with the possible exception of the three Baltic states. Responding
to growing political demand, the Moscow academic community has produced a
number of theoretical versions of a neo-imperialist scheme, aptly labelled the
'Monrovsky Doctrine'.

---

31 Speaking on Russian Television on 28 February 1993, as quoted by Lepingwell (1993c, p.17).

32 On the intrigue surrounding Lebed's nomination see Parkhomenko (1992b). Lebed himself
claimed that his appointment marked a shift toward a more assertive policy for which Moldova was
a testing ground. (See *Moscow News*, no. 27, 5 July 1992.)

33 Iver Neumann (1994) has indicated one important exception. The decision to give support to
Moscow's traditional clients in Tadzhikistan and deny it to then-President Iskanderov (which duly
resulted in the fall of the latter) was taken in early November 1992 with the active participation of
the Russian Foreign Ministry. Neumann concludes that this marked the end of the non-interference
course and was 'an important nail in the coffin of the romantic Westernizing interlude in Russian
foreign policy'.

This idea of growing challenges for Russia's security coming from the 'near abroad' was instrumental for building a remarkably broad consensus on the disorderly domestic political arena. Certainly, none of the newly independent neighbours was taken as a hostile power; it was the internal instability and ethnonational conflicts in these states that were widely perceived as posing a threat to Russia's external interests and threatening to spill over inside its borders. This consensus included also an assumption that while Russia should rely on political and economic instruments wherever possible, it should not refrain from using military force where necessary.

The most remarkable intellectual attempt to define regional priorities and thus to limit Russia's aspirations was undertaken by Alexandr Solzhenitsyn (1990) in the twilight of the Gorbachev era in a long tirade against democratic modernization in general and the All-European House concept in particular. His 'grand design' – repeated with fresh vigour in his address to the State Duma in November 1994 – was to include in the new union around Russia only Ukraine, Belarus and Kazakhstan, since there would be no resources for anything larger.[34]

Another powerful idea stemming from the same Slavophilic root claims that Russia has special responsibility for some 25 million ethnic Russians who since December 1991 have suddenly found themselves residing in 14 'foreign countries'. There is no space here for elaboration on this widely discussed topic which since mid-1993 has become the most important one in the Russian foreign policy agenda.[35] What deserves mention is that it was the military who discovered the sensitivity of the 'Russians Abroad' issue back in mid-1992, when the Foreign Ministry was reluctant to accept even the modest recommendations from the Council on Foreign and Defence Policy.[36]

The military leadership found in the 'Russians Abroad' issue a perfect legitimation for its action in Transdniestria and tried to exploit it against the Baltic states, insisting on a link between troop withdrawals and the alleged discrimination against the Russian population. Accordingly, the Draft Military Doctrine (1992) identified as a possible *casus belli* the violation of the rights of Russians and 'those identifying themselves ethnically and culturally with Russia' – a definition that confused the then-moderate nationalists in Moscow and alarmed many Western experts.[37] But during 1993 emphasis on this issue was gradually

---

34 One direct political proposal from this scheme was to withdraw from Tadzhikistan and establish a new border between the 'Slavic Union' and the Muslim world along the southern boundaries of Kazakhstan. Another derivative was to 'amputate' Chechnya as a 'gangrenous limb'; Solzhenitsyn insisted on recognizing its status as an independent state after the war erupted in December 1994. See his interview with *Argumenty i Facty*, no. 1, 1995.

35 The report 'Russians in the Near Abroad' (1993) produced by the Gorbachev Foundation made an accurate early political diagnosis. For a good overview see Teague (1994), but the most comprehensive and in-depth study is Kolstoe (1995). My abridged analysis can be found in an article in the PRIO series 'Conflicts in the OSCE Area' (Baev, 1995a).

36 Thus, the report 'Strategy for Russia' (1992), arguing that the new Russian diaspora was actually an important asset for Moscow's 'enlightened post-imperial course', called for the creation of a special ministry with responsibilities for building stable ties with the Russian communities.

37 Fedor Shelov-Kovedyaev (1992b) carefully avoided this charged issue in his report mentioned above. Malcolm Mackintosh (1994), rather typically, takes the old wording as absolutely relevant for the new doctrine.

reduced as inappropriate. And in 1994, against the background of Yeltsin's repeated pledges to protect Russians 'not by words but by deeds', the military preferred to stick to the modest definition from the new Doctrine: this reduced the case to 'suppression of rights, freedom and lawful interests of Russian citizens'.[38]

Perhaps for Russia's concerned neighbours this did not sound sufficiently reassuring since, as Charles Dick (1994, p. 499) has put it: 'It is exceedingly moot as to whether Russia really has come to terms with their independence.' Still, there are reasons to assume that the military leadership and particularly the General Staff indeed tried to withdraw from a commitment on which they were hardly able to deliver. One reason is conflicting regional priorities in Russia's strategic and political thinking. In 1992, for the military it was indeed defence *à tous azimuts*. Contingency planning shifted from Transdniestria to Tadzhikistan and from Kaliningrad to the Kuril Islands. By mid-1993, the necessity of more concentrated efforts was recognized, and the focus of attention was placed on the Caucasus. The reasons for this will be analysed in greater detail in Chapter 5; it is the discord with the political thinking that is of relevance here.

In mid-1993, the latter – after the benevolent negligence of 1992 – started to assume a maximalist stance, claiming 'special rights and responsibilities' on the whole territory of the former USSR. This indiscriminate 'blanket approach' (in the words of Renée de Nevers, 1994, p.45) continued in 1994 – a good example being President Yeltsin's address to the UN General Assembly in September. However, the combination of Solzhenitsyn's 'Slavic Union' and the 'Russians Abroad' issue implicitly brought with it certain regional priorities: Eastern Ukraine and Crimea, Belarus, Northeastern Estonia and Northern Kazakhstan – hence the invariably nervous reaction in Kiev, Tallinn and Alma-Ata to every 'Russians-protective' statement in Moscow.

By mid-1994 it had become evident that the difference between the political and military courses concerned more than just regional priorities. After a short period of active interventionism in the second half of 1992, the military authorities became increasingly aware of both the risks involved and the limited resources available. Gradually they arrived at the conclusion that attempts to assume ultimate security responsibility in the disorderly space of the former USSR were not corresponding particularly well with Russia's current military posture. A more cautious and pragmatic military course made a sharp contrast with self-assertive and at times aggressive foreign policy rhetoric.[39]

On the surface this rhetoric seemed shallow and empty: at least nothing real was done for the 'Russians Abroad', and attempts to introduce the standard of dual citizenship in the CIS, which some analysts linked directly to the provision of the new Military Doctrine (Lepingwell, 1994c, p. 74), were not really consistent. But

---

38 Paul Kolstoe has drawn my attention to the fact that during 1994 the military newspaper *Krasnaya Zvezda* was perhaps the only major periodical that did not publish a single leading article on the 'Russians Abroad' issue.

39 The shift in Russia's foreign policy is often ascribed to pressure from the military and the necessity to 'neutralize' Zhirinovsky. I have argued against the first assumption in Baev (1994f), and Suzanne Crow (1994, p. 3) has made the point that the importance of the Zhirinovsky factor should not be overestimated: he has actually 'become a scapegoat for policies for which Russian officials would like to avoid responsibility and a foil for those who would like to continue calling themselves liberals'.

it is important to remember that the Soviet political tradition – which is still very much alive – is based on the pivotal importance of words. Adopting the new rigid political style, the Kremlin actually introduced a new nationalistic discourse which was more active and perhaps more comprehensible than the previous liberal-democratic one. In a paradoxical way, it is only the name 'Liberal-Democratic Party' that remains of the abandoned ideals, whereas the rhetoric of its leader Vladimir Zhirinovsky has now been taken over by Yeltsin and his entourage.

One might have expected a more sober military approach to prevent these words from becoming deeds, but then this should also serve to maintain the integrity of the Army. Deep cuts in the defence budget and the failure to pursue military reforms actually made the 'minimalist' course unsustainable. The severe crisis into which the Army sank in 1994 and growing tensions in the military leadership made it tempting for the Defence Ministry to abandon its cost-ineffective pragmatism and gamble with a 'small-and-successful' war. The military intervention in Chechnya dramatically changed the political landscape in Moscow. On the one hand, all the risks and consequences of the neo-imperial course were dramatically revealed – and the massive shift in public opinion left Zhirinovsky with only a handful of supporters. On the other hand, the democratic camp failed to build a politically meaningful anti-war coalition and only became more disorganized. The Chechen war aroused new doubts and concerns among Russia's neighbours about both Moscow's current intentions and its ability to control the internal chaos.[40] They certainly saw new evidence for the conclusion that the diminishing power and shrinking resource base only made Russia's behaviour more unpredictable. But fortunately, one factor that had figured quite high in the 'neighbour' relations in 1992–93 was now quite substantially downplayed – nuclear weapons.

2.4 Uncertainties of the Nuclear Dimension of Security

By early 1995 not much evidence could be mustered to justify such characteristics as 'crucial' or 'paramount' in speaking about the role of nuclear weapons in Russia's security. The strategic importance of the nuclear 'triad' has diminished drastically with the dismantling of the structures of confrontation; political efforts to claim some 'special privileges' referring to nuclear status are too importunate to be convincing; and even the non-proliferation agenda as related to the NPT Review/Extension Conference was not particularly demanding. Still, many well-qualified experts have come with warnings that, caught in the current turbulence, Russia could retreat to far more extensive political and military reliance on nuclear instruments (Arbatov, 1995c; Konovalov, 1994).

Indeed, while the transfer of the nuclear responsibilities from the USSR to Russia went unbelievably smoothly, and a series of agreements with Belarus, Kazakhstan and Ukraine in 1993–94 formally removed the residual obstacles, thousands of nuclear warheads still remain hostage to unpredictable political

---

40 These concerns were spelled out by Nursultan Nazarbaev, President of Kazakhstan, in an interview with *Moskovskie Novosti* (see Nazarbaev, 1995a).

developments. What further increases the uncertainty related to Russia's nuclear posture is the lack of consistent thinking; this is too obvious to be presented as an analytical conclusion, and could rather be taken as a point of departure. Russia inherited from the USSR the peculiar coexistence of various elements of nuclear thinking which used to provide a certain flexibility in arms control and buildup.[41] Three key elements could be identified as Symbols, Bargaining Chips and Weapons – and each of them went through significant changes, driven by its own internal logic.

Symbols traditionally came in two opposite categories (plus and minus), but they underwent a sort of 'positive evolution': fewer evils and more assets. Emphasis on the advantages of nuclear status is certainly justified in political terms – after all, there is not much else to support claims for the 'Great Power' role.[42] Less understandable is the diminishing public concern about the risks related to the nuclear complex; even recent accidents at nuclear facilities (like the explosion at the Tomsk-7 nuclear processing plant in April 1993) have failed to revitalize the 'Chernobyl syndrome'.

Bargaining Chips, used so skilfully by Gorbachev, were drastically devalued during hectic negotiations on START II.[43] Already in early 1993, Russian negotiators started to discover that there was not much left for further trade-off; they had done their best to secure US financial support for implementing the agreed cuts, but the political value of possible new reductions was now much lower. Actually, it was Ukraine who converted most directly its nuclear warheads into 'bargaining chips' in seeking to play Russia against the USA – and rather wisely winding up this potentially self-damaging game by January 1994. And in early 1995, Russian politicians saw the other side of the coin when the USA started to press for cancelling Moscow's nuclear deal with Iran, threatening to discontinue its support for Russia's nuclear disarmament.

Weapons were always the most obscure part of Soviet nuclear thinking. Notwithstanding the sophisticated calculations of the esoteric 'big strategy', every regiment commander in the Soviet Army routinely planned exercises for operations on a nuclear battlefield, and every Air Force pilot was trained to deliver a nuclear weapon on target. At the same time, in the strategy of deep offensive operations conducted by concentrated armoured formations (the best-known variant being the concept of 'operational manoeuvre groups'), nuclear exchanges were considered more of a problem than a solution.[44] This can explain why the

---

41 The most ambitious effort to integrate the various elements into a comprehensive concept was undertaken in the IMEMO and presented in the Yearbooks *Disarmament and Security* for 1987, 1988 and 1989. For a project conducted at the Institute of Europe see Baev et al. (1990).

42 For an early proposal to increase political reliance on the nuclear instrument see Karaganov (1992a).

43 Alexei Arbatov (1993a, p. 21) responds with bitter criticism: 'The treaty negotiations were conducted in a confusing and disorderly policy-making environment. It is difficult to know who the authors of specific decisions were, and why and how decisions were made.'

44 Beatrice Heuser (1993, p. 444) confirms in her research of the documents on the Warsaw Pact doctrine: 'None of the plans for the late 1970s and the 1980s, among those that have made their way to the Potsdam archive, speak of a first use of nuclear weapons by the Warsaw Pact without relating it to NATO first use preparations.'

Soviet military gave whole-hearted support to Gorbachev's denuclearization initiatives. But by the mid-1990s this attitude has changed to the opposite, as the Russian military have begun to develop a distinct inferiority complex.

Some new perceptions of the nuclear weapons – as Weapons – could be found in the new Military Doctrine, though its language is often so vague as to be nearly incomprehensible. It was the absence of the 'No-First-Use' principle that was immediately picked up by the Western mass media, though this old hypocrisy from the Brezhnev era (which even Gorbachev failed to make trust-worthy) hardly deserves any mourning and in any case was never taken seriously. But the proclaimed adoption of a 'normal' deterrence concept based on 'a mea-sure of uncertainty about a nuclear response to an aggression' (Grachev, 1994a, p. 4), indicated a trend toward increased use of the nuclear 'multiplicators' to compensate for conventional weakness. While in the USA many influential voices are arguing for conventional high-tech responses to new security chal-lenges, among the Russian military there is an understanding that this alternative is not available, nor is it likely to be in the foreseeable future.[45]

Therefore, one can easily find a certain parallelism in political and military thinking that are both changing in the direction of increased reliance on nuclear forces. On the other hand, there is also a deep perceptional gap since for the for-mer it is mostly about Symbols and for the latter, Weapons. This gap reveals itself in different ways in the two key areas of nuclear relations: with the USA and the West in general; and with the new independent states and Ukraine in particular.

As far as the West is concerned, the initial political project was to build a func-tional nuclear partnership already in the near future. The first phase inevitably placed emphasis on reductions in both strategic and non-strategic arsenals, sup-plemented with some structural links involving re-targeting, establishing new 'hot-lines' on operational levels, reducing alert status, etc. But by mid-1993, the difficulties in implementing such ambitious commitments started to mount, blurring the prospects of further developments.[46]

On the surface, the stumbling block was the issue of ratification of START II in the Russian Parliament, where opposition to what was perceived as elimina-tion of the very foundation of Russia's 'Great Power' status was indeed increasing.[47] This pro-nuclear campaign actually rendered hollow President

---

45 Paul Nitze (1994) has argued: 'The Gulf War offered a spectacular demonstration of the potential effectiveness of the smart weapons used in a strategic role.' But he admits that this lesson was not universal: 'The question remains, whether other powers, such as China and Russia, have come to this conclusion.'

46 It was the recognition of the lack of serious progress that drove Fred Iklé and Sergei Karaganov to bring together prominent American and Russian experts in order to develop a joint initiative. The project indeed produced a convincing programme for nuclear partnership (see *Harmonizing the Evolution . . .*, 1993), though somewhat ironically it was published the same month as the new Russian Military Doctrine was released.

47 Vladimir Lukin, Chairman of the International Affairs Committee of the State Duma, insisted in Spring 1995 that there was no need to rush ratification of START II, and that Russia should not waste its 'last-resort argument' until the issue of NATO enlargement could be clarified (interview in *Segodnya*, 28 March 1995).

Yeltsin's far-reaching proposals for further nuclear reductions – as presented in his address to the UN General Assembly on 26 September 1994 – which in any case did not seem to have had the benefit of serious thinking.[48] And the Russian government itself was by no means reluctant to play the nuclear 'trump card', especially in its uneasy relations with NATO. During the heated debates on the Partnership for Peace programme, Moscow repeatedly cited its nuclear status as an irrefutable argument for special privileges. But even the symbolic contacts between Russia and NATO's Nuclear Planning Group as envisaged by draft partnership programme were frozen when Kozyrev refused to sign it in December 1994. And the implicit threats to bring nuclear arguments into the NATO enlargement debate (making an 'asymmetrical response') were reminiscent of an express-comment of a Russian Security Council official on the nuclear aspects of the new Military Doctrine: that they were aimed at keeping the East European states 'out of the orbit of NATO and the WEU' (Foye, 1993b; Konovalov, 1994).

Obstacles to nuclear partnership also littered such fields as theatre defence against ballistic missiles, where competition had eliminated earlier cooperative projects (Keeny, 1994; Savelyev, 1994), and non-proliferation, where the US attempt to dissuade Russia from a nuclear deal with Iran failed to outweigh its financial lucrativeness. But all issues related to nuclear relations with the West felt only a minor impact from the Russian military, which remained reluctant to bring back nuclear Weapons on the agenda and preferred to leave the Symbols to the politicians.

The picture of nuclear relations with the new independent states in the CIS framework looks remarkably different. If in the new capitals, particularly in Kiev, the nuclear issue was enmeshed in political struggle, in Moscow from the very beginning it had been much less politicized but substantially more militarized. Back in early 1992, Russian politicians had few doubts in considering mind-boggling ideas about splitting up the nuclear heritage, finally settling on the compromise of a collective CIS nuclear 'umbrella'.[49]

The Russian military never subscribed to this compromise, instead pursuing a straightforward course of undivided control. The first and – with the wisdom of hindsight – decisive step here was the brilliantly organized operation on the withdrawal of all tactical nuclear weapons from Ukrainian territory in May 1992. This deserves a place in the annals of Russian military history. The next step was to secure control over the nuclear 'button'; the Russian Defence Ministry successfully blocked all attempts from CIS Commander-in-Chief Air

---

48 Only a few days before Yeltsin's visit to the USA, the Pentagon delivered its Nuclear Posture Review, concluding that further cuts in strategic and non-strategic arsenals could be envisaged after full implementation of START I and START II, but would in any case remain conditional on political developments in Russia (Starr, 1994).

49 Sergei Rogov (1993b) expressed the feelings in expert circles after the CIS summit in March 1992 when Moscow was only one step away from agreeing on 'nationalization' of the property of Strategic Forces: 'Such irresponsibility and incompetence could be explained only by the fact that the documents were being prepared in a hurry, without participation of experts . . . One cannot but be struck by how superficial was the attitude of Russia's leaders to the nuclear problem.'

Marshal Shaposhnikov to amend and clarify the initial agreement on the status of the Joint Strategic Forces. It was in May 1993 that the Russian military leadership decided that the situation was ripe for a decisive breakthrough and issued a statement that Russia should assume sole responsibility: 'The Joint Command, as well as the CIS, is not a state and cannot have the right to control and use nuclear weapons' (ITAR-TASS, 13 May 1993). The final decision to disband the Joint Command came at the meeting of the CIS defence ministers on 15 June 1993. General Grachev waited no longer than one day to send a special group to remove the 'nuclear suitcase' from Shaposhnikov, even though the latter had been authorized to keep it by the CIS Council of Heads of States (see *Moscow News*, no. 30, 1993).

As a result of this bureaucratic coup, for the first time in nuclear history, thousands of warheads and delivery systems came under exclusive control of the military. To be sure, in formal terms President Yeltsin is duly accompanied by an officer with the electronic 'key', but as the incident with a Norwegian meteorological missile in January 1995 illustrated all too clearly, real control is in the hands of the General Staff.[50] Accordingly, it was the military leadership that was ultimately responsible for the protracted nuclear negotiations with Ukraine in 1993 to early 1994.

In retrospect, one cannot but question whether the real goal of the Russian military was to denuclearize Ukraine. On the surface of it, there was a sustained pressure in which two main themes recurred: that Ukraine was unable to provide proper maintenance and service for nuclear weapons; and that Ukraine had attempted to establish 'positive operational control' on the ICBMs by breaking launching codes. While the first accusation was indeed well-founded, it was equally applicable to Russia itself.[51] As for the second accusation, which received a lot of alarmist attention in the Western mass media (see, for example, 'Ukraine Near Control . . .', 1993), it bluntly ignored the fact that since mid-1993 Kiev had discontinued any attempts to establish real control over nuclear weapons due to technical obstacles and financial costs (Orlov, 1993b).

For many Russian experts it was fairly obvious that the scheme of 'existential deterrence' would not work here: under no circumstances could Ukraine pose a nuclear threat to Russia, because of the inflexible and unbalanced structure of its strategic forces (Grigoryev, 1993). The best Ukraine could possibly obtain would be a quasi-nuclear status, quite possibly delegitimized by the international community. And Russia would have acquired a usable superiority vis-a-vis its weak and isolated rival, with plenty of opportunities for non-deterrable nuclear threats, first of all on the tactical level (Kincade, 1993). Well aware that

---

50 Despite the proper notification, that missile launch triggered the 'red' alarm. President Yeltsin had to interrupt his weekend relaxation in order to activate his personal control system, following the instructions of Defence Minster Grachev. Commenting on this episode, Nikolai Devyanin (1995), the chief designer of the nuclear launch system, blamed the 'owners' of the 'black suitcases' for not modernizing the whole system which remained based on the concept of pre-emptive strike, thus leaving very little time for cross-checking the alarm signal.

51 The Bellona Report prepared by Thomas Nilsen and Nils Bøhmer (1994) gives a highly accurate description of these problems.

'Nucraine' – to borrow the term from *The Economist* ('You'd Be Nervous . . .', 15 May 1993) – would be a far more serious security challenge to Europe, to the international non-proliferation regime and even to the USA than to Russia, the Russian military leadership sought to exploit its key role in the negotiations in order to reap some political dividends.[52]

It was Ukraine itself that denied the possibility of developing this game into a real strategic intrigue, by agreeing to sign the Trilateral Agreement with Russia and the USA in January 1994. And when newly elected President Kuchma, after some hesitation, confirmed Ukraine's commitments in August and persuaded the Ukrainian Parliament to ratify the NPT in November, the whole issue was basically resolved. From the point of view of the Russian military leadership, the area of nuclear relations with the new neighbours was reduced to practicalities related to obtaining some valuable strategic assets, such as the SS-25 mobile ICBMs from Belarus or the 19 most modern Tu-160 strategic bombers from Ukraine.

In general, since mid-1994 the nuclear dimension of Russia's security has become increasingly marginalized. On the political side, there is a growing awareness of the limited usefulness of the nuclear trump card for the demands of 'Great Power' status, and diminishing opportunities for building a nuclear partnership with the USA and NATO. On the military side, incentives to compensate for the rapid erosion of conventional forces by tactical re-nuclearization are countered by the assessment of the marginal usefulness of nuclear weapons in most potential conflicts. There is, however, also a negative side to this lessened attention to the nuclear posture: with it comes negligence of the exponentially growing risks involved in maintaining the nuclear complex. In fact, Russia now poses such a nuclear threat to itself that its nuclear status is becoming unsustainable and unfeasible.

2.5   Conclusion

The years 1991–94 were a period of unprecedented shifts in Russia's security perceptions. And it is not only the amplitude and the dynamics of these shifts that are so striking. That perceptions in the political elite and in the military leadership differed drastically is nearly a commonplace; indeed they followed different trajectories in their evolution, but by 1994 they had become remarkably compatible. In 1995, neither the political nor the military mindsets underwent serious new adjustments (the pre-elections fever was not helpful for drawing lessons from Chechnya) – and both developed a gap with the new reality which called for setting internal priorities in resource allocation and paring down external ambitions.

At the starting point in 1991 the political elite operated with an assessment of a dramatic reduction in all security challenges; in this new non-threatening

---

52 Russian Defence Minister Grachev persistently brought this subject into the agenda of his meetings with Western counterparts and particularly with the US Secretary of Defense. (See Lepingwell, 1994a.)

environment the West became the main potential ally and nuclear partner. The military stubbornly continued to see NATO as the potential enemy, but were much quicker in recognizing the new security risks in Russia's Near Abroad. They made deliberate efforts to establish control over nuclear relations with the newly independent states, first of all with Ukraine. Disillusionment in political circles as to the perspectives of partnership with the West, and the devaluation by the top brass of NATO's intentions and ability to intervene in the former USSR were a kind of parallel development. The outcome of both was to concentrate on Russia's vital security interests in the Near Abroad.

This conclusion, however, does not imply that there was a complete convergence in security perceptions. Among Russia's political elite, a sober assessment of potential risks has often been mixed with and even subordinated to ambitions to restore if not the empire then the sphere of dominance, to acquire control without responsibility, to maximize the advantages of the nuclear status or at least to play this game to get more public support. Within the military leadership, the corporate interests of preserving the integrity and internal cohesion of the Army have been the main driving force, dictating a more balanced and pragmatic approach to the conflicts in the Near Abroad. At the same time, the military leaders increasingly harbour the desire to compensate for the dislocation of the conventional power by bringing back nuclear weapons. It is among the military authorities that disregard of the international norms related to the use of force flourishes, thus undermining the whole political framework for stability in the geopolitical space of the former USSR. Clausewitz's invisible hand is drafting the military–political scenarios for the future; while those may be preferable to the designs of aggressive nationalism, the lack of democratic alternatives should give grounds for worry.

PART II

BEING MORE SPECIFIC

At this juncture, I would like to be more specific.

> Pavel Grachev, Russian Defence Minister, speaking about the irrelevance of the 'flank limits' of the CFE Treaty at the NATO Headquarters, Brussels, 24 May 1994.

> (Grachev, 1994a)

3
The Feasibility of Political Control of the Army

3.1 Introduction

The lack or even the very existence of political control of the Russian Army is a topic widely discussed among Russian experts and in Western strategic studies alike. Russia seems to be setting a unique pattern among the post-Communist states. If – though this hypothesis is now looking increasingly improbable – Russia is still moving towards a democratic model, then it is a prerequisite to have efficient political control embodied in such institutions as a civilian Ministry of Defence and parliamentary committees to supervise the military budget. If, on the other hand, Russia is slipping into the more habitual authoritarian model, rigid central control of the military structures is crucial to make this work. In fact, neither is happening in Russia at the moment, nor are there convincing reasons to believe that the Army is planning a coup d'etat to establish its own control of politics.

It does, however, seem possible to speak about a sort of coexistence between the military, trying to secure professional sovereignty, and politics, where various forces are trying to pull the Army to their side. Despite other forays, the main area of interactions and conflict between the two is economics, or more specifically the budget; and it is here that we should seek the answer to the question of how durable this state of coexistence actually is.

3.2 Political Transformations and the Politicization of the Army

At several crucial junctures in Russia's recent history, it was the Army who determined what the direction was to be. Obvious examples here are the two mini-revolutions in Moscow, with the outcomes decided by a few thousand men and a few tanks: the abortive coup in August 1991, and the assault on the White House in October 1993. Less obvious examples could be when the military leadership chose Yeltsin against Gorbachev in December 1991, thereby tilting the balance of the fate of the entire USSR; and when the Minister of Defence (certainly forced by political pressure) decided to start the war against Chechnya in December 1994, marking a crucial watershed in post-Communist reforms. In Chapter 5, I will also argue that the Army's decisions concerning peace-making operations were the main factor in setting the key political guidelines for Russia in the Near Abroad.

From these examples, however, we should not draw the conclusion that the Army has become an independent policy-maker. That the Army was forced to make certain political choices is one thing, but none of these choices could qualify as interference or intervention.[1] Not that the widely used – especially by the military leadership – slogan 'the Army is outside politics' necessarily holds that much water; but the fact of being 'inside' and making certain decisions does not mean being the determinant force.[2] The hasty retreat of the Army from the political arena – after appearing on it in such a dramatic way in October 1993 – suggests that the seemingly self-evident dilemma – political control of the military or military control of politics – could in fact have two negative answers. In December 1994 and January 1995 strong resistance in both the high command and the rank and file against the war in Chechnya unleashed a new wave of speculation about an 'imminent' coup, but already by late February the 'military opposition' had become marginalized.[3]

In the following pages I develop a twofold argument: (a) that the two main obstacles for establishing efficient political control over the Army were the weakness of political institutions and the extended professional independence of the military; (b) that the main factor that has prevented the military from going into politics is, paradoxically, the politicization of the Army.

The first assumption is based on the distinction between subjective and objective control, as defined by Samuel Huntington in his classic *The Soldier and the State* (1957). Subjective control involves consistent efforts on the part of the political leadership to penetrate the Army through special mechanisms and to guide its behaviour. Objective control means an accord between the political and military elites in which the former has supreme authority and the latter acknowledges it but enjoys broad professional autonomy. Huntington's conclusion, as elaborated by Kolkowicz (1967, 1984), was that objective control in various forms was typical of democratic societies, while totalitarian and particularly Communist regimes relied primarily on subjective control.

This conclusion has been challenged by several analysts (Colton, 1979, 1990; Gustafson, 1990); here John Lepingwell's analysis (1992) is perhaps most convincing. He argues that while some elements of subjective control (first of all the Main Political Administration) were indeed used by the CPSU, objective control still played the key role. Lepingwell's major postulate is the congruence of values in the two elites, and indeed the conflict of values – as identified by Kolkowicz – remained an analytical construct backed up by scant empirical evidence; in

---

1 Otto Latsis (1993a), liberal *Izvestia* columnist, argues against a common misunderstanding of what constitutes military interference in politics. He insists on a narrow definition: a decisive action against the political leadership. This would completely acquit the behaviour of the Army in all the cases mentioned above.

2 The Army's role in deciding single-handedly the outcome of the October 1993 crisis provoked an avalanche of speculation concerning its future as a major influence on political decision-making. See Arbatov (1993c), *The Economist* ('Yeltsin Regrets', 9 October 1993), Fitchett (1993), Foye (1993g) and Odom (1993); for a different view see Taylor (1994).

3 While many analysts rushed to blame the military for the war, Richard Woff (1995b, p. 20) got it right: 'To its credit, virtually the entire Russian high command opposed the operation from the beginning, believing it violated the Russian constitution.' (See also Galeotti, 1995.)

retrospect, all that could be discovered were some minor differences related primarily to the cultivation of military professionalism.[4] The Soviet political
leadership from the mid-1960s (learning its lessons from Khrushchev's conflict
with the military elite) up to the mid-1980s granted the top brass exclusive
authority within its domain, as long as this remained duly limited. This
arrangement actually placed industrial interests ahead of military ones (and the
Military–Industrial Commission de facto above the General Staff) which in
turn led to the gradual hyper-militarization of the state. Perestroika was initially
simply an attempt to restore the viability of the socialist model by reducing the
military burden. This attempt was not only hopeless, it was self-defeating, since
by then the Soviet Union 'did not have a war machine, it was a war machine',
as Christopher Donnelly (1992, p. 30) reiterated. In the course of Gorbachev's
suicidal struggle with this war machine, the elements of subjective control over
the Army were eliminated, and the two main foundations of objective control – the military monopoly on decision-making as related to the Army, and
the congruence of core goals – were shattered.

The military leadership saw a direct threat to its fundamental values coming
not so much from Gorbachev's disarmament initiatives as from his flagging
ability to control political developments. By late 1990 only two options were left
open: to force Gorbachev to take a rigid course, or to opt for another leader.[5] An
unholy alliance with the KGB bosses was contracted in order to pursue the first
option, and only when it proved to be fruitless was KGB guidance accepted in a
desperate attempt to oust the President/General Secretary. Herein lay a paradox:
on the one hand, the military leadership wavered too long before overstepping
the bounds of the professional code of conduct, but on the other hand, the officer corps was not at all ready to follow. The failure of the August coup resulted
in a severe crisis in the Soviet Army which for some time was quite out of
control, in both political and military terms.

Even in the euphoria of his triumph, Russian President Yeltsin recognized that
Gorbachev could not be definitely ousted without the consent of the Army. So he
promised to the military leadership the one thing that could secure this consent – that the all-Union integrated military structures would be preserved.[6] And
the top brass at that moment were too disoriented to question the feasibility of an

---

4 To Lepingwell's eloquent though intrinsically academic arguments this author can add his personal experience from joining the Communist Party in the late 1980s while working in a military
institute.

5 Gorbachev, drifting backwards in late 1990, promised at a meeting with over 1,000 officers to
make significant corrections to his course (Foye, 1990). He gave serious consideration to the petition
signed by several top generals in December to declare a state of emergency in some critically unstable
areas and dismissed Shevardnadze's dramatic warning about dictatorship as too emotional. But
when the military decided to push the still-hesitant leader by staging the clash in Vilnius in January,
Gorbachev instead retreated to political compromises with the leaders of the republics.

6 Gorbachev appealed to the military leaders on 10 December, arguing that the Commonwealth
which had been improvised a few days earlier by Yeltsin, Kravchuk and Shushkevich would
inevitably involve splitting up the Army (which was true). Yeltsin, appearing on the same podium the
next day, promised to pay proper attention to the problems of the Army but refrained from any
mention of civilian control.

arrangement which implied an Army without a state. It is hard to say how seriously Yeltsin took his commitment but he certainly invested some political efforts in this doomed project. Perhaps already in early 1992 the military had developed some second thoughts on the dissolution of the USSR, but by that time it had become an irreversible *fait accompli*. Moreover, the ground for developing these thoughts into something meaningful was undermined by the snap decision taken by the majority of officers in Kiev, Odessa and Carpathian military districts: to swear the new oath of allegiance to the newly declared Ukrainian state.

Perhaps the first months of 1992 provided a unique 'window of opportunity' for establishing a new political control over a disorganized Army in search of a mission and a master. In retrospect, one might argue that some elements of subjective control (enlisting into various 'reform groups' the young officers involved in the Democratic Russia movement) could have been introduced to facilitate the transition, but the main emphasis was necessarily the creation of a civilian Ministry of Defence.[7] Relying more on his political instincts – which were telling him that the Army would not be a real problem for some time but could very soon become an invaluable ally – Yeltsin preferred to evade this Herculean work. A justification was readily available – the need to concentrate on the economic reforms embodied in Gajdar's 'shock therapy'. And the latter was instructed to ignore for the time being the fact that lavish spending on the Army (but not on the defence industries) was incompatible with his pattern of financial austerity.

In early May 1992 Yeltsin signed the decree 'On the Creation of the Armed Forces of the Russian Federation' which stated:

> In order to prevent loosening of the command and control of the troops, those should be conducted through the structures of the former Ministry of Defence and the General Staff of the USSR until the central mechanisms of the military administration of the Russian Federation are formed.[8]

This made it clear that the superficially reshuffled military bureaucracy was to remain quite unreformed – and quite unaccountable. As Richard Sakwa (1993, p. 311) pointed out: 'Russia ultimately was forced simply to rename the Soviet Army the Russian Army, and thus incorporated the worst as well as the best of the old traditions.' Lost was the opportunity to establish effective political control over the Army: Yeltsin himself could hardly have harboured any illusions that his decree 'On Assuming the Responsibilities of the Commander-in-Chief' signed the same day would provide for such control.[9]

---

7 Some preliminary work had been done in Russia's State Committee on Security and Defence. Back in autumn 1990, the Deputy Head of this Committee, Vitaly Shlykov, mentioned, at an international seminar at the Institute of Europe, Moscow, plans to employ several hundred experts and administrators in this quasi-Ministry. The year 1991 saw more of such paperwork, but by December the Committee had a staff of 18 people. (Personal records.)

8 This package of military decrees was published in *Krasnaya Zvezda*, 9 May 1992.

9 Christopher Donnelly (1992, p. 37), one of the best analysts of the post-Soviet military, has written that 'large bureaucratic institutions continue to function irrespective of the lack of government, and the largest and most cohesive of these institutions is the armed forces. As of mid-1992, the armed forces hierarchy was increasingly determining its own agenda.'

What started to emerge in Moscow from mid-1992 was a sort of coexistence between the political and military institutions. For the military leaders, expanding and securing their sphere of professional sovereignty became the fundamental goal. The primary task was identified as to eliminate any internal opposition and thus deny the politicians any future possibilities of subjective control. This was accomplished by forcing many of the young democratically oriented officers to retire.[10] Then the top brass started to play – with an acumen no one expected from such a gung-ho paratrooper as General Grachev – on the growing controversies between the President and the Parliament.

It could be said that the Law on Defence, approved in September 1992 by the Parliament after lengthy debates, provided for rather rigid state control of military structures, despite the last-minute withdrawal of the stipulation that the position of Minister of Defence could be occupied only by a civilian. But bureaucratic in-fighting in and around the newly created Security Council reduced its ability to perform any actual control functions to mere paper-pushing. As for legislative control, especially on the budget, the military leadership managed to sidestep it, demonstratively taking sides with the President.[11]

By late 1992 it was becoming clear that the very basis for objective control was missing: a new set of values had crystallized in the military elite – and one remarkably different from what had been proclaimed as the foundation of the 'transfigurated' democratic Russia (primacy of the law, good-neighbourliness, respect for human rights, etc.). Now the new core values of the Russian military could be described as survival of the Army itself; preserving its key missions and upgrading its status in the society; restoring Russia's 'Great Power' status; enhancing internal stability; and consolidating the sphere of influence in key areas of the Near Abroad.[12] These were values easy to translate into political objectives. The Army started to urge politicians to pursue them, at times taking the initiative in its own hands.

In early 1993, President Yeltsin began to embrace the political agenda proposed by the Army, at least as far as the last three of the core values were concerned. His increasing inability to deliver on the first and primary objective – survival of the Army – was somewhat compensated by deliberate efforts

---

10 Vladimir Lopatin (1992), one of those young reformers, wrote bitterly: 'It is done now what Yazov has failed to do: the faith in the Army in the possibility of reforms is undermined; the opposition to conservative generals from the young officers demanding changes is eliminated; those who started the fight for reforms (like General A. Vladimirov) are expelled from the Army.'

11 Grachev put things remarkably straight in a June 1993 interview: 'A couple of times I was called to the Supreme Soviet. So I had to repeat to them my message – spare the Army your political squabbles. But I have regular contact with the President. Every day' (Grachev, 1993).

12 Many Western experts are inclined to include 'strong nationalistic sentiments' as one of the core values (see Lepingwell, 1992, p. 547). The Russian military leaders' campaign for protection of the 'Russians Abroad' in late 1992 seemingly supports this interpretation. But, as will be shown in more detail in Chapter 7, this campaign was instrumental in achieving other goals. Actually, the split of the former Soviet Army along republican borders greatly increased the ethnic homogeneity of the Russian Army. Nationalism – never deeply rooted in the officer corps – became even less relevant.

to reassure the military elite of his readiness to protect its interests.[13] These efforts could never qualify as control-building: perhaps a better term would be loyalty-buying, which also included salary raises by Presidential decrees, conferring the rank of general on long lists of candidates, etc. Nor were results long in coming: when the critical test was set in early October 1993, the tanks not only arrived to back the President but indeed blasted the Russian White House, raising dramatically the threshold of political violence.

Why did the Army accept this political role? This question has in fact been analysed thoroughly by several prominent Western experts (Desch, 1993; Foye, 1993f; 1994f; Taylor, 1994), so few new perspectives can be added here. The easy part of this question concerns the choice between the two sides: indeed the erratic behaviour of the Parliament, the low public standing of its leaders (including 'shadow' Defence Minister Achalov), its legislative encroachments on the Army's interests (e.g. the Law on Military Service from February 1993), even the pseudo-democratic slogans with which it embarked on the final confrontation with the President – all made the Parliament an unacceptable partner for the military leadership. More difficult actually is the question of why the Army went so far: natural as it was for the top brass to take sides with the President, it was obviously less so to seek to crush his opponents with tanks. What looms beyond the analysis is an assumption about a carefully planned crisis. Such planning would have involved making a very precise calculation of an amount of street violence far from threatening the state powers but sufficient to urge the Army onto the stage. It would have also taken into account a very high probability that the crisis in its course would run out of control – as indeed it did. However implausible, such an assumption at least offers some explanation of an otherwise inexplicable situation.[14] And that the Defence Ministry took hours to reach the final decision to bring in troops testifies to doubts about crossing this Rubicon. A retreat to the purely professional niche after performing the role of gendarme would have seemed highly unlikely.[15]

It was widely expected that the Army would present an impressive bill to the rescued politicians; Michael Desch (1993, p. 473) included in the list: increased military spending, only minor cuts in the size of the military, greater military

13 At a meeting with the High Command on 10 June 1993, Yeltsin praised them for restoring control, rebuilding cohesion and raising morale in the Army. Vice President Rutskoi, in a counterattack, charged that the armed forces were in a disastrous state and accused the President of ignoring the most important of the new values. However, he himself had very little to offer. (See Foye, 1993a.)

14 With the wisdom of hindsight, it is possible to find a loophole that could have allowed the Army to avoid direct involvement: indeed, the chaotic assault on Ostankino was repelled by the MVD troops and by the morning of 4 October the rebellious forces retreated to the White House (see Taylor, 1994, p. 28). But the shock of seeing the centre of Moscow seized by an ecstatic crowd of some 10,000 extremists and hooligans with OMON nowhere in sight, could have been healed only by extraordinary measures.

15 Michael Desch's (1993, p. 487) footnote remark 'I suspect that they were holding-out for concessions from Yeltsin rather than hesitating', ascribes too much perfidy to the top commanders who were well aware that the majority of the officer corps would strongly disapprove 'gendarmerization'. Accusations from the President's Office that the generals were 'paralysed into inaction' perhaps go too far on the other extreme.

autonomy, a harder line on certain domestic and foreign policy issues, and in general a greater voice for the military in the policies of the Yeltsin government. Indeed, some voices in the Army clamoured for rewards (notable in this chorus was General Burlakov, Commander of the Western Group of Forces). Moreover, the new Military Doctrine which was approved only one month later could be interpreted as formal confirmation of new privileges for the Army (Foye, 1993g). But in real terms the military leadership failed to extract anything of substance from the President, and the new doctrinal guidelines provided no hedge against further cuts in the military budget.[16] Actually, the commanders of the Army – contrary to the many predictions of their impending accession to the political Olympus – were far more concerned about restoring shattered cohesion in the officer corps. They clearly wished to be able to leave that tragic day behind.

To explain why the Army was unable to obtain any lasting dividends from its ultimate performance and retreated with such haste from the political arena, we need to look into the issue of politicization of the Russian Army. Stephen Meyer (1991/1992) has proposed a useful model for this process which includes both the enabling factors (glasnost and democratization; the collapse of CPSU authority; the rise of semi-democratic legislatures) and motivating factors (the rise of anti-military currents in society; poor living and working conditions for officers; the explosion of nationalism; the rise of republican power and the decline of the centre; threat of dissolution of the Union). Meyer concludes that politicization reached its peak in August 1991; thereafter, 'military professionalism, built over decades, was being destroyed' (p. 28).

While the first half of this conclusion is unquestionable, the second half was perhaps formulated too categorically. Immediately after the abortive coup, the new military leaders discovered that the now-politicized and demoralized Army was nearly uncontrollable. The only way to prevent its further disintegration was to reverse the trend and strike back hard against politicization. This meant banning any party activities in the ranks; it also meant the forced retirement of those who had been personally involved in political campaigning – in this case, the committed democrats (Clarke & Reisch, 1992). Gradually, some of the enabling factors (such as wooing the Army) came to naught, while those related to disintegrative trends – being as relevant for Russia as they had been for the USSR – sometimes developed the opposite effect and encouraged the comeback of military professionalism.

The Army's leaders were skilful in playing on the controversies between the President and the Parliament: but they also took care to hold up the slogan 'the Army is outside politics' and to declare its 'neutrality' in the internal

---

16 Stephen Foye, whose brilliant analysis is based on the paradigm of the high political profile vs low professionalism of the Russian Army, insists that the impact of the 'top brass' on Russia's foreign policy after October 1993 indeed increased. (See Foye, 1993g, 1994f.) But much of his evidence appears circumstantial, while there are strong reasons to believe that Yeltsin's new course was rather a product of his own deliberate attempt to embrace and co-opt the nationalistic trend. The only real litmus test for measuring the pressure from the Army is its share of resources, but Foye while acknowledging the 'fundamental contradiction' between the 'appetite of Russia's generals' and the pattern of reforms, has stopped short of admitting the negative result.

confrontation.[17] All too soon, however, the need to make a choice during the October crisis recalled the spectre of politicization. The Army saw its fragile integrity threatened by many splits: within the military leadership, between the central authorities and regional commanders, inside the ranks, etc. In the ensuing weeks, the Ministry of Defence made extraordinary efforts to restore the chain of command, avoiding any cadre changes and using the approval of the Military Doctrine as its main trump card. Still, the credibility of the Yeltsin regime was seriously undermined, as was shown convincingly by the parliamentary elections in December 1993.[18]

Through most of 1994, the military leadership maintained its efforts to keep the Army out of politics. The relative stabilization on the political arena was indeed helpful. Defence Minister Grachev's 'strong recommendation' that members of the military should not stand for parliamentary elections also bore fruit, minimizing the influence of various self-appointed 'political commissars'. One consequence of this broad de-politicization was that the Army's loyalty to the President remained a touchy question. Yeltsin had to rely on the complete personal dependence of Pavel Grachev; primarily he sought the solution by giving more power to his own Security Service, which in Autumn 1994 marched triumphantly onto the political arena. Even Moscow's experienced political analysts were taken aback when presidential bodyguards raided the office of MOST-Bank (which had sponsored independent mass media) and when the head of the Security Service extended his authority to such areas as arms exports and the transfer of high technologies (Parkhomenko, 1995). By comparison, the Army indeed seemed to be 'outside politics' despite its occasional involvement in the officially proclaimed 'battle' against organized crime.

The only military figure who persistently remained outside this reassuring picture – other than Defence Minister Grachev, who had to confirm again and again his closeness to the President – was General Lebed, Commander of the 14th Army in Transdniestria. His far-reaching statements and provocative interviews were apt reminders that the cancer of politicization of the Army had not been cured but simply pressed under the surface; the politicians would always deny responsibility for bringing the tanks onto the streets but would certainly try to do it again (Simonsen, 1995a). Just how close Lebed was to the truth became clear in late 1994, when the dynamics and logic of various intrigues in the centre prompted policy-makers to seek an 'easy solution' somewhere on the periphery. Waging a 'small-and-successful' war in Chechnya seemed the obvious

---

17 Such a line remained much more attractive for the majority of officers than the militant anti-Yeltsin course declared by the Officers Union headed by Stanislav Terekhov. While this semi-official organization claimed a membership of some 30,000 officers, further events revealed it as a minor group operating on the fringes of the military community (Foye, 1993g).

18 There were plenty of speculative reports that the Army voted predominantly for the ultra-nationalist platform of the Liberal–Democratic Party headed by Vladimir Zhirinovsky. No reliable statistics exist, but there is no doubt that in those electoral precincts with a high proportion of military voters, support for the LDP was more than the national average of 22.8%. Yeltsin admitted that about one-third of the servicemen voted for Zhirinovsky; in fact most estimates put the figure close to 40% (Felgengauer, 1993a). Noteworthy is that another 20% of the military voters supported the Communist Party. For useful comments see Brusstar & Jones (1995).

choice. Many in the military leadership and perhaps even Grachev feared that this unpopular and costly campaign would bring the already weakened and demoralized Army to the verge of disaster; paradoxically, however, the political influence of the Army was not strong enough to prevent blundering right into it. And this war – much like the Crimean War in 1855, and World War I in 1917, and the Afghan War by the mid-1980s – eroded the support base of the regime and put under question its survivability, but this time the Army found itself at the very centre of politics.

3.3 Political Leaders and the Military Elite

In so centralized a state as Russia, where crucial decisions often depend on a 'smoke-filled-room' deal struck by a handful of actors, the style of personal relations between the Kremlin and the top brass is an essential subject for analysis. Indeed, the key to understanding the decision-making about the Chechen War – incomprehensible as it was – should be sought rather in personal matters than in strategic interests. Central here is how relations among key players influence the relations between the two sets of bureaucracies.

Gorbachev inherited from the stagnant Brezhnev years a Party–military union based on wartime friendships, boon companionships and family ties so tight that it took several years to find a weak link. The chance arrived when a total dark horse – the young German Mathias Rust – landed his Cessna next to the Red Square in May 1987, providing a legitimate cause for sacking the Minister of Defence and prompting a major reshuffling in the ranks. Gorbachev's choice in this situation was perhaps one of his gravest mistakes. The necessity of kick-starting the reforms in the Army called for an able and resourceful leader.[19] Instead, Gorbachev, seeking guarantees against the danger of military opposition, preferred General Yazov – a man whose main merits were an inability to think big and a reluctance to take responsibility for risky decisions. As an additional precaution, this 'controllable' Defence Minister was supplemented by an inexperienced Chief of General Staff; it was not until late 1990 that Gorbachev started to discover that even such weak figures as Yazov and Moiseev could become dangerous under heavy bureaucratic pressure.[20]

Yeltsin certainly tried to learn from Gorbachev's mistakes. By August 1991 he had several high-ranking military men on his side, while Vice President Rutskoi, as an Air Force Colonel, was courting the officer corps. Yeltsin was also quick to welcome newcomers, and Air Marshal Evgeny Shaposhnikov became his

---

19 Christopher Donnelly (1989, p. 122) pointed out two years later: 'There was still quite a lot of dead wood amongst the High Command and at middle (formation command) levels, in contrast to the recent appointment of some very young and bright commanders.'

20 Actually, it did not take a serious effort to strip Gorbachev of power, but real leadership was necessary to confront Yeltsin, who by then enjoyed broad public support. The only man among the military who was ready to go the whole way in the coup was perhaps the Commander-in-Chief of the Army, General Varennikov. In 1994 he declined the amnesty declared by the Parliament and in August appeared in court alone – to be acquitted 'in the absence of any crime'. For praise for his determination see 'Russian General . . .' (1994).

trusted plenipotentiary in the market of military relations with other, suddenly independent republics.[21] But when the question of appointing the first Russian Defence Minister came to a short-list choice, Yeltsin found out that personal loyalty was not enough to make his protégé General Kobets an acceptable candidate.[22] For several weeks the democrats in Yeltsin's entourage cherished the idea of a civilian Defence Minister, and Andrei Kokoshin advertised himself as a front-runner. But Yeltsin wisely decided not to alienate the Army (perhaps due to a presentiment that he could soon need its support), and Kokoshin had to console himself with the position of Deputy Defence Minister.[23]

Although by no means an obvious choice, General Pavel Grachev emerged as the only candidate acceptable to all partners in the amorphous coalition that ruled Russia in early 1992. For the democrats, his refusal to participate in the August coup was a convincing testimony; for the reformers, the 44-year-old Commander of the Airborne Troops was a representative of the new generation in the Army; for the military, the decorated Afghan war veteran looked like the leader they so desired. Certainly, there were also many senior officers in the Ground Forces and in the General Staff who were stunned by such leap-frogging, but their dissatisfaction was hardly a serious political factor at the time. More important were the glowing testimonials given to Grachev by Vice President Rutskoi, who took close to his heart the comradeship among the Afghan veterans.

From the very beginning, serious doubts were expressed by some civilian and military experts on the new Minister's ability to handle the extremely complex responsibilities – and with time the grounds for them only increased.[24] As Stephen Foye (1994f, pp. 3–4) eloquently put it, 'Grachev's relative youth and his rather narrow and specialized background appeared to have left him ill-prepared intellectually for managing not only one of history's greatest and most painful strategic retreats but also for overseeing the restructuring and reinvigoration of an army left in tatters by the wrenching historical changes of the preceding five

---

21 Shaposhnikov's further political evolution brought him to the camp of the radical democrats; and in the December 1993 elections he joined the list of the Russian Movement for Democratic Reforms, which failed to cross the 5% threshold. For an example of a remarkably distorting analysis ascribing to him 'Bonapartist' ambitions see Nguyen (1993).

22 General Kobets tried to counter arguments on the shortcomings of his career in the Rear Services by a series of 'conceptual' articles. (See, for example, Kobets, 1992.) After the nomination of his rival Grachev, he disappeared from the political frontline; in June 1993 Yeltsin made him a Deputy Defence Minister and in the midst of the October 1993 crisis he briefly resurfaced, pushing for resolute measures against the opposition (Sokolov, 1993; Taylor, 1994, p.25). But throughout the bitter arguments and split in the high command about the Chechen War, Kobets was nowhere in sight.

23 He coped surprisingly well with his portfolio of economic and technological policy (capitalizing on his academic background on the US military–industrial complex) and managed to avoid responsibility for the severe crisis in armaments procurement (see Kokoshin, 1994; Woff, 1994a). In several critical situations, he demonstrated loyalty to both the President and the Defence Minister (see Foye, 1993e). It is only his habit of 'thinking big' on strategic matters in interviews that perhaps betrays his further career ambitions (see Kokoshin, 1993, 1995).

24 Russian periodicals frequently quoted unnamed military sources describing Grachev as 'possessing the intellect of a regiment commander' and 'incapable of thinking at a level higher than the division'. Stephen Foye (1993a) has presented a good overview.

years.' But it may well be that for many in Yeltsin's entourage these concerns spoke rather in favour of the new Defence Minister, in much the same way as Yazov's narrow-mindedness had been his main attraction for Gorbachev.

If there were indeed expectations among Yeltsin's advisers about how 'controllable' Grachev would prove, he wasted no time in disappointing them. His first bold step was to assemble a team of Afghan war veterans and put them in key positions in the Ministry, pushing elderly bureaucrats into retirement. This reshuffling hardly made his critics in the military hierarchy any happier, but at least it enabled the Defence Ministry to act decisively (albeit not necessarily rationally) in the burning conflicts in the Near Abroad, political considerations notwithstanding.[25]

Quite soon Grachev also had to make a political choice that would eventually decide the outcome of the tug-of-war between the President and the Parliament. Putting aside his sentimental feelings toward Rutskoi, Achalov and even Lebed, Grachev judged accurately that the only man who could guarantee his survival on the top of the hostile military hierarchy was the President. Already in October 1992 he started to act accordingly, convoking a meeting of the Defence Ministry Collegium and obtaining from it a declaration of loyalty to the President as Commander-in-Chief. In early March 1993, Grachev and his deputies had a meeting with Yeltsin where they allegedly demanded that he take 'resolute measures' in order to end the power struggle; this information was conveniently leaked to the international press, most probably by the presidential team that was sending up a series of trial balloons before the first attempt to introduce 'special rule' (Higgins, 1993). At that time Yeltsin was forced to retreat due to the defection of several close allies including Yuri Skokov, Secretary of the Security Council. Grachev, however, remained on his side, and even had the courage to blame the Parliament for the crisis when he addressed it in plenary session. And each of these pro-presidential moves was rewarded by increases in officers' salaries, 'positive' budget corrections, promotions, etc., which allowed Grachev to prove to the 'neutralists' in the ranks that his course was indeed beneficial to the Army.

The final test of the Army's loyalty came in September–October 1993. In the earliest phase of this crisis Yeltsin carried out a smart manoeuvre, telling the military exactly what they wanted to hear: they should continue their professional business 'as usual' and not respond to 'provocations'. This allowed Grachev to turn 'neutrality' into the pro-presidential line. When the violent unrest in the capital left only military means to restore order, the Army – or rather the Tula, Taman and Kantemirov Guards Divisions based outside Moscow – delivered on the Minister's commitments.[26] With time, the circumstances of this tragedy became only more muddled: there were conflicting reports on the controversies

---

25 This led Stephen Foye (1994f, p. 2) to make the point that Grachev's nomination 'was one of the first manifestations of a schizophrenia in the policies of the Russian government that was to emerge with increasing clarity in the months that followed'.

26 Grachev bluntly dismissed rumours of his wavering and claimed that the Army had 'rallied like never before, became more united and manageable'. He was especially insistent on belittling the role played by General Kobets. See, for example, the sharp comments from his press conference by Igor Chernyak (1993). As Brian Taylor (1994, p. 13) puts it in his remarkably accurate description: 'Grachev felt that he and the military had narrowly avoided a catastrophe.'

among the military leadership, dubious explanations of the late arrival of troops; the President's own memoirs may have explained the charged atmosphere in the Kremlin corridors but did little in the way of providing the facts.[27] The amnesty declared by the Parliament in February 1994 removed the opportunity to clarify what had actually been planned in this crisis and where it had run out of control.

The genuine panic in Yeltsin's entourage during the hectic night of 3 October is in itself a testimony that Grachev was not one of the crisis managers and that others set the stage for him to act. Nor could there be any doubts on Grachev's part – his previous choices had linked his survival inseparably to that of the President. The explanation for ambivalences in the Minister's behaviour (he kept telling the President that the troops were arriving from mid-day 3 October, while they actually entered Moscow in early morning of 4 October) should be sought rather in his uncertainties whether the troops would follow the combat order. Hence his decision to bring in Moscow battalions from three 'palace guard' divisions and several other elite units that all had enjoyed special presidential attention.[28] By the dawn of 4 October the tanks had arrived in front of the White House: this perhaps marked the peak in Grachev's career. Subsequent political developments, however, were to reveal both the very tenuous basis of the victorious alliance between the President and the Defence Minister, and the growing isolation of both within their respective institutions.

Yeltsin sought to legitimize his victory by declaring a referendum on the hastily redrafted new Constitution and by the parliamentary elections in December 1993. But the heavy vote behind the statist-nationalist platform of Zhirinovsky and the questionable approval of the Constitution (again due to the endorsement by Zhirinovsky) were compelling testimony that Russian society rejected the programme of democratic reforms.[29] Yeltsin tried some cabinet reshufflings, but by and large this was a case of sailing without any sense of purpose except his own survival. The relative political stability through most of 1994 allowed the consolidation of new political forces over which Yeltsin had no control. His powers were becoming illusory, rendering his leadership irrelevant.[30]

---

27 The style of the President's prose speaks for itself: 'I was trying to bring my combat generals out of their state of stress and paralysis. I saw that the army, despite all the assurances of the defence minister, for some reasons was not able to come quickly to Moscow's defense and fight the rebels . . . The army, numbering two and a half million people, could not produce even a thousand soldiers, not even one regiment could be found to come to Moscow and defend the city. To put it mildly, the picture was dismal' (see Yeltsin, 1995, pp. 275–276). Tatyana Tolstaya (1994, p. 7) is severe: 'Yeltsin's final battle with the Parliament is the largest and murkiest part of his "autobiography". Everything having to do with it is lies and innuendoes.'

28 As Mark Galeotti (1993b, p. 539) accurately points out: 'Little demonstrates the essentially haphazard and ad hoc nature of the pro-Yeltsin forces' response [more] than the composition of the Defence Ministry's contingent.'

29 Reports on voting in the Army were contradictory; Yeltsin admitted only that one-third of the servicemen supported Zhirinovsky. One undeniable fact was that the strongest vote for the latter came from precisely the units involved in the October events. (See Sherr, 1994.)

30 Lilia Shevtsova (1994b, p. 6), one of the sharpest analysts with unquestionable democratic credentials, pronounced the verdict: 'This is the logic of the development of any ruling regime free from societal control: it turns into a self-propelling force that either takes leaders hostages or changes them at will.'

Grachev found himself in an even worse predicament. As early as September–October 1993, a group of high-ranking military officials had openly distanced themselves from the Minister. Leaders of this group were General Kolesnikov, Chief of the General Staff, and General Gromov, First Deputy Defence Minister. The former commanded a lot of respect among the bureaucrats; the latter, with his Afghan reputation and high political profile, had a strong support base among the field officers.[31] Grachev's position against them was seriously undermined by the fact that in 1994 he was unable to secure the requested military budget, not to mention delivering any salary increases, social benefits, etc. This was seen as evidence that he had accomplished the mission prescribed by the politicians and henceforth had lost any influence in the Kremlin. Grachev's only chance was to compromise Kolesnikov in the President's eyes. And indeed, this he managed to do, through the so-called 'Version One' – the sensational fabrication of a plot to overthrow Yeltsin that hit the headlines in March 1994.[32]

But in a few months' time the blow to Grachev turned out to be devastating. It came from the anti-corruption campaign, which the majority of the Russian political elite had tended to dismiss as nonsense. Claims and counter-claims on bribery were widely used during the noisy quarrels of 1993, but after the elections the issue ceased to be relevant, leaving the general impression that the political class was corrupt beyond redemption. Actually, it was then Vice President Rutskoi who first raised the question of corruption in the Western Group of Forces (WGF) in spring 1993, and the Defence Ministry felt obliged to stand firm against these political accusations.[33] Another reason for this bureaucratic self-defence was the bitter reflections of the fierce anti-Army campaign in the mass media during late perestroika.[34]

Pursuing this protective course, Defence Minister Grachev in mid-1994 insisted on making General Burlakov, commander of the disbanded WGF, yet another Deputy to himself.[35] That was to prove a disaster. While it was perfectly

31 Gromov failed to arrive at the decisive meeting of the Defence Ministry Collegium on the night of 3 October. This is hardly surprising, in view of his 'clean record' from the August 1991 coup. For the most comprehensive analysis of his biography see Wilcox (1994).

32 Kolesnikov was named as one of the plotters; this seemed plausible because of rumours about his impending resignation that had leaked from the Defence Ministry in February. See the leading article in *Moskovskie Novosti* with the telling headline 'Nice Gesture? Or Resignation of the Chief of the General Staff?' (Zhilin, 1994b).

33 Yury Boldirev, then Head of the State Control Department, resigned when Grachev persuaded Yeltsin to cancel the investigation in the WGF. In a later interview in *Izvestia* (4 November 1994) he said that in November 1992 he had reported personally to Yeltsin on the findings and submitted a report together with a draft of an 'appropriate' edict (see Boldirev, 1994).

34 On Gorbachev's uncertain attempts to use glasnost as a tool for pushing reforms in the Army, see Holloway (1989/1990).

35 Besides investigative journalism (see, for example, Zhilin, 1994c), astonishing examples of corruption in the ranks were presented in the report of General Nosov, Chief Military Procurator, published in *Moscow News* ('Army: Everything for Sale', 1994). Sergei Yushenkov, Chairman of the Committee on Defence of the State Duma, went public with a harsh critique of Burlakov's nomination, calling it a 'disgrace for the Army'. In an unprecedented instance of insubordination, General Lebed refused to allow a commission headed by General Burlakov to inspect the 14th Army, calling the latter 'a common swindler' (see *Moskovskie Novosti*, no. 40, 1994).

possible to deny new allegations, a bomb that killed a journalist involved in the investigation marked a point of no return. Burlakov was hastily dismissed 'in order to protect the honour of the Armed Forces', but that failed to pacify the infuriated mass media or to satisfy the parliamentary investigation, which focused on the Defence Minister personally.[36] Yeltsin's ambivalent confirmation of his confidence in Grachev did little to make the situation any better.[37]

It stands to reason that the coming thunder forced Grachev to join the gamble with a 'small-and-successful' war in Chechnya initiated by the Federal Counterintelligence Service (FSK) and the Ministry of Interior. This intervention will be addressed in more detail in Chapter 6 and in the concluding chapter, but the sharp split in the military leadership which it catalysed should be mentioned here. For any military man – with or without a strategic mind – it was probably all too clear that this adventure would be neither small nor successful. Throughout summer 1994, Grachev had made every possible effort to avert the war (including brokering a ceasefire which was in turn broken by the FSK), so his infamous 'give-me-one-regiment-and-two-hours' bravado should not be taken as the plan for the campaign.[38] By the late autumn, Grachev's field for manoeuvre had narrowed to two options: either to join the 'party of war' (in which the key figures were Stepashin, Director of the FSK and Erin, Minister of Interior) and confront his own domain; or to go against the 'presidential line', with uncertain support from the rank and file. And the fierce anti-corruption campaign had left Grachev totally dependent on the presidential entourage – effectively denying him an opportunity to consider the second option.[39]

One opposing voice was fairly certain: in mid-November, General Gromov had gone public with an open criticism of the attempt to disguise Russian troops as the Chechen 'opposition'.[40] Gromov stressed that the Army was unprepared for this large-scale operation but would inevitably be held responsible for the outcome. In order to deny Gromov the best opportunity to consolidate the 'dissidents', the Defence Ministry Collegium was completely excluded from handling the operation, but further events proved that the anti-war position had even wider support in the military leadership than Grachev feared. Deputy Defence Minister General Valeri Mironov (1995) firmly stated his opposition, and even Grachev's most trusted deputy General Georgi Kondratyev (who was in charge of the assault on the White House in October 1993) took the 'No' side.

---

36 Richard Woff (1994b, p. 21) perhaps got it right: 'The case against Gen. Grachev is that he is too much Yeltsin's tool and mouthpiece.'

37 Responding to charges in the mass media, Yeltsin called Grachev 'the most able and respected Minister', which invited new critical salvos. But in a few weeks, addressing the annual meeting of senior officers, Yeltsin neglected to mention his Minister at all, which was interpreted as an indication of forthcoming sacrifice.

38 Grachev made this statement during the press conference with the Danish Defence Minister on 28 November 1994.

39 As Mark Galeotti (1995, p. 51) concluded: 'Marginalized in Moscow, despised within the officer corps, Grachev proved too weak to resist the official line for long.'

40 Major General Boris Polyakov, commander of the elite Kantemirov Guards Tank Division, submitted his resignation in November in protest at the FSK 'hiring' officers from his division to do 'contract jobs' in Chechnya (see Woff, 1995a, B36-4).

Commander of the Airborne Troops General Evgeni Podkolzin, who in November came with his own plan for a strike operation, was infuriated by the organization of the campaign and the heavy losses; First Deputy Commander of the Army General Eduard Vorobyev refused to take control of the operation (Zhilin, 1995). Unbelievably poor planning of the invasion was in itself the best testimony that the General Staff had had little (if any) part in it. Chief of *Genshtab* Mikhail Kolesnikov kept a low profile and refrained from taking sides with the opposition, but he was careful to deny responsibility.[41] Kolesnikov's master-plan was aimed at taking the *Genshtab* out of the Defence Minister's control and making it a 'presidential institution'; this innovative idea captured public attention in February–March (Arbatov, 1995a).

This plan may have looked like innocent bureaucratic restructuring, but it actually involved a major reform of the military hierarchy. Relieving the Defence Minister of any direct control over troops essentially meant making him responsible primarily for the budget and the military–industrial complex, while the General Staff would acquire a new political role. The first consequence involved sacking Grachev, who was obviously unsuited for the new role – and this again raised the question of whether to try a civilian or go for another military leader. This option had been widely discussed during the previous autumn (Woff, 1994a) but Grachev held on, declaring that generals would never obey orders from a civilian since no such thing had ever happened in Russia (Kryuchek, 1994). This argument sounded less than convincing after Grachev's own notably poor command in Chechnya, but the real question actually was about the 'controllability' of a new military chief, i.e. the head of the *Genshtab*. While Andrei Kokoshin perhaps appeared all right for an 'economy-oriented' Defence Minister, Mikhail Kolesnikov's loyalty to the formal Commander-in-Chief was indeed questionable, and no other figure was readily available. Relying primarily on personal bonds and dependence to keep his team moving, Yeltsin shied away from the decision that could have meant a step toward a post-Yeltsin period. Grachev, against all odds, again held his position and was given carte blanche to crush the 'military opposition'; during March, Generals Gromov, Kondratyev, Mironov and Vorobyev were either forced into retirement or moved to obscure positions. General Lebed – another vociferous critic of the war in Chechnya and of Grachev's personal role in waging it – submitted his resignation in May.

This hardly 'normalized' relations between Yeltsin's entourage and the military elite, but direct political intervention on the part of the latter was prevented – at least, for the time being.[42] The 'top brass' had a war to deal with;

---

41 Actually, when the *Genshtab* became involved in conducting the campaign in late January 1995 and Lieutenant General Kvashnin, First Deputy Chief of the Main Operational Directorate, took control of planning, Russian troops started to capture Chechen strongholds one by one. And the operational plans released at the high command meeting in late February showed none of the 'improvisations' of the first month of the war. (See Woff, 1995c.)

42 Grachev also survived the Budennovsk crisis in June, when a unit of Chechen fighters penetrated deep into Stavropol *krai* and took several thousand civilian hostages. Erin and Stepashin lost their jobs for their dismal performance, but Grachev – despite his several quite irresponsible statements – was not even reprimanded. See the leading article in *Moscow News*, 7–13 July ('Grachev Saved . . .', 1995).

indeed this was a war which brought the Army into such a crisis that extraordinary efforts were needed to handle it. But a new round of political battles was in the offing – and the newly retired and still active generals could be counted on to take an active part in it .

3.4   Military Reform: Small Steps to Nowhere

The dramatic political changes of Autumn 1991 created a wave of new expectations concerning a military reform for which Gorbachev had never had either the time or the stomach. Several breathtaking radical projects were quite seriously discussed in the Russian leadership – which, after the defeat of the Communist Party, had been showing some symptoms of an omnipotence complex. But in a matter of months this enthusiasm gave way, not to a more realistic approach, but to the complete abandoning of any consistent efforts at reform.

The programme for a new Russian Army as formulated by several military reformers included such steps as: (a) radical reduction of the Armed Forces to a level of 1.5 million men, maybe as low as 1 million; (b) rapid professionalization of the Army and the abolition of conscription; (c) restructuring the main elements of the Armed Forces, including merging the Air Defence Forces and the Air Force, elimination of the Strategic Directions (TVD) command level, and creation of Mobile Forces; (d) transforming the Defence Ministry into a civilian structure responsible primarily for the military budget (Kobets, 1992; Lobov, 1993; Lopatin, 1992). One stumbling-block was the clearly unilateral 'Russia-goes-its-own-way' character of this programme, which was in contradiction to plans to preserve as much as possible of the integrated military structures in the CIS framework (Lobov, 1993). With all the unavoidable disagreement on priorities and proceedings, there had remained a common point of departure that the Army would never be able to reform itself, so strong and sustained political guidance was taken as a prerequisite.

To shoulder the enormous burden of this reform, President Yeltsin had to make a choice between two basic managerial models. The first one was to rely on a new team of experts who would build from scratch a civilian Defence Ministry, in much the same way as Yegor Gajdar and his team had attempted to destroy *Gosplan* and other old economic superstructures. The second one was to rely on a devoted high-ranking military reformer who would mobilize and organize the internal 'revolutionary' forces.[43] Rejecting the first option for fear that real political control could alienate the military, and unable to find a reliable reformer in the ranks, President Yeltsin ended up by effectively burying all plans for major reforms.

When General Grachev moved into the office of Defence Minister in May 1992, it was presumably with a single file entitled 'Mobile Forces' in his brief-case.

---

43 Stephen Peter Rosen (1991) has proposed a model according to which political leadership could initiate necessary changes in the military bureaucracy by promoting a resourceful military innovator who would overrun the internal resistance by creating new career opportunities for the younger generation. For a useful analysis see Kaufman (1994).

The problems related to this file will be addressed in more detail later, but the emptiness of his 'Radical Reform' folder makes it impossible to put all the blame on bureaucratic resistance. Grachev's mandate as provided by the President was to restore the controllability of the Army and secure its loyalty, but not to reform it. Accordingly, the key issue for the remainder of 1992 and for early 1993 was to rescue as much as possible from the collapsing military structures of the Soviet Union. This essentially meant that Russia entered into possession of the Soviet Army writ small on the level of combat units but – since the 'savings' started in Moscow – with basically the same swelled administrative apparatus.

To satisfy the public demands for radical changes, the newly created Defence Ministry hastily came forward with a reform plan developed in the General Staff.[44] The *Genshtab* – which, aside from some changes at the top, had managed to preserve itself – became the main bastion of conservatism. The 'go-slow' approach was not necessarily that bad at the time, but led directly to a critical accumulation of military problems by late 1994. With the wisdom of hindsight, we can say that the current crisis was built into the original reform plan, which covered the 7-year period up to the year 2000 and was divided into three stages.[45]

Phase One was obviously a preliminary one; by the end of 1993 the basic inventory of the Armed Forces was to be completed and more detailed plans for further reforms should be elaborated. During this time the necessary reductions related to the division of the Soviet military structures among 12 new independent states (three Baltic states refused to be listed as heirs) were to be completed, and unavoidable withdrawals should be planned properly.

Phase Two extended up to the end of 1995 and primarily included the numerical reduction of the Armed Forces to the level of 1.5 million. Envisaged structural changes included the elimination of the TVD command level, the establishment of the Mobile Forces Command and the beginning of the reorganization of the Ground Forces from the army-division to the corps-brigade structure.

Phase Three involved the most serious transformations to be conducted by the year 2000. On the macro level, the key issue was the merger of the Air Defence Forces and Strategic Rocket Forces (much reduced according to the START agreements) into the Air Force. On the operational level, the idea was to abandon the system of military districts and establish instead four to six joint strategic commands, starting with geographically remote Far Eastern MD and Transbaikal and Siberian MD (the latter two could be integrated into one

---

44 The plan was quite compatible with the Draft Military Doctrine, which postulated a continued military threat from NATO and paid remarkably little attention to low-intensity conflicts. This inability to recognize new threats which by then had materialized in a number of violent conflicts could only be attributed to the desire to preserve the core mission of the Army and thus to maintain its main structures.

45 The outline of the plan first appeared in *Krasnaya Zvezda*, 21 July 1992. General Barynkin, Head of the Main Operational Directorate of the General Staff, explained its provisions in much detail during a series of parliamentary hearings on the Law on Defence in June–August. (Personal records.)

strategic command).[46] This phase would also involve the complete withdrawal of all Russian troops from foreign countries and re-deployment according to new strategic plans.

What was particularly advantageous about this plan, from the viewpoint of the military leadership, was that it allowed for some breathing-time, which was indeed necessary due to uncertain assessments of both requirements and capabilities. Credit should be given to the new team in the Defence Ministry which managed to minimize the external influence on the military structures and establish reliable lines of internal control remarkably quickly. Top-level transformations were basically completed by early 1993; one of the new (and perhaps unexpected) features proved to be a more 'militarized' or maybe 'operationalized' Defence Ministry.

The whole military-economic area, including relations with industry, was placed under control of Deputy Defence Minister Kokoshin and thus not only separated from the military structures per se, but relatively isolated and later – due to severe budget cuts – marginalized.[47] Hence the split in the former monolithic military–industrial complex, into the Army as such and the defence industries which were left to struggle with the problem of conversion.[48] A further consequence of this split became apparent by late 1994: the increasing technological backwardness of the Russian Army due to lack of funds for procuring the modern weapons still being produced en masse by the monster-plants.[49] This rendered irrelevant the emphasis in the reform rhetoric (typical since Gorbachev's 'reasonable defensive sufficiency') on quality instead of quantity. It furthermore revealed how empty was the claim in the new Military Doctrine of 'utilizing the latest achievements in technology to create armaments of new generations ahead of competitors' ('Basic Provisions . . .', 1994).

By early 1993, bureaucratic consolidation of the Defence Ministry started to generate tension in relations with the General Staff, which during the previous reshufflings had acted as a system-preservation mechanism protecting the 'essential cores' of the Army (Kaufman, 1994). Besides being 'the brain of the Army', the General Staff is authorized to exercise operational command over all units in the Armed Forces through the Main Staffs of their five major branches

---

46 Defence Minister Grachev explained this plan during his visit to Far Eastern and Siberian MD in April 1993. An interesting point was that the commander of the new formation (holding the position of Deputy Defence Minister) would have more control over and responsibility for the forces. See Lepingwell (1993a, b). These plans were confirmed in principle but no progress was reported during Grachev's later visit to this area in October 1994.

47 Actually, the parts of the Russian Defence Ministry currently (early 1996) under Deputy Minister Kokoshin form a mechanism resembling the Western model of defence ministry.

48 While the drama of conversion cannot be followed in this book, one recent piece of analysis marked by both keen insight and bold generalizations deserves mention. This is Shlykov (1995).

49 Sergei Rogov (1994a) perceptively pointed out that the mass production of relatively modern weapons in Russia was a sort of postponed reaction to 'Reagan's bluff' of the early 1980s, when several ambitious research projects were launched in the USA but then discontinued. Russian defence industries continued to implement similar projects non-stop. The Defence Ministry contributed to this crisis by delivering its procurement orders to the enterprises early in 1994, i.e. before the defence budget was approved. As a result, by the end of the year some 3,000 billion roubles were unpaid, causing some 400 military plants to halt their production lines and another 1,500 to work part-time.

(Mackintosh, 1994).[50] But Defence Minister Grachev aspired to retain operational control in his own hands. In fact, he established a separate chain of command under his Deputy General Kondratyev, due to the latter's responsibilities for crisis situations and peace-keeping operations.[51] Moving further into the domain of the General Staff, Grachev took under personal supervision the buildup of the 'frontline' North Caucasus Military District. Already by mid-1994, however, it had become obvious that his ambition to be in charge could hardly compensate for his lack of ability. Grachev's poor performance in handling crucial budget problems and his flagging reputation among the ranks convinced President Yeltsin to establish more direct links with the General Staff and upgrade its chief General Kolesnikov to a full member of the Security Council (Galeotti, 1994b). But this 'palace intrigue' stopped far short of giving the *Genshtab* anything like a free hand in proceeding with reforms which by then had become urgent even for the most conservative career bureaucrats in uniform.

These intra-system disturbances hampered the implementation of the initial reform steps planned for the first phase. Moreover, political pressure forced the military authorities to upgrade the priority given to the issue of withdrawal from foreign countries. The Defence Ministry was made responsible for accelerating redeployment not only from East Germany, but also from the three Baltic states (for an analysis of the intrigue involved, see Chapter 7) and besides faced the necessity of evacuating troops from Azerbaijan.[52] Attention – maybe nervously but quite understandably – was concentrated more on the 'Out' than on the 'In' side of the withdrawal process. Indeed, it may have come as a surprise that this unprecedented 'homecoming', which involved moving more than 50 divisions to Russian territory, resulted in a net decrease in the real strength of the Army. Even the redeployment of the first-line divisions from East Germany, which had considerable financial support from the erstwhile 'hosts', with very few exceptions ended up with an overall loss of combat readiness.[53]

---

50 As Christopher Donnelly (1992, p. 30) has pointed out, the Soviet/Russian concept of the General Staff follows closely the Prussian model. However, Donnelly went perhaps too far with the assumption that 'The General Staff not only designed the armed forces, it also defined the threat and determined the direction for the militarization of the entire nation. More to the point, the General Staff alone did this.' The problem was that this concept which indeed implied a 'complete monopoly of authority on military matters', had been implemented in full only when the General Staff was headed by such able leaders as Marshal Ogarkov or Marshal Akhromeev. In the late 1980s, Gorbachev deliberately reduced its role to mere database and broker among powerful branches.

51 Kondratyev, in turn, relied primarily on the Airborne Troops Command. A special position of Deputy Commander of Airborne Troops for Peace-keeping was established in late 1992; General Staskov, appointed to this position in October 1993, maintained direct command and control lines to all 'hot spots', except Tadzhikistan. (See Woff, 1995d.)

52 Benjamin Lambeth (1995, p. 94) recognized this: 'It [the Russian Army] also has recently concluded one of the most extensive and least appreciated force withdrawals in recent times, namely its voluntary and, in the view of many officers, humiliating return home from three generations of forward deployment in Eastern Europe and the Baltic states.'

53 Thus, the 10th Guards Tank Division redeployed from Magdeburg to the bare steppes of Voronezh *oblast* by Autumn 1994 had its T-80 tanks permanently parked while personnel were busy building barracks. Soldiers and sergeants who had been eager to sign contracts to serve in Germany immediately broke them off in Russia; many young officers handed in their resignation. (See A. Kolesnikov, 1994.)

The easiest way to address the problem of disorganized and combat-unworthy units was to disband at least half of them; indeed during 1993 three tank divisions and 16 motor rifle divisions were excluded from the official records. On their base, seven new style motor rifle brigades were formed, thus marking a first step towards new structures (see *The Military Balance* . . ., 1993–1994, pp. 96–97). Debate on this transition remained rather marginal, so the implementation of a new idea – as too often in Russian history – started before it had been properly thought through.[54] Some further reductions in the number of units were conducted during 1994: one tank division and four motor rifle divisions were disbanded, and four new brigades were formed (see *The Military Balance* . . ., 1994–1995, p. 110). Not only was the tempo of unit reshaping now slowing down, but the lack of a consistent blueprint was becoming more of a problem as many of the new brigades remained ill-equipped and poorly trained units with unspecified combat missions.

Another avenue exploited by the military leadership was the consolidation of control over all paramilitary forces. Speaking to the Parliamentary Committee on Defence in May 1994, Chief of the General Staff Kolesnikov pointed out that the Federal Counterintelligence Service, the Ministry for Emergency Events, the Federal Agency of Government Communications and the Presidential Guard had de facto now created their own armies (Rahr, 1994). Kolesnikov emphasized that the budget could ill allow retention of all these formations which together had 4 million men 'under arms'. Two months later, Grachev put forward a proposal to subordinate Border Troops as well as railroad, construction and civil defence forces to the Ministry of Defence, thus permitting better distribution of scarce resources. This proposal was bluntly rejected by the Security Council, which strongly favoured strengthening the Border Forces; its commander General Nikolaev (former Deputy Chief of the General Staff) was even made a full member of the Council directly answerable to the President (Foye, 1994l). Actually, by late 1994 the central control over various paramilitary formations was looser than ever before. The presidential Security Service was perhaps the most striking example, but even inside the Armed Forces, the Defence Minister's ability to exercise control over the elite *Spetsnaz* units subordinated to the GRU had become rather questionable (Clark, 1995).

None of these organizational changes, however, managed to arrest the erosion of morale in the Army. Long since forgotten were the early reform ideas about 'human rights of the servicemen' (Lobov, 1994, p. 77), about humanization and democratization of the whole atmosphere in the Army; moreover, crime and violence in the barracks were flourishing. Defence Minister Grachev found no better way to build a 'fighting spirit' than to launch a major propaganda offensive. In spring 1993, he started to proclaim from every rostrum that 'a

---

54 There were also more specific proposals concerning changes on the tactical level from the battalion-regiment-division structure in the Army to a supposedly more flexible battalion-brigade one. For a useful discussion of this issue see Hall (1993). Such opponents of the new structure as Army General Gareev (1992) provided no better counter-argument (except reference to the experience of World War II) than accommodation difficulties since many facilities and barracks were regimental-size.

psychological turning point' had been reached and that the bulk of the troops were fully combat-capable due to resumed normal training.[55] Certainly, this was exactly the message which the political leadership wanted to hear. At a meeting with senior officers in June 1993, President Yeltsin eagerly joined in the self-complimentary campaign, praising the Army for its role as guarantor of external security and internal stability.[56]

If this campaign was a success anywhere, it was primarily among Western security experts, who had been seeking to prove that there still existed a military threat from the East.[57] From the Russian perspective, the somewhat schizophrenic nature of this rhetoric was all too obvious, especially if held up against the forecasts of catastrophic consequences of financial cuts and the disastrous situation with the draft, uttered by the same military leaders quite often in the same breath (Lopatin, 1993). It indeed does not take in-depth expertise to conclude that training was substantially reduced if not a single division-size field exercise was conducted during 1993–94. And for the thousands of houseless officers serving in the 'combat' units with few if any soldiers, Grachev's self-serving exorcism sounded perhaps less than overwhelmingly convincing.[58]

By late 1994 the failure to implement or even launch a comprehensive reform programme had created a dangerous dilemma: either further cuts in the military budget (unavoidable in the protracted economic depression) would push the Army from degradation to disintegration; or the military leadership would secure 'proper' financing, thereby pushing the country into economic catastrophe. Grachev proved unable to deliver the second option, but the presidential entourage preferred to ignore the first one. Speaking at a meeting of senior officers of the Armed Forces in mid-November 1994, President Yeltsin declared that 'the Armed Forces are becoming proper for Great Russia'. Adding some criticism, he pointed out certain serious deficiencies and pronounced himself 'not completely satisfied' with the level of combat readiness, but neglected to make any mention whatsoever of military reform (Korotchenko, 1994). However, this was a not problem that could simply be ignored. General Lebed (1994a) – with all his reputation of a maverick – in a few days sent a strong warning that if the huge body of the Army should be left to decompose, the state would not go unpunished.[59]

It was only after the disastrous New Year (1995) assault on Grozny that the

---

55 In an interview with *Nezavisimaya Gazeta*, Grachev (1993) declared that his meetings with junior officers had convinced him that with 'a new faith in the future of the Russian Army' they were able to concentrate on combat training which had been forgotten since 1988.

56 For Yeltsin's remarks see *Krasnaya Zvezda*, 11 June 1993. A penetrating analysis of the background of the whole campaign can be found in Foye (1993c).

57 Thus, Malcolm Mackintosh (1994, p. 537) argued that credit should be given 'to those professionals who have provided their state with some viable form of military machine with such limited precedents and resources'.

58 General Podkolzin, Commander of the Airborne Troops, complained that of 9,500 officers in his troops, 6,500 did not have flats. His conclusion was bitter: 'If we do not have money to feed our soldiers and to give houses for our officers, all talk about the on-going military reform is just empty' (Podkolzin, 1995).

59 Calling for concentrating the best intellectual efforts on preventing the catastrophe, General Lebed blamed Grachev personally for presenting some minor and unavoidable structural changes, and even the introduction of a new uniform, as real reforms.

real scale of the disaster in the Armed Forces became clear. A new round of spec-ulations about military reform boiled up – and again waned. For many experts it was only too obvious what the policy-makers refused to admit – that the sole answer was to entrust the fate of the Army to a new team of leaders who could make meagre resources into a lever of reform.

3.5   Military Budget: Reform Instrument or Control Lever?

Details and technicalities like those discussed above are rarely a subject for political discussions. Quite often the whole issue of military reform is reduced to two interlinked questions: how much – men and money – is enough?

Russia inherited Armed Forces of about 2.7 million, of which 2.1 million were within her borders (Lepingwell, 1993b, p. 12). In July 1992, the reshuffled Russian Ministry of Defence produced its first proposal to reduce the total strength of the Army to 2.1 million by 1995. But no one in the General Staff was able to provide an accurate estimate of what was available, or to argue convincingly what was needed. Hence the lack of confidence in the debates on the Law on Defence which was approved by the Parliament in September 1992. According to this Law, by 1 January 1995 no more than 1% of the pop-ulation should be serving in the Armed Forces. This essentially introduced a ceiling of 1.5 million. Not until February 1993 was the general inventory more or less accomplished; keeping the details to himself, Grachev announced that the authorized strength of the Russian Armed Forces was 2.34 million, while alternative estimates of its actual strength gave a figure of 1.8 million and several months later only 1.5 million (Lopatin, 1994).

Until spring 1993, the Defence Ministry had been too preoccupied with the problem of the many troops arriving in Russia from abroad to be concerned about this discrepancy. Acknowledgement of its real scale came together with the Law on Military Service, approved by the Parliament in February 1993 against the objections of the military authorities. This Law not only reduced the duration of compulsory military service from two years to 18 months but also introduced a series of exemptions which would allow some 84% of potential draftees to avoid conscription. Already after the spring draft of 1993, the Russian Army had a manpower deficit of some 910,000 soldiers. The real disaster came in the autumn, when two batches of conscripts – some 580,000 men – were demobilized, while only 150,000 were available for the draft.[60] In turn, this figure had to be reduced by 25–30% due to draft-dodging, which had become a common and non-punishable practice not only in many republics, but also in Moscow.[61]

---

60 Immediately after the vote was taken, Chief of the General Staff General Kolesnikov issued a warning that the situation in the autumn could become critical. (See his interview in *Segodnya*, 23 February 1993.) In June 1993, the Defence Minister complained in greater detail that 'there are 1,814,000 men of draft age in the country but 1,515,000 of them have legitimate rights to deferment'. He also added that up to half of those drafted were taken by the Border Troops and the Ministry of Interior. (See Foye, 1993c.)

61 In late November 1993, only about one-third of those eligible for draft in Moscow reported at the enlistment offices (see *Izvestia*, 23 November 1993). According to official military figures, some 70,000 young men evaded the draft in 1993 (see Foye, 1994b).

Aside from complaints, the only real attempt to reverse this debilitating trend was undertaken by the military leadership in November–December 1993, when Defence Minister Grachev on several occasions stated that an Army of 1.5 million 'would be fine for a compact state without such vast borders', but that Russia needed at least 2.2 million men in its Armed Forces. Nobody in the government dared to object, keeping in mind the invaluable support rendered by the Army during the October crisis, but on the other hand, nothing was done to meet the new demands except one presidential decree permitting the draft of students attending technical schools (Ermolin, 1993; Falichev, 1993).[62] The military leadership had to face the fact that the conscription system was fundamentally flawed and damaged beyond repair (Felgengauer, 1993b). For several months, officials avoided any comments on the manpower problem. Not until early March 1994 did they present a final estimate that gave the actual strength of the Army as only 60% of the authorized level of 2.34 million (Foye, 1994a). *The Military Balance* (1994–1995, p. 109) gave a figure of 1,714,000, emphasizing that 'no combat formations, including airborne and the divisions earmarked for peacekeeping, have more than 75% of their authorised strength and roughly 70% of divisions have less than 50%'; according to my own estimates, by early 1994 the Russian Army had shrunk to less than 1.2 million (Baev, 1994a).

By that time, many in the Russian military leadership had finally realized that the argument about the strength of the Army essentially concerned not millions of men in uniform but billions of roubles in the budget. Throughout 1992, the financial demands of the military leadership had been satisfied by and large, although their spending habits were obviously incompatible with the chosen economic reform strategy known as Gajdar's 'shock therapy'. But as *The Economist* put it, 'Mr Yeltsin may be gambling that he can best protect his reform programme by not confronting his opponents head-on' ('Yeltsin Turns Nasty', 1992).

In 1993, the situation with the military budget started to get more tense. Defence Minister Grachev and his civilian Deputy Minister Kokoshin found it difficult to communicate with Finance Minister Fedorov, Deputy Prime Minister Gajdar and other reformists, so they tried to make President Yeltsin the lobbyist for the Army. In June 1993, Yeltsin announced that the military budget for 1993 would be increased from 3.5 trillion to 5.35 trillion roubles. The Defence Ministry was not satisfied and one month later put forward a figure of 8.8 trillion, which after bitter debates with the Finance Ministry was reduced to 6.35 trillion. The main military newspaper *Krasnaya Zvezda* in July published a series of articles with the clear message that the military budget was not the place to look for savings – an argument that the 'Guns of October' certainly made more convincing. Nevertheless, Deputy Finance Minister Pochinok, sparing no

---

62 This decree was expected to provide only some 2,500–5,000 new recruits, so the whole draft pool for autumn 1994 was estimated at 250,000 men (Rogov, 1994a). A much further-going step would be to draft college students as had been done in the late 1980s, but as Stephen Foye (1993g, p. 50) pointed out, 'Any significant increase in the army's share of the nation's human or economic resources, particularly in light of Russia's mounting economic crisis, could revive the animosity that many in the civilian professional class manifested toward the military bureaucracy in the late 1980s.'

compliments for the Army, made it blatantly clear already in late October that no financial rewards should be expected, and that the 1994 military budget would remain on the same level of about 5% of GDP (Foye, 1993g).

Both Gajdar and Fedorov resigned in a matter of months, but the thrust of the warning remained. The Defence Ministry was told to submit the absolute minimum as its financial request (which turned out to be some 80 trillion roubles); in the draft budget proposed by the government in March 1994 this was more than halved (to 37 trillion). Deputy Defence Minister Kokoshin immediately sounded the alarm on the catastrophic consequences since the Army would have to demobilize some additional 400,000 men (Bush, 1994). The battle of the budget continued up to early June, when the State Duma approved the final figure of 40 trillion. President Yeltsin withdrew his earlier promises, instead offering the confusing advice to use some 'non-budgetary appropriations' (Lepingwell, 1994b). Grachev had no other choice than to announce three days later that the authorized strength of the Armed Forces would be reduced to 1.9 million men by 1 October 1994 (Foye, 1994i).

It was clear that the military leadership lacked a consistent approach in adapting to financial austerity. In strategic planning the crucial problem was the allocation of meagre resources between maintenance, procurement and R&D, whereas for the top brass the most relevant question concerned salaries. President Yeltsin himself gave highest priority to the salaries issue – hoping thereby to buy the support of the Army. Back in mid-1993, some officials had been astonished to discover that 'a platoon commander receives more than a professor, and a teaching surgeon earns ten times less than a regiment commander'.[63] Yeltsin laid on more bonuses on the eve of his September confrontation with the Parliament, and by the end of 1993 a lieutenant in the Airborne Forces was earning some 70,000 roubles a month (about $60) and twice this amount when serving in a 'hot spot' (Gordon, 1993).

This relatively high income was the main incentive for signing contracts and staying in the Army as a professional after the compulsory service. A sergeant in Tadzhikistan or Transdniestria could expect a contract salary of 100,000 rbl, while the average wage in the industrial sector was estimated at 33,000 rbl. This 'over-paying' was not without success, and the plan for 1993 to attract some 100,000 contract servicemen was indeed fulfilled. But expectations that such 'professionalization' would compensate for the manpower deficit proved misplaced. In late 1993, Defence Minister Grachev had to admit that few contracts had been signed for the combat units, while the majority of new 'professionals' had signed up for rear and administrative posts. In January 1994, President Yeltsin signed a decree authorizing the Army to recruit an additional 150,000 contract soldiers, but no further financial allocation was provided. High salary remained the only way to attract sign-ups, but the available budget hardly allowed over-paying to continue.[64] By spring 1994 the official figure for contract servicemen in the ranks was 160,000 and the

63 These facts were presented by Sergei Stepashin in an interview to *Segodnya*, 18 May 1993.
64 On 10 March 1994 the leading military newspaper *Krasnaya Zvezda* published an advertisement for contract recruits, announcing that salaries began at 110,000 roubles.

guideline for the end of the year was set as high as 400,000, i.e. 32% of the army's soldiers and sergeants.[65] In view of budget realities, this plan could be characterized as quite utopian.[66]

It is indeed ironic, as Stephen Foye (1994d) has observed, that in a matter of a few years the debates on the all-volunteer army had made a complete turn-about. In 1990, many liberal security experts argued against the draft system and for the 'professional' model, while military conservatives insisted that the cost would be prohibitive. In 1994, the military leadership – which by no means could be called liberal – started to consider the alternative of contract service, but the remaining reformists in the government refused to finance it. Sergei Rogov (1994a) tried to break this circle, arguing that instead of an Army with an actual strength of some 1.7 million (of which 1 million are professionals – officers and warrant officers) Russia should have a professional Army of some 1.2–1.3 million (with a normal ratio between officers and privates like 1:3). This, he pointed out, would cost the same and maybe even less.[67]

The problem with financing was more than just the size of the military budget. No less important was its closed character, a feature obviously inherited from the Soviet past. As Rogov put it, 'All discussions of reform are senseless as long as the budget request from the Defence Ministry is presented on one page.' The blunt refusal of the military authorities to provide any details on expenditures, even to the Parliament, led Sergei Yushenkov (1994), Chairman of the Committee on Defence of the State Duma, to comment that the closed character of the military budget was the main source of corruption in the Army since 'huge sums of money are distributed without any control, at the will of the "top brass" who are pushing for unjustified increases'. (Yushenkov has also found – to his sorrow – that it made corruption charges very difficult to prove.) Back in 1992, several experts insisted that 'past experience tells that it is impermissible to leave the military budget under control of the ministries even if they are headed by true democrats; independent external control should be established' (Luboshits & Tsimbal, 1992).[68] The only real attempt to change the structure of the budget was undertaken by Andrei Kokoshin (1993), who sought to introduce a system of procurement based on flexible 5–year programmes roughly copied from the US model, but severe cuts in the funding allocated for new contracts and general lack of financial predictability made such innovations

---

65 Chief of General Staff Kolesnikov described the emerging mixed system of manning as 'most optimal' and assumed that it would permit 90–95% of the non-officer positions to be filled by the end of 1995. See his interview with *Krasnaya Zvezda*, 1 February 1994.

66 As total budget revenues for 1994 proved considerably lower than expected, the level of actual financing of the military budget was only 60%, which made the actual figure of military spending as low as 35 trillion roubles. Only in late November did the special governmental commission agree to increase the financing to 70% of the original budget. See Borodulin (1994).

67 What was hidden in Rogov's proposals was the necessity to retire some 700,000 officers, which for the military establishment was nearly a suicidal option. While the officer corps certainly was shrinking, the main component of this trend was not senior retirement, but massive resignation of junior officers, making the Russian Army remarkably top-heavy.

68 They also proposed basing budgetary calculations not on the models of different wars but on the models of containment, the main criterion for which should be conflict prevention.

nearly senseless.[69] If in 1993 the military industries accepted a long postpone-
ment of payments (by the end of the year the accumulated debt had reached 8
trillion roubles), by 1994 they had started turning down orders from the
Defence Ministry and the situation began to get out of hand (Shlykov, 1995).

Given the lack of political involvement in the 'forgotten' military reform (as
Rogov himself put it), these proposals were doomed to remain a voice in the
wilderness. It looked as if the political leadership had decided to let the multi-
plying military problems 'eat' themselves up, thus minimizing the risks related to
loose control over the Army. The first draft military budget for the 1995 financial year, released in August 1994, allocated only 40.6 trillion roubles to the
'National Defence' section (for initial analysis see Galeotti, 1994b); in the final
version delivered to the State Duma in October the figure was increased to 45
trillion. Though this made up a hefty 22% of the state budget, it was only about
one-half of the 83 trillion requested by the Ministry of Defence as its minimum
'survival' level.[70] In a situation of unpredictable inflation and unstable financing,
fixed defence expenditures at the level proposed by the government would translate into a 50% decrease in real terms (Rogov, 1994a). That means that the
envisaged reduction of the Armed Forces to 1.469 million men by the end of
1995 was an optimistic assumption. Addressing the State Duma in mid-
November, Defence Minister Grachev called the new budget 'ruinous'; on
several other occasions he referred to it as 'criminal'.[71] Perhaps surprisingly, the
most realistic assessment came from General Lebed: 'on the one hand, the budget allocations for defence are much lower than the lowest level of requirements
of the Armed Forces, but on the other hand, they are far beyond economic
limits' (Lebed, 1994a).[72]

Neither complaints nor imprecations could change the financial reality; but
instead of making the cuts in defence spending into an instrument for transforming the military structures, the political leaders allowed them to become a
highly destructive weapon. Unable to reform itself, the Army had to face the fact
that its very structure was unsustainable. But instead of undertaking at last
some structural changes, rescue efforts since early 1995 have been centred on
increasing the number of soldiers. Grachev, acting with a renewed mandate

---

69 Thus, the government budget for FY 1995 allocated only 8.5 trillion roubles for procurement
and 2.5 trillion for research and development. Sergei Rogov (1994a) pointed to the inevitable destruction of the scientific potential concentrated in the military–industrial complex and called for the
development of special long-term programmes (for example, on conversion) outside the military
budget.

70 This coincided with a sharp drop in the rouble against the dollar (known as 'Black Tuesday'),
so the Information Directorate of the Defence Ministry issued a special statement in *Krasnaya
Zvezda* denying any connection and calling financial injections in the defence sector a 'myth' (see
'Financial Injections . . .', 1994).

71 The figures were left practically unchanged when the 1995 budget was finally approved in mid-
March 1995. But by then the war in Chechnya had made the budget provisions all but hollow;
according to preliminary estimates, in January the direct costs of the operation in themselves were
about 13 billion roubles a day. (See 'The Total in Writing', 1995.)

72 He also argued for a thorough civilian, primarily parliamentary control of the budget that 'will
make it possible in 2–3 years to raise a cohort of politicians able by their level of competence to take
the position of the Minister of Defence'.

from the President, declared that reductions below the level of 1.7 million were 'intolerable' and that having a professional non-conscript Army was unfeasible – hence his demand to amend the Law on Military Service.[73] In Spring 1995, special legislation was pushed through the Parliament, allowing the duration of compulsory military service to be extended from 18 to 24 months and permitting the draft of college students. But with no additional financial allocation, this numerical increase only added to the appalling problems of supply, housing, training, etc.[74] Already in mid-1995, military authorities started to complain that they could not buy enough food for the Army and that by winter many garrisons in the North could simply starve – but heard only the advice to borrow some money in commercial banks (Yakovleva, 1995).

In real terms, the only solution to the seemingly deadlocked problem of not enough roubles for an undermanned Army could be a thoroughly detailed request from the General Staff for additional funding for numerical reductions. This would involve creating a special pension fund for a massive retirement of senior officers and generals, allocating extra funds for disbanding some 25 tank and motor rifle divisions, covering expenses for new redeployment of personnel and equipment to the bases and facilities in need of upgrading and modernizing. Such a programme – despite a rather impressive price tag – could probably find broad political support. But by all evidence, electoral battles and military intrigues would guarantee that even the 1996 budget would not include such an approach, thus dooming the destructive underfinancing of the Russian Army to continue.

3.6   Conclusion

By late 1994 the whole issue of political control over the Army had acquired a dramatic character. While President Yeltsin was inclined to reduce it to a question of the personal loyalty of the Defence Minister, the latter now realized what had long been evident to every general who tried to prevent his skeleton division from selling arms for food and to every lieutenant who submitted his resignation – that the key military structures had become unsustainable. In this situation, political control over the Army meant first and foremost setting sound guidelines for the military reform. This was indeed a matter of survival. Instead, the Army found itself pushed into the quagmire of war in Chechnya.

Even leaving the moral aspects aside, this war posed several questions directly related to the main subject of this chapter. Why did the Army enter into this war and wage it in such a devastating way? Why did the political leadership, relying more and more on military means, invest so little effort in modernizing them or at least keeping them usable? In essence, if the military force is indeed such a

---

73 Grachev delivered a lengthy speech at the meeting of the High Command held on 28 February. His presentation of the Chechen war justified and praised the Army's performance but offered few conclusions on the necessary reforms. (See Grachev, 1995.)

74 Many liberal commentators were quick to point out that the envisaged increase in manpower available to the Army combined with a decrease in financing could only worsen the situation. (See Arbatov, 1995b; Latsis, 1995.)

useful political instrument, why did the reform not take place and why was the deterioration allowed?

As to the first of these questions, it may seem that the generals' obedience to this hopeless and senseless warfare order was a proof of efficient political leadership. But perhaps a more accurate diagnosis would be that the demoralized Army simply lacked the cohesion to resist. And those generals who saw the inevitable defeat all too clearly were also aware that any attempt to act decisively on their side would involve the risk of splitting the Army. So they kept their personal protests limited to resignation – and this allowed the Defence Minister, who had no other choice than to devote himself to this war, to conduct large-scale purges in the high command, aimed at eliminating even the shadow of a 'military opposition'. Speaking in late January 1995, General Lebed made a bitter prediction: 'If the Defence Minister manages to get rid of Gromov, Mironov and other opponents, the leadership of the Defence Ministry will certainly become more united. But this does not preclude that it will make decisions as a result of which Russia will finally lose the army' (Lebed, 1995b).

Indeed, once at war, the Army mobilized all its energy and resources – as it had done so many times in the past – and went for victory with no regard for the losses. But the war could not bring any solution to the Army's problems – even the military budget was not increased by a rouble. And the inability of Yeltsin's entourage to produce any sound plans for restructuring and revitalizing the Army was patently obvious, despite his promise to 'control privately the military reform'.[75] There was little of substance in the President's February Message to the Federal Assembly, except for promises 'to transform the explosive energy of the conflicts into a potential for forthcoming changes in the Army'.[76]

This negative conclusion still does not explain why the military reform was never implemented. This chapter has provided several specific answers concerning why the military bureaucracy was unable to reform itself, why policy-makers gave priority to the loyalty of the top military echelon instead of supporting reformists, why there was never enough money to start meaningful reforms, etc. But in a broader sense, the issue of military reform should be seen as yet another part of the overall problem of the development of reforms in Russia. And, as of early 1996, the general picture does not look very encouraging.

The democratic reforms have produced a Constitution which envisages a powerless Parliament together with an unaccountable executive branch controlled by an unimpeachable President. The economic reforms have produced a landslide economic decline and a weak and worthless rouble. Nothing resembling a middle class has emerged in Russian society, with one-third of the population slipping below the poverty line while a handful of 'New Russians' are shamelessly demonstrating their enormous fortune. Actually, only in three spheres is

---

75 Yeltsin made this remark during a ceremony at the Tomb of the Unknown Soldier on 23 February, adding that 'We should do everything so that our army feels itself confident' (INTERFAX in FBIS-SOV-95-036, 23 February 1995).

76 Yeltsin declared his intention to elaborate reform guidelines 'in a few months' time' and to set up a permanent presidential commission for developing those, but little evidence of any intensive work had appeared by the end of summer. (See 'On the Effectiveness . . .', 1995.)

there anything like booming development: in the independent mass media, in private banking and in organized crime. But all three of these have long had significant internal potential for growth, and to a substantial degree are feeding one another. In all areas that needed focused and sustained governmental efforts – land reform, or the reform of the judicial system, or conversion of military industries – the results are pitiful.[77]

Military reform is but one more case in this long list. Feeling the pressure to resolve some burning issues, the government always sought 'quick fixes' – the withdrawal of hundreds of thousands of troops from Germany and the three Baltic states is the best illustration. Similarly, facing the need to employ military force, policy-makers invariably went for easily available instruments, giving some salary increases as reward. With the law routinely neglected and decision-making concentrated in a very narrow circle, everything seemed possible for the rulers in the Kremlin but nothing actually was.[78] The personal union between President Yeltsin and Defence Minister Grachev is just one element of the political regime which has emerged in Russia as a result of the internal crisis that culminated in October 1993; and this regime by its very character remains unable to implement any strategic reform plans. The results of the parliamentary elections in December 1995 confirmed that the Yeltsin regime had lost support among the population; but since it was the Communist Party who mobilized the protest vote under anti-reform slogans, the chances for dynamic and realistic leadership have hardly increased.

That means that the Army will have to wait until the new Russian President (to be elected in June 1996 – and a big question mark is involved) appoints a new Defence Minister who in turn can present a reform plan which could find political support in the new Parliament. It is sadly apparent that this starting point for reforms will be much worse than back in early 1992. The question is whether the badly shattered military structures can in fact survive such a delay. Every day that is lost for the reform process contributes to making the alienated military leadership into an uncontrollable political force, as well as turning Russia's emerging civil society against the Army.

---

77 With an eye on the forthcoming elections, in the summer of 1995 the leaders of Russian democratic parties were bitter in their criticism of the results of reforms. Yegor Gajdar (1995b) has admitted that the 'capitalism' which has emerged in Russia is 'disgusting, criminal and socially unjust'. Grigory Yavlinsky (1995) has pointed to the undemocratic pattern of reforms as the main source of alienation in society, which in turn led to slowing down and curtailing of reforms after mid-1992.

78 Paul Goble has recalled this Dickensian metaphor in a recent article (Goble, 1995b).

4

Europeanizing the Russian Army

4.1 Introduction

'Europeanization' may mean many different things – even for one and the same Army. Among the topics discussed above, the ongoing numerical reductions are bringing the Russian Army somewhat closer to European standards (except as to professionalization, since a non-conscript army is by no means the model typical in Europe); also in terms of the share of the national wealth allocated for defence Russia now could be compared to other European states, whilst the USSR always was a thing apart. But in terms of civil–military relations (including the issue of political control over the military) Russia today is not one step closer to Europe than it was at the beginning of reforms in early 1992.

This chapter – taking as its point of departure that the gap remains unbridged – focuses on the problem of establishing stable relations between the Russian Army and various European security institutions. Such relations in themselves are – or at least are meant – to serve further transformation of the enormous military machine which Russia inherited from the Soviet Union. So 'Europeanization' is taken here in a much narrower sense than reforming the Army by European standards, and means primarily building bridges. Two main issues here are arms control, which not only imposes limitations but also creates numerous links between national armies of all European states; and military-to-military contacts, which are the main way of exploiting the transparency developed at the negotiating table in order to build partnership. The issue of the current international profile of the Russian Navy comes separately, with a narrow focus on the Northern Fleet and its role in the Barents Initiative.

4.2 Implications of Arms Control

Sorting out the initial problems related to the Soviet military heritage, the Russian leadership soon discovered that whatever the spontaneous reductions, international commitments to limiting armaments still mattered. The idea was to make arms control instrumental in dividing this heritage in line with what were Russia's interests. Accordingly, various opportunities were explored in order to influence the behaviour of both newly independent states and former adversaries, using the arms control levers. Nuclear relations were of pivotal importance here; they have been briefly discussed in Chapter 2, as detailed analysis would have required another book. In the following pages the focus is on conventional forces.

One initial advantage Russia enjoyed over other newly independent states was the experience and expertise concentrated in the Foreign Ministry and several think-tanks. This allowed Moscow to move remarkably fast, drafting in Spring 1992 a proposal on distribution of the Conventional Armed Forces in Europe (CFE) Treaty limits among 'European' republics. The key issue was to persuade Kiev to abandon its 'privatization' approach, which envisaged setting the ceiling for each country according to what it had on its territory (thus, Ukraine would be able to retain 4,500 tanks, and Russia in its European Military Districts 6,000 tanks). Moscow's counter-proposal as presented by General Kobets introduced the concept of 'integral criteria' (size of territory, population, length of borders) which would leave Russia with 7,114 tanks as against only 2,877 for Ukraine (Burbyga, 1992).[1]

What made this 'big-brother' proposal relatively convincing was the precedent of using a similar criterion for distributing the general allocation for the Warsaw Pact among former member-states – although most of them were highly loath to being mentioned in this context.[2] Russia also tried to mobilize some pressure from the West through the newly created North Atlantic Cooperation Council (NACC) where the High Level Working Group (HLWG) was created.[3]

All these efforts failed to overcome Ukraine's stubbornness, demonstrated in all its glory at the Commonwealth of Independent States (CIS) summit in Kiev in March 1992 (Rogov, 1993a, pp. 4–6). After that event, the pressure from the HLWG came rather on Moscow, so in about 6 months – being profoundly concerned about preservation of the CFE framework – Russia agreed to settle for less-than-favourable terms.[4] The final agreement was signed at the CIS summit in Tashkent (hence known as the Tashkent Accord) on 15 May 1992. Combat aircraft was the only area where Russia secured for itself a clear superiority , but it had to agree to give additional helicopters to Ukraine and some other participants (see Table 4.1). It would seem that by that time the Russian leadership had arrived at the conclusion that the quarrels with Kiev were essentially senseless. For one thing, Ukraine would not be able to maintain an army at the level set by the ceilings; and the preliminary plans for reductions in Russia itself indicated that even

---

1 Another proposal developed in the General Staff Academy was presented by General Danilovich (1992). The key idea was to create the CIS strategic equipment reserve where some 10,000 tanks would be stored, while Ukraine could have up to 3,000 tanks and Russia, 8,500 tanks. The proposed sharing of combat aircraft was rather different: some 500 would go to the CIS, Russia would retain up to 1,300 and Ukraine would get only 300.

2 Primarily for this reason, the three Baltic states decided against participation in the CFE, but the Russian troops on their territory were included and provisions were made for inspections.

3 As Jonathan Dean (1994, p. 300) argues, 'Western negotiators did a good job in rapidly and effectively urging Soviet successor states to sign onto the CFE Treaty . . . and in informing officials of the new states, some of them completely new on the job, of the obligations of their government under the treaty.'

4 Jane Sharp (1993, p. 599) has emphasized that the Ukrainian leadership had reasons to consider the CFE Treaty as 'a useful vehicle to engage the West in support of Ukrainian claims to what it considered to be its fair share of the former Soviet military assets', especially since in the final analysis 'Ukraine's entitlements are higher than any other former WTO state except Russia and more than the sum of entitlements for Poland, Hungary, Slovakia and the Czech Republic, a preponderance of military capability that was disconcerting to defence planners in Budapest and Warsaw.'

Table 4.1   *USSR Successor-states' Holdings of Treaty-limited Equipment (TLE) and Ceilings as Settled by the Tashkent Accord*

	Tanks	ACV	Artill.	Aircr.	Helic.	Total
Armenia						
1992	258	641	357	0	7	
1994	129	346	225	6	13	
1995	102	285	225	6	7	
Limit	220	220	285	100	50	875
Azerb.						
1992	391	1,285	463	124	24	
1994	279	736	354	53	6	
1995	285	835	343	58	18	
Limit	220	220	285	100	50	875
Belarus						
1992	2,263	2,776	1,384	650	82	
1994	3,108	3,414	1,584	378	78	
1995	2,348	3,046	1,579	348	78	
Limit	1,800	2,600	1,615	260	80	6,355
Georgia						
1992	850	1,054	363	245	48	
1994	41	51	7	2	1	
1995	39	49	27	2	1	
Limit	220	220	285	100	50	875
Moldova						
1992	155	402	248	0	0	
1994	0	133	138	31	0	
1995	0	190	129	27	0	
Limit	210	210	250	50	50	770
Russia						
1992	10,604	17,338	8,107	4,161	1,035	
1994	7,493	13,466	6,069	3,921	954	
1995	6,696	11,806	6,240	3,283	872	
Limit	6,400	11,480	6,415	3,450	890	28,635
Ukraine						
1992	6,204	6,394	3,052	1,431	285	
1994	5,394	5,803	3,725	1,460	270	
1995	4,768	5,187	3,407	1,276	270	
Limit	4,080	5,050	4,040	1,090	330	14,590

Figures for each state are the declared holdings at the time of signing the Tashkent Accord (May 1992), on 1 January 1994, on 1 January 1995 and the limit as envisaged by the Accord.

Sources: 'Weapons in Europe Before and After CFE', *Arms Control Today*, June 1992, p. 32; *The Arms Control Reporter*, 1994, 407.B.501; *The Arms Control Reporter*, 1995, 407.B.515

the low ceilings allowed more than enough. But what was becoming more important for Moscow was to fix equally low levels for Armenia, Azerbaijan and Georgia and thereby partly demilitarize the Caucasus conflict area.

It was symptomatic that none of these three agreed to take a commitment on the maximum level of its army in the Negotiations on Personnel Strength conducted in Vienna. These negotiations resulted in a 'politically binding' agreement (also known as CFE 1A) signed on the first day of the CSCE summit in Helsinki in July 1992. Unlike the ceilings adopted at the previous negotiations, the limits on personnel in the Army and Air Force (Naval Forces were excluded as well as interior troops) were unilaterally declared and actually not subject to negotiation. Russia took this opportunity to claim a ceiling of 1,450,000 men, which by far exceeded the real strength of its forces based west of the Ural Mountains.[5]

When the CFE Treaty formally entered into force in November 1992 (implementation including inspections started by mutual agreement after the CSCE Helsinki summit in July), the first problem related to physical destruction of the treaty-limited equipment (TLE) became evident. Russia raised the issue at the Joint Consultative Group, arguing that the agreed procedures of destruction involved prohibitive costs. Thanks to support given by Germany, permission was granted to use cheaper methods.[6] This made it possible to meet the first treaty deadline, according to which during the first year 25% of the reductions should be carried out.[7] Later, Russia and Belarus indicated on several occasions that unless special international aid were provided (preferably through a special disarmament fund), they could not meet the second deadline, according to which another 35% of the redundant TLE should be destroyed by November 1994. Nevertheless, this target was also successfully achieved, and by 1 January 1995 about 60% of the total Soviet Union destruction liability of 23,400 TLE had been accomplished by the successor-states.[8]

Perhaps a more serious problem related to the first and second phases was the some 2,000 TLE (of which 600 were tanks) missing from official records. Most of this derived from the failure of Armenia and Azerbaijan to declare actual holdings and simply take any commitment on TLE destruction. According to Russian estimates from May 1993, Azerbaijan should scrap 195 tanks and 939 ACVs, and Armenia 159 ACVs.[9] Both countries insisted that their actual holdings were

---

5 The figure was provided only days before the Helsinki summit and immediately after the Russian Parliament had ratified the CFE Treaty. Ukraine committed itself to a much more modest ceiling of 450,000 men. (See Feinstein, 1992.)

6 Russia also proposed simply allowing the equipment to rust and then verifying its uselessness by inspections, but the Western partners felt that this method went too far (see Walking, 1995). For details on destruction methods see Koulik & Kokoski (1994, pp. 31–33).

7 By November 1993, Russia had scrapped 804 tanks, 2,368 ACVs, 173 artillery systems, 324 combat aircraft and 25 strike helicopters. Ukraine had destroyed 603 tanks, 630 ACVs and 175 combat aircraft. (See Lachowski, 1994, p. 570.)

8 General Zhurbenko, First Deputy Chief of the General Staff, provided the information that by 17 November 1994 Russia had duly destroyed 1,953 tanks (61% of the envisaged cuts), 4,328 ACVs (79%), 397 artillery systems (60%), 726 aircraft (71%) and 60 helicopters (61%). (See FBIS-SOV-94-233, 5 December 1994.)

9 Russian estimates were based on the assumption that all TLE left on the territory of a particular state was the responsibility of its government, while Azerbaijan claimed that much had been captured by uncontrolled rebel groups (see 'CFE Treaty: Consequences for Russia', 1992). The level of combat losses in Nagorno Karabakh remained beyond any assessment though, strictly speaking, those could not be counted as destruction of the TLE. According to IISS estimates, in early 1994 Azerbaijan had 279 tanks and 820 ACVs, and Armenia 120 and 410 respectively. For ACVs, these figures are slightly higher than those officially declared to the CFE information exchange (Table 4.2). (See *The Military Balance*, 1994–1995, pp. 80–81.)

much lower than the agreed ceilings. The suspiciously low figures provided by Georgia were also impossible to verify due to ongoing fighting in Abkhazia and general unrest in the country. In fact, that led to all but formal exclusion of the Transcaucasus from the CFE area, implicitly confirmed after the exchange of information on the second stage of implementation in December 1994.

Many parties to the CFE tended to take this 'black hole' as an unfortunate local disturbance, but it inevitably involved more serious problems that could threaten the whole Treaty. The epicentre of these problems lies in the North Caucasus, but the name of the issue is 'Flank Limits'. This is a provision introduced in the CFE Treaty after strong pressure from NATO, and against Soviet objections that were finally lifted only weeks before the signing ceremony.[10] What is particularly complicating about Article V is that it sets one accumulated limit for two different flank zones (Northern and Southern) thus covering on the 'Eastern' side Bulgaria, Romania, Moldova, Armenia, Azerbaijan, Georgia, one military district (MD) from Ukraine (Odessa), and two from Russia (Leningrad and North Caucasus). By the time of signing, the Warsaw Pact was already defunct, so the sum for the group of states was purely artificial and Bulgaria and Romania made their own calculations, carrying with them nearly 50% of the overall flank limit. The next division involved the newly independent states; the Tashkent Accord gave Russia less than half of the former Soviet limit, which was to be further divided between the Leningrad MD and North Caucasus MD.[11] That meant that Russia had to divide about 10% of all tanks, ACV and artillery systems allowed for its active units between the two military districts that together cover approximately a half of its European territory (Map 4.1).

The Russian military actually had little say in all this, since all these calculations had been completed before the Russian Defence Ministry was formed (see 'CFE Treaty: Consequences for Russia', 1992). By autumn 1992, the military leadership concluded that it could live fairly comfortably with all conventional arms control limitations, especially since the destruction of the redundant TLE (as well as the agreed destruction of military equipment that had been moved beyond the Urals in 1990–91) had by and large been removed from its sphere of responsibility. Some thought was also given to the fact that even in the mid-term perspective the CFE Treaty could become more restrictive on the Western side if NATO were to increase its membership while keeping the same ceiling on major weapon systems (Arbatov, 1995c).

The problem arrived after Defence Minister Grachev announced his intention to build a 'frontline' military district in the North Caucasus, with an envisaged strength of about 600 tanks, 2,200 ACVs and 1,000 artillery pieces.[12] Spring 1993 saw a series of complaints about the 'unfair' and 'discriminatory' character of the

---

10 For penetrating analysis of the CFE intrigue see Dunay (1991).

11 Thus, Russia was allowed to retain 1,300 tanks (of which only 700 in combat units), 1,380 ACVs (580), and 1,680 artillery systems (1,280). Aircraft and helicopters were excluded from the flank limitations as inherently mobile (see Table 4.2).

12 That meant the need to have in the flank zone 400 tanks, 2,429 ACVs and 820 artillery pieces more than allowed, but without violating the overall national ceiling.

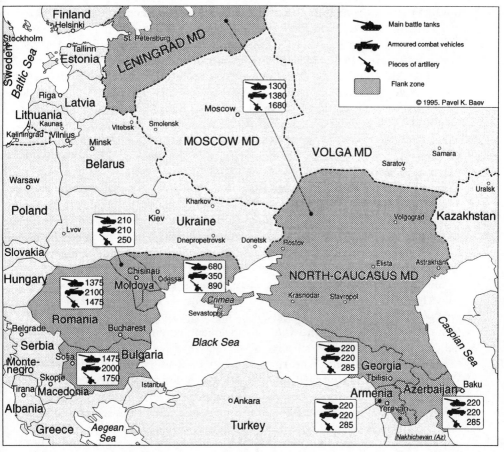

Map 4.1 *The Flank Zone and the Ceilings on Tanks, ACVs and Artillery Envisaged by the CFE Treaty*

flank limits, accompanied by preliminary manoeuvres in the Joint Consultative Group (JCG). In June Grachev raised this issue at the meeting with US Defense Secretary Les Aspin, but found little understanding, and even less when he visited Ankara in July (Starr, 1993). But this did not prevent President Yeltsin from sending letters to key Western partners in September (in the midst of the gathering political storm in Moscow) calling for the suspension of Article V of the CFE Treaty and warning about possible 'adequate unilateral measures . . . including those that wouldn't respond fully to the spirit of the Treaty'; this was followed by a formal démarche at the JCG (see Clarke, 1993b).[13]

The rationale for the Russian position was the obvious irrelevance of the basic CFE two-bloc approach. In the current situation it had become discriminatory against Russia, which was the only state (except Ukraine, which basically supported the Russian claim) affected by Article V. Russian negotiators pointed

---

13 For the text of the démarche of 28 September see *The Arms Control Reporter*, 1993, pp. 407.D.85-86.

out that the Treaty provisions actually implied a heavy concentration of weapons in Kaliningrad *oblast* (to the growing concern of Poland and the three Baltic states) (see 'On the Implementation of the Treaty on Conventional Armed Forces in Europe', 1993). The military authorities on their side tried to make it clear that Moscow had no intentions of a 'Western orientation' of the Armed Forces deployment and argued that the costs of re-deployment could be reduced by putting into use the available infrastructure in the South (Kolesnikov, M., 1994). The final argument was about the fundamental change of circumstances which involved direct threats to Russia's vital security interests that could be averted only by strengthening the military grouping in the North Caucasus MD (Grachev, 1994b; Lachowski, 1994, pp. 571–573).

Predictably, the strongest reaction against the Russian démarche came from Turkey, which urged its allies to rebuff any attempt to lift flank limits, since the latter would only serve to re-establish Russian military domination over the Caucasus (Batur, 1994). What made Turkey's position less convincing and even invoked a double standard was the fact that during the CFE negotiations it had insisted on the exclusion of the south-eastern part of its own territory, referring to military threats from Iraq.[14] On these grounds Turkish objections perhaps could have been overruled, but the absolute majority of the CFE participants opposed any 'opening' of the Treaty, insisting that setting a first precedent could lead to dismantlement of the whole arrangement, making re-ratification in the national parliaments impossible.[15]

Russia was not at all disheartened by this opposition, especially since the Western partners encouraged Moscow to seek solutions within the limits of flexibility of the Treaty. That is why Defence Minister Grachev, addressing NATO Defence Ministers in Brussels in June 1994, raised the issue of postponing the implementation of Article V at least until 1996 in a soft way remarkably different from the previous démarche: 'When addressing the question of joining the Partnership for Peace programme and taking formal commitments on cooperating with NATO in the cause of improving the European security system, I think Russia can rightfully expect a different policy stand on Paragraph 5 in the CFE Treaty. Leaving this issue unresolved would merely indicate that the bloc-type thinking of Cold War years has in no way been abandoned by everybody' (see Grachev, 1994a, p. 7).

While investing serious diplomatic efforts in expanding the 'limits of flexibility', Russia exploited the available avenues for circumventing flank limits. One possibility was to recategorize some troops as 'internal security forces', which would make it possible (according to Article XII of the CFE Treaty) to deploy up to 600 additional armoured infantry fighting vehicles in the area. For

---

14 Therefore, the concentration of some 35,000 Turkish troops for the military operation in Northern Iraq in March 1995 was outside the CFE Treaty area.

15 There were only a few proposals on accommodating Russia's needs. Thus, Jonathan Dean (1994, p. 303) argued in favour of a temporary increase for peace-keeping operations. Lee Feinstein (1993, p. 25) indicated the possibilities of extending the implementation date for Article V and increasing the number of weapons allowed for internal forces. Jane Sharp (1994) proposed that the CFE map should be redrawn so that all Russian territory would be in the same zone. It was Richard Falkenrath who, in spring 1995, produced a most comprehensive overview of all possible options.

this purpose a special North Caucasus Internal Troops District was established by Presidential decree of March 1993. From the military viewpoint, however, this was not a very satisfactory solution since the integrity of control was split; besides, the central question concerned tanks and artillery. The possibility of exploiting the special provision for naval infantry and coastal defence (related to Article III) was blocked by the heated dispute with Ukraine over the division of the Black Sea Fleet.[16] Another loophole was the provision in Article V itself on the temporary deployment to the flank area of an additional 153 tanks, 241 armoured combat vehicles and 140 artillery pieces. That certainly was not much but could prove helpful in local emergency situations – albeit not on the scale of the war in Chechnya that started in December 1994.[17] The only thinkable solution for the conflict area in and around Chechnya was to exclude it completely from the CFE zone – but this was an alternative US Defense Secretary William Perry refused to consider during his talks with Grachev in Moscow in early April 1995 (see Clarke, 1995b; Felgengauer, 1995a).

Yet another reserve option was to convince the three Transcaucasian states to reduce their holdings (thus amending the Tashkent Accord), raising Russia's ceiling by the difference (Clark, 1994). But Armenia, Azerbaijan and Georgia all had intentions of building up their national forces (Table 4.2). They resisted this pressure rather successfully, applying for support to Turkey and other Western partners. Only in March 1995 did Tbilisi yield to Grachev's pressure and agree to transfer to Russia the part of its quota that at the moment was not 'covered' – but this protocol seemed to have a rather shaky legal foundation, falling short of what the Russian Defence Ministry needed to 'legalize' its newly created 58th Army in the North Caucasus.

One fundamental problem has remained: while it is perfectly possible for the former adversaries and the former allies to block Russia's requests, implementation can hardly be enforced. Spring 1995 saw a considerable debate in the West on the 'flank issue', but the bottom-line was that as the deadline drew nearer, Russia would eventually comply and the problem would disappear all by itself.[18] This lack of understanding and cooperativeness on an issue that may be secondary to most European states[19] but directly affects Russia's vital security interests contributed to the 'Versailles' perception of the CFE Treaty. Observing this trend, Richard Falkenrath (1995, p. 133) warned:

---

16 Russia could deploy up to 662 tanks, 990 ACVs and 872 artillery systems in naval infantry/coastal defence units. But this would involve changing the unilateral legally binding statement made by the USSR in June 1991, according to which this equipment was subject to the flank rules.

17 The US State Department issued a special statement that the war did not in any way violate the CFE Treaty since the flank limits were not yet in force and temporary deployments were allowed. No reference was made to the requirement for notification of such military activity.

18 Col. Jeff McCausland (1995), Department of National Security & Strategy, US Army War College, speaking at an IISS seminar in London in March 1995, came with a strong warning that the issue had very little chance of being resolved in time.

19 Norway can justly claim the flank issue as a prime concern since the military grouping on the Kola Peninsula is effectively limited. It seems possible that Russia may lift these concerns by retreating to the early Warsaw Pact proposal on two separate limits for Northern and Southern Flanks (200 tanks, 150 ACV and 1,000 artillery pieces were indicated as the limit for the northern part of Leningrad MD).

Table 4.2   *Treaty-limited Equipment in the Former USSR's Part of the Southern Flank*

	Tanks			ACV			Artillery		
	'94	'95	L	'94	'95	L	'94	'95	L
Armenia[1]	129	102	220	346	285	220	225	225	285
Azerb.[1]	279	285	220	736	835	220	354	343	285
Georgia[1]	41	39	220	51	49	220	7	27	285
Moldova[1]	0	0	210	133	190	210	138	129	250
Ukraine[2]	1838	na	680	1600	na	350	1554	na	890
Russia	662	na	1300	1485	na	1380	1176	na	1680
incl:									
Tr-Dn	121	121	—	180	180	—	129	129	—
Tr-C	310	310	—	490	490	—	726	726	—
NCauc	231	na	—	815	na	—	321	na	—

Abbreviations: na, data not available; L, limit established by the CFE Treaty; Tr-Dn, Transdniestria; Tr-C, Transcaucasus; NCauc, North Caucasus.

[1] Figures for Armenia, Azerbaijan, Georgia and Moldova are those officially declared as holdings on 1 January 1994, 1 January 1995 and the ceilings as settled by the Tashkent Accord (May 1992).
[2] Figures for Ukraine are the estimates of the IISS *Military Balance*, 1994–1995. Limits for Ukraine cover only Odessa Military District.
[3] Figures for Russia are the estimates of the IISS *Military Balance*, 1994–1995. Limits for Russia are for both Northern and Southern flanks. Of them, 600 tanks, 800 ACVs and 400 artillery pieces are required to be in storage. By 1 January 1995, Russia had in the whole 'flank area' 2,158 tanks, 4,550 ACVs and 2,444 artillery pieces.

Sources: *The Military Balance*, 1994–1995; *The Arms Control Reporter*, 1995.

> Juridical arguments do not dictate political reality in Moscow, a point which should inform how the West responds to Russia's position on the flank rules . . . Russians are convinced that the flank ceilings are too low for their strategic needs. They may be wrong, but no amount of argument is likely to change their minds, and no policy toward the flank problem is likely to change their behavior in the Caucasus.

As the dispersed team of disarmament experts in Moscow failed to convince the political elite that the CFE Treaty would serve Russia's security interests in the mid-term perspective,[20] or to make it instrumental for the military reform, arms control lost its role as the key policy handle with which Gorbachev could enforce dramatic cuts.

Gradually, the whole attitude towards arms control in Moscow has changed. Increasingly it is perceived as irrelevant and unfair, not only in the military leadership but also by many politicians.[21] There is also a perception that while

20 Alexei Arbatov (1995c), who found himself very much a voice in the wilderness in the State Duma, argued in mid-1995 that making some short-term sacrifices in order to meet the CFE requirements would open the way for a follow-on agreement that could consolidate Russia's strategic gains. (See also Rogov, 1994a.)
21 Thus, Vladimir Lukin, Head of Committee of International Affairs of the State Duma, issued a blunt statement that the CFE Treaty did not answer Russia's security interests. He formulated a clear-cut dilemma: either the West would agree to revision of the Treaty or Russia would have to abandon it. (Interview to ITAR-TASS, 10 January 1995 in FBIS-SOV-95-007.)

NATO is really interested in preserving those elements of the arms control regime which allow it to keep Russia down, its own military preparations are affected only to a minor degree. Moreover, as new evidence that NATO was bent on proceeding with enlargement despite Russia's objections started to arrive in late 1994, a few remaining Russian experts discovered that this would 'automatically destroy the CFE Treaty' (Konovalov, 1994). Indeed, the 'CFE–NATO' link is built into the structure of the Treaty, which fixes equal levels in five categories of armaments for two groups of states: NATO and the former Warsaw Pact, while the state-wise distribution of the ceilings was to be decided within each group. Direct expansion of one group at the expense of another (as with the DDR) could be accomplished only with the consent of all parties (see Dunay, 1991, pp. 85–90). On the one hand, this gives Russia some new bargaining-chips that could be used both in settling the 'flank issue' and in reducing the holdings of the key Western powers (that is, if new NATO members were to be placed under the same ceiling).[22] On the other hand, if Russia should stick to an uncompromising approach toward NATO enlargement, this would certainly provide Moscow with a legitimate cause to declare the Treaty null and void.

It may be that until NATO enlargement is practically decided, no such dramatic action as complete withdrawal from the CFE Treaty will take place. But the very amount of official, semi-official and personal statements – that at first were trial balloons and then perhaps contained a good portion of bluff – has now acquired such political weight that some voluntaristic revisions of the CFE provisions are nearly certain to be made.[23] Russia's political leadership is still interested in solving the problem without major complications, which is why some 'understanding' expressed by US President Clinton at the Moscow summit in May 1995 was interpreted as readiness to accommodate Russia's demands (Freeland & Clark, 1995). These expectations soon proved false and the perceived lack of flexibility on the Western side only increased the pressure for greater emphasis on unilateral steps. It is indeed quite difficult to expect that the *pacta sunt servanda* principle would stand towards international agreements when inside the country the law is commonly neglected and the Constitution commands very little respect.

The situation around the CFE Treaty in summer 1995 called for some urgent measures, but the balance of various interests seemed so delicate that no one could come up with any meaningful initiative. Obviously, neither Russia nor any other participant in the CFE Treaty was interested in damaging this cornerstone of European security. But President Clinton's attempt to find some face-saving solution for Moscow proved too vulnerable to criticism for 'appeasing' Russian neo-imperialism and too uncommitted to generate a new consensus in NATO.

---

22 Evgeny Kozhokin, Director of the Russian Institute of Strategic Studies, insisting that the CSCE summit had revealed that the CFE Treaty became 'jarringly anachronistic', proposed to seek support from the East Central European countries in revising it and negotiating a new agreement. (Interview to RIA Novosti, 22 December in FBIS-SOV-94-249-A.)

23 As Christopher Donnelly (1992, p. 40) warned back in mid-1992, 'It is very difficult to generate any enthusiasm about implementing the CFE agreement. However important this might be to Western military and political leaders, their counterparts in the former Soviet Union have so many other concerns that CFE has retreated into the background.'

While the solution was not that difficult to invent – suspension of Article V supplemented by some unilateral legally binding statement from Russia on new ceilings and verification seemed the most promising avenue – only major multilateral investments of political capital could secure it. At the time of writing, it is still far from being clear whether intensive discussions during the series of NATO meetings in autumn 1995 would provide for such an investment and produce any meaningful compromise proposal. What actually is at stake, is that a clash over a clearly peripheral issue might endanger the really central element of the CFE: transparency and confidence-building, including extensive contacts and exchanges between the Russian Army and its European partners.

4.3 The Russian Military and Partnership for Peace

The uneasy relationship between Russia and NATO makes a multi-chaptered saga that could easily fill the rest of this book. Military-to-military contacts are but one strand: they can be separated from the whole story to a degree but still retain their own logic and dynamics. It can even be argued that these contacts are the very core of the relationship while the loud political eulogies and even louder quarrels are but surface trimmings. The early 1990s did see some attempts at 'politicizing' the Atlantic Alliance in terms of expanding its economic, scientific and environmental activities according to Article 2 of the Washington Treaty. But it soon became clear that in these fields there is very little if any niche for NATO. By contrast, the traditional military dimension of its activities allows new and unique opportunities for expansion, thus keeping the Alliance in business even after its fundamental purpose has vanished.[24]

Moreover, in some areas military-to-military contacts go beyond the NATO framework, one obvious example here being arms control verification. Hundreds of Russian officers have travelled across Western Europe conducting inspections and thousands are involved on the receiving end also gaining first-hand experience from direct contacts with NATO colleagues. The starting point for all this was the INF Treaty (1987) with its breakthrough to extensive on-site verification. At the time it was confined to bilateral US–USSR exchanges; it was only the CFE Treaty (1990) that made them truly multilateral. This also allowed NATO to position itself at the very hub of verification activities, making its electronic database available for all participants and adopting the policy of joining each East–on–East inspection (*The Arms Control Reporter*, 1994, pp. 407.B.502, 407.B.508).[25]

As CFE negotiations in 1989–90 moved into the final phase, many 'civil strategists' in Moscow recognized the importance of securing a new prestigious

---

24 As far as Russia and the rest of the former USSR are concerned, this niche was broader. The years 1994–95 saw a spate of such untraditional NATO activities as a seminar on the Lake Baikal environment, or a workshop on the Climatology of the Black Sea.

25 For a detailed description of NATO's Enhanced Cooperation Programme see Nedimoglu (1994).

role for the anxious Soviet military leadership. The easiest way seemed to promote close cooperation between a few dozen top generals in Moscow and their Western counterparts.[26] The message was duly received by those American security experts who had been giving serious consideration to the vulnerability of Gorbachev's regime vis-a-vis the Army. It was Robert Blackwill who initiated the most ambitious 'Program for Russian General Officers' at the John F. Kennedy School of Government at Harvard University, which was followed by similar programmes at RAND Corporation, Brown University and elsewhere.[27] NATO followed the example somewhat hesitantly, hosting the first special course at its Defence College in Rome in October 1991.

The problem with these initial contacts was that they inevitably were narrowly oriented on the Soviet military leadership – and then this whole cohort (including such key generals as Akhromeev, Lobov, Moiseev, Lushev, Gareev) was literally wiped out in late 1991, taking with them quite a number of loyal officers in the colonel ranks who also had had an opportunity to taste the West. So the whole programme of exchanges had to be started anew in early 1992, and this time the focus was more on the emerging military leaders with the ambitious (but hardly novel) goal of 'winning their hearts and minds'. According to Graham Allison (1993, pp. 156–157), this included: direct exposure to Western society, which would increase understanding of common interests; the establishment of personal relationships with their Western defence and military counterparts, which would build mutual recognition of military professionalism and expertise; a continuing relationship, which would guarantee a lasting effect and consolidate the positive influence.

The main problem with implementation was resources – both financial and political. In the 1993 financial year, funding for Russia in the US International Military Education and Training (IMET) programme increased more than fourfold. That made it possible to establish (on the base of the famous Russian Institute in Garmisch-Partenkirchen, Germany) the George C. Marshall European Center for Security Studies as an academic institution under the United States European Command (see Cohen, 1995).[28] These US efforts were duly supported by NATO and also by special programmes in several European think-tanks, such as Stiftung Wissenschaft und Politik (Ebenhausen). With the wisdom of hindsight we may note that this increase could by no means be sufficient to involve the '1,000 potential leaders' in anything more than occasional meetings. Those were staged mostly under the auspices of the North Atlantic

---

26 Academic experts in Moscow were cautious not to publicize such recommendations too widely, leaving the initiative to their Western colleagues. Perhaps the only one who tried himself to build bridges to the military was Andrei Kokoshin, then Deputy Director of the USA & Canada Institute.

27 As Graham Allison (1993, pp. 151–152) pointed out later, the courses at Harvard, workshops and seminars 'constitute several times as many direct contact hours between members of the American national security community and General Staff officers as the military-to-military exchange programs managed by the entire US government'.

28 Russian Defence Minister Grachev was invited for the inauguration of the Center but did not arrive until a few hours after the ceremony was over, which provided a peculiar illustration to the address of US Defense Secretary Les Aspin: 'It can promote militaries that are responsible to democratically elected governments.' (See Barry, 1994, p. 328.)

Cooperation Council (NACC) but this was pretty much the limit of this organization's activity.[29] The real key to success would lie in the sustainability of steadily expanding efforts – and this was proving to be hard to deliver.

Already in late 1993 military-to-military relations started to run into serious political trouble. While the Russian military leadership tried to keep a low profile during the first NATO enlargement crisis (September–October 1993), many politicians sought to present the Army as the main opponent. The same went for the bitter quarrels on the issue of military withdrawal from the Baltic states – which, in fact, went according to schedule and was completed by August 1994. The heated debates on Russia's status in the NATO Partnership for Peace Programme were also primarily a political exercise, though General Grachev made several unfortunate contributions to them as well as to the Baltic issue.[30]

Political tensions bedevilled also the implementation of ambitious plans for joint military exercises, once considered one of the most promising avenues for involving the Russian military in practical relations. Minor communication problems were formally cited as an explanation for the non-participation of Russian troops in the first two joint exercises: *Cooperative Bridge* (12–16 September 1994, Poland) and *Cooperative Spirit* (21–28 October 1994, the Netherlands). Less easy to dismiss were the political obstacles to the first US–Russian joint peace-keeping exercise in the Volga Military District originally scheduled for July that year. It took only a few critical comments in the State Duma to persuade President Yeltsin to reconsider the plan; thereupon he ordered the Defence Ministry to hold 'additional consultations' with Washington (Foye, 1994g). The military leadership refused to flirt with the opposition and insisted on maintaining the cooperative contacts. Eventually, the exercise was held in September with 250 troops from each side participating, but publicity was kept to the absolute minimum. Since the prime importance of this military get-together lay in its symbolism, it was indeed a non-starter.[31] It came as little surprise that Russia refrained from participating in *Cooperative Nugget* (August 1995, Louisiana, USA) and observed with visible irritation the joint US–Ukrainian naval exercises in the Black Sea in July 1995 (Semena, 1995).

Another promising 'window of opportunity' for extensive military-to-military contacts, particularly involving junior officers, concerned stationing the

29 As Douglas Clarke (1995a, p. 27) has argued: 'The NACC was little more than a forum for dialogue and consultation, spawning a plethora of meetings, visits, courses, seminars, and colloquia. It was soon perceived as having more form than substance . . .'

30 Thus, in mid-April 1994 after NATO airstrikes near Gorazde, Grachev publicly announced that 'recent events in Bosnia-Herzegovina have shown that this concept remains in words only' and called for an approach based on Russia's own views on partnership with NATO. Even worse, he threatened that Russia might consider reinforcement of its forces in Estonia if the policy of 'apartheid' towards ethnic Russians were to continue. (See Foye, 1994h.)

31 US experts were far more keen to comment on this exercise, seeing it as a litmus test for further partnership. And the accusation of General Ladygin, Chief of the Main Intelligence Directorate (GRU), that the 27 US aircraft flown to Russia for the exercise were packed with electronic surveillance equipment, was taken quite seriously. (See Lambeth, 1995.)

Western Grouping of the Russian Armed Forces in Germany. Both the local authorities in the new Eastern Länder and the leadership of the Bundeswehr deserve credit for their efforts in engaging the Russian troops in various professional, social and environmental activities.[32] All the same, morale in this 'lost legion' eroded rapidly due to corruption, tax evasion, commercial activities related to unaccounted-for military stocks, arms smuggling, etc.[33] What made the atmosphere in the ranks particularly favourable to such clandestine 'business activities' was the fact that many officers arrived in Germany seeking a sort of respite after serving in numerous 'hot spots' including Afghanistan in the not-too-distant past. In any case, what was positive in this exposure to Western society was discontinued after 31 August 1994 when the last troops were withdrawn from Germany, to be placed in unprepared garrisons inside Russia where reflections on the role and status of the Army in the 'civilized' world were of very little relevance indeed.

As of mid-1994, signs of frustration were becoming visible in Western policies as related to 'Europeanization' of the Russian Army. Perhaps it was the increasingly tense political relations between Russia and NATO that promoted impatient questions about the results of these military-to-military contacts far too early – actually before the latter had been established on a proper scale. As the second 'enlargement crisis' started to unfold in late 1994 – marked by the 'twin peaks' of Kozyrev's scandalous refusal to sign the partnership programme in Brussels in November and Yeltsin's sharp warning about the 'Cold Peace' at the CSCE summit in December – the Russian military made it clear that they were not ready to swallow their objections. US Defense Secretary William Perry, visiting Moscow in early April 1995, had to take as a response for his manoeuvres Grachev's message: 'NATO's expansion will undoubtedly force us to take counter-measures'.[34] Such an irreconcilable opposition made it very difficult indeed to secure funding for continuing exchanges, seminars, joint projects, etc. in the US Congress.

On the other hand, NATO's new partners and candidates for membership from East Central Europe were eager to demonstrate the tangible results of military reforms, vying with one another for priority attention from Brussels (Donnelly, 1995). Pointing to the 'cost-effectiveness' of investments in military-to-military contacts, Poland, Hungary and other prime candidates came forward

---

32 At the same time, opposition from Bonn forced the USA to cancel plans for joint manoeuvres with Russian forces in Germany which had been provisionally scheduled for November 1993. (See Lachowski, 1994.)

33 Russian mass media gave extensive coverage of these problems. See, for example, a series of articles 'Generals in Business' in *Moscow News* (nos 24, 34, 38). In October 1994, investigative journalism claimed its first victim when Dmitri Kholobov from *Moskovsky Komsomolets* found a bomb instead of documents in a briefcase given to him by a 'source'. Massive resonance from this terrorist act forced President Yeltsin to relieve General Matvei Burlakov, former commander of the Western Group of Forces, of his new duties as Deputy Defence Minister 'with a view to protect the honour of the Armed Forces and their supreme command'. (See FBIS-SOV-94-212.)

34 The suspension of CFE Treaty implementation was named first among possible 'counter-measures' and indeed seemed more feasible than the creation of new military groupings in 'danger-prone directions' and strengthening of military ties in the CIS. (See Pogorely, 1995.)

with solid applications for further allocation of funds for the 'Atlanticization' of their armed forces.[35]

With this East European enthusiasm as a basis for comparison, it was easy to discover a 'lack of consistent high-level determination on the Russian side to engage in this program' (Callaghan, 1993, p. 167). This lukewarm attitude could in part be explained by the focus on the issue of political control over the military, deliberately inserted by Western programme-designers. While for the Polish or Hungarian officers this was indeed a necessary re-education, the Russian generals did not find it particularly relevant. Defence Minister Grachev himself had serious communication problems in contacts with his colleagues, as the only warrior amidst a clutch of civilians. Neither were the Russian top brass keen to enter into elaborate discussions on financial matters, since the structure of their budget remained secret and its sheer size had become heart-rending.

As for the debates on the military doctrines and strategies which had seen such a promising start in the late 1980s, their focus had been shifted in the direction of 'peace operations' since early 1993. In this field the differences in approaches were indeed striking. While the Western partners definitely preferred to keep exchanges to the traditional kind of peace-keeping (presumably until they could sort out among themselves the differences in views on humanitarian intervention, peace enforcement, etc.), to the Russian warriors this concept remained foreign and fundamentally irrelevant. They saw peace-keeping as just one element of operations in low-intensity conflicts; to them, such activities as observation and monitoring were closely linked with raids, ambushes and search-and-destroy. (See Chapter 6.3 for more details.) Western ambitions to educate Russians in newly established peace-keeping centres failed to take into consideration the educational effect of quite a few field operations under way in the former Soviet Union.[36] Since early 1995, Russia's military intervention in Chechnya has made any dialogue in this field into a senseless exercise.

The proliferation of first-hand knowledge about former adversaries – as the central focus in military-to-military contacts – was not necessarily helpful in destroying traditional 'enemy images'. Many Russian officers had a chance to see with their own eyes that the NATO armies were undertaking cuts in parallel with rearmament, and that the newly created Rapid Reaction Forces were being oriented outside the old defensive lines. At the same time, severe cuts in the funds allocated for procurement and research in Russia clouded the perspectives of its technological modernization, revitalizing the old spectre of inferiority, especially in such areas as high-precision weapons, communication and intelligence.[37] Unlike

---

35 It was a different question that these investments were made without any coherent perception of a desired result. As Asmus, Kugler & Larrabee (1995) have pointed out, the political decisions on enlargement were taken up for consideration with no connection to the changes in military strategies and postures.

36 A Russian officer was heard to comment in Garmisch: 'You are only talking peace-keeping – we are doing it all the time.'

37 Addressing the State Duma in November 1994 on the eve of the Chechen war, Defence Minister Grachev claimed that only 40% of the armaments of the Russian Army could be classified as 'modern' and by the year 2000 this figure could be down to 10%. 'There is no other army in the world in such a disastrous situation', he concluded. (See Parkhomenko, 1994.)

most other clichés used so widely in the current political campaigning, it is true that the damage being inflicted today will take years if not decades to repair.[38] Growing irritation and anger in the Russian officer corps make fertile ground for suspicions that what the West is attempting to do is to make military-to-military contacts instrumental in downgrading the suspicious 'partner' into a second-grade military power with no chances of recovery.

But perhaps the main reason why military-to-military contacts have not been a success is the rapidly deteriorating social infrastructure of the Russian Army. Poor housing, insufficient and irregular salaries, uncertain prospects for retirement – all these look bad enough even without comparing them with conditions in the West. In such a situation the rare opportunities to see for themselves that the status of the military in the 'civilized' societies is indeed very different would only add to the frustration in the Russian officer corps. Simply providing the proper hospitality on the receiving end of the contacts was a problem, to say nothing about 'saving face'. And if there ever had been any expectations on the part of the Russian military leadership that direct contacts with the former adversaries could help in solving social problems, perhaps already by 1994 they must have discovered that fund-raising efforts in this field were hopeless. As Benjamin Lambeth (1995, p. 98) put it: 'There is a particular need for both militaries to advance beyond perfunctory goodwill exchanges for education or other intangible goals (which some Russian generals now dismiss as "military tourism") toward interaction that can address real problems and concerns facing the two institutions.' But what reads on the American side as somewhat nostalgic and wishful thinking, on the Russian side is rapidly becoming a mockery, if not deception. Indeed, the perception that NATO's concept of partnership is actually 'getting something for nothing', providing 'photo opportunities' while demanding serious strategic concessions, would seem not completely groundless.

4.4 The Russian Navy and the Barents Initiative

From the late 1980s, the Soviet Navy was at the forefront of bilateral contacts with the US Navy, sending its ships on visits to Norfolk and San Diego and greeting American ships in its own bases, exchanging Naval Academy delegations, etc. In the early 1990s, these contacts were expanded to include the key European NATO countries, and a series of passage and search-and-rescue joint naval exercises was conducted. Noteworthy among them were the NATO naval exercises in the Baltic Sea in June 1993, where Russian, Polish, Swedish and Lithuanian combat vessels joined in. All these intensive relations were meant to allow the consolidation of a new international profile for the Russian Navy, which by its very nature had long been the most 'Europeanized' branch of the Armed Forces. The Russian leadership also found this international profile quite

---

38 Deputy Defence Minister Kokoshin (1995) has persistently argued a point in which the 'if' seems less and less positive: 'If the vast potential I have spoken about has not been realized in the next few years, the threat of Russia turning into the global backwoods scientifically and technologically – with all the negative consequences for the country's defence capabilities arising therefrom – will become real.'

useful, sending in October 1992 several combat ships to join the international naval force in the Gulf which was to observe implementation of the UN sanctions against Iraq.

What gradually made this positive picture less and less convincing was the accumulating underfunding of the Russian Navy. General Grachev's team in the Defence Ministry had very little understanding of the 'blue water' strategy, and from the very beginning took the naval programmes as an obvious target for savings. Shipbuilding was affected immediately; in 1992, for the first time since the reign of Peter the Great, Russia failed to begin construction of a single warship (Clarke, 1993a, p. 30). However, even the slowed-down accomplishment of projects launched in the early- and mid-1980s meant that new modern ships were still entering into service.[39] But as the budget cuts became really severe in mid-1993, the Navy entered a period of accelerating degradation.

By all evidence, this process has developed faster and has reached further than the corresponding degradation of the Army, but without arousing any real concern in the centre. Naval experts had always been a rather isolated caste, and their attempts to broadcast an alarming message were not particularly convincing (see, for example, Zubkov & Vinogradov, 1994). Many 'civil strategists', arguing at length about the military reform, reduced the arguments about the Navy to a mere sentence or two (Rogov, 1994a). In a peculiar way, political attention in Moscow has been concentrated on the two fleets that in fact were of very little strategic importance: the Black Sea Fleet, which remained a subject of heated disputes with Ukraine, and the Baltic Fleet, which had to withdraw from its bases in Liepaja, Latvia and Paldiski, Estonia. But it was the ocean-going, strategically pivotal Pacific and Northern Fleets that were hardest hit by the abrupt change of fortune. The degeneration of the Pacific Fleet was marked by several spectacular explosions at ammunition depots, and also by the tragic incident at one of its training camps where several new draftees died of starvation. Moscow's only response to these alarming signals was to replace the Fleet's Commander-in-Chief, against the protests of many officers (Reznik, 1994). Here, however, our further analysis will concentrate more on the problems of the Northern Fleet. Those have more of an international dimension, and the European neighbours are more involved in the search for solutions.

In the past the Soviet Northern Fleet used to enjoy most-privileged status, justified by the fact that all of the most modern strategic nuclear submarines (six *Typhoon* class and seven *Delta* IV class) were based in the fjords of the Kola Peninsula.[40] This strategic status was not altered, indeed perhaps it was even strengthened, by the START I and START II Treaties. Today, however, these privileges are certainly gone for good.

The 'weak point' of the Northern Fleet was always maintenance and support. Only nuclear submarines were provided with sufficient basing facilities, while major surface combatants could never find a proper pier and had to fix their

---

39 According to *The Military Balance in Northern Europe, 1994–1995* (pp. 30–35), between January 1994 and January 1995, two strategic submarines (SSBN), one nuclear submarine (SSN), one aircraft carrier (*Kiev* class), two cruisers (*Kresta II* class), and 16 frigates were commissioned.

40 For an accurate assessment of discrepancies in political, military and naval hierarchies of fronts see Tunander (1989, Chapter 10).

anchors in the middle of fjords and keep their engines going in order to provide electricity. According to Northern Fleet Headquarters, only 22% of the necessary maintenance was provided in 1993 (*Murmansky Vestnik*, 2 December 1993); in 1994 this figure presumably fell even lower. As a result, most combat ships have become inoperative since early 1994. The aircraft carrier *Kiev* was scrapped in 1994, and the *Admiral Gorhkov* followed in 1995. As for the one remaining and relatively young aircraft carrier, the *Admiral Kuznetsov*, up to mid-1995 it was waiting for the modification of Su-27 fighters (Su-33) to make a permanent squadron of deck aircraft. Although the training programme was not completed, in December 1995 the *Kuznetsov* was sent to show the flag in the Mediterranean.[41] The number of vessels in the Northern Fleet has been more than halved since the late 1980s, but still over one-third of the ships in its present combat order were built before 1970 and with the available level of maintenance are unable to sail in the open sea (see Nilsen & Bøhmer, 1994, p. 19). Severe fuel shortages have further reduced the number of days at sea (provided primarily by the nuclear submarines) to the absolute minimum.[42]

Another debilitating problem for the Northern Fleet concerns personnel. Living conditions in its remote bases were never satisfactory, but with the growing shortage of basic supplies they have become simply impossible. Junior officers are refusing to demonstrate the traditional staunchness and in increasing numbers are seeking early retirement. As for the sailors, the Defence Ministry, facing a general deficit of draftees, is giving priority to manning the Mobile Forces and some other elite units – and so is sending to the Northern Fleet several times less than its due. Only a few ships have more or less complete crews, on many others the lack is acute. For example, the teams operating the nuclear reactors are reduced from the required 6 to only 2.[43] High professionalism, always a trade-mark of the Northern Fleet, is disappearing even faster than rust is corroding the hulls of recently proud combat vessels.

The scale of the problem is indeed immense, and there has seemed very little hope that Moscow would pay any attention to this politically insignificant periphery.[44] But recently some solutions have been found in an area unique for North-Western Russia: regional cooperation with its Nordic neighbours. The so-called 'Barents Initiative' was launched at the January 1993 meeting of the foreign ministers of Russia, Norway, Sweden and Finland in Kirkenes, Norway. This is a

---

41 For details see *The Military Balance in Northern Europe*, 1994–1995. On the *Kuznetsov* in the Mediterranean, see Litovkin, 1995b.

42 April 1995 saw a rather large-scale Northern Fleet exercise in the southern part of the Barents Sea with several submarines and surface combatants participating. Admiral Yerofeev, Commander of the Northern Fleet, used this opportunity to declare his fleet combat-ready (see his interview with ITAR-TASS in FBIS-SOV-95-065), but nearly all his vessels spent the rest of the spring–summer season at their moorings.

43 This assessment is based on information from the travel report to Murmansk by my PRIO colleague Robert Bathurst, who has been conducting a networking project in this area.

44 Some Western analysts insist that the Northern Fleet is 'still one to be taken seriously and watched with care' (Downing, 1995, p. 245). But the conclusion about 'preserving and developing its critical capabilities in the expectation that it might be required to conduct more robust forward defence operations at some time in the future if political and economic conditions permit' looks like a mixture of traditional over-estimations with rather hypothetical assumptions.

project focused on promotion of cooperative links between the northernmost provinces of the four countries in fields like economy, trade, ecology and tourism.[45] Military cooperation and some other sensitive issues (such as border disputes) were deliberately left out of its framework, but Nordic researchers have explicitly pointed out that in its foundation lies a security-building concept (Kjølberg, 1994).

Indeed, without a benevolent attitude from the Northern Fleet leadership no international contacts would be possible in the Murmansk *oblast*, not because of the 'closed' status of many cities, but primarily because of the traditionally high political profile of the naval authorities. For decades, they had the decisive say in any matter which could even implicitly involve military activities – and the Kola Peninsula still is one of the most militarized territories in the world. Certainly, this role has changed dramatically in recent years, and as the flow of resources from Moscow ebbed away the Northern Fleet found itself more and more dependent on supplies from local sources. This can explain some of the readiness to lift at least to a degree the veil of secrecy and permit potential international sponsors to visit the formerly forbidden fjords. The rapid development of regional trans-border relations led to further political marginalization of the military authorities, it is true, but at least some financial spillover from the relatively flourishing civilian economy has allowed the fleet to make some ends meet.

Today the most urgent problem that really cries for international solutions concerns the decommissioned nuclear submarines. Some 50 submarines built in the 1950s and 1960s were retired before 1992; 20 more were decommissioned in 1992–93 and a further ten in 1994–1995, including two *Yankee* class strategic submarines built in the early 1970s. This brought the total number of nuclear submarines in line for scrapping to 80; and at least 15 more are considered to be in less than full operational service with only a skeleton crew. Only some 20 submarines have had their nuclear reactors emptied of the spent fuel, and the capacities for disposing of this fuel are very limited.[46] The whole technological process of removing reactors from submarines and scrapping them is extremely costly, and the meagre resources allocated from the defence budget are by no means sufficient.[47] The Barents Initiative, with its strong environmental focus, would seem to provide a useful framework for attracting international efforts at solving this potentially disastrous problem.

Norway, as the main driving force behind the Barents Initiative, also initiated the parallel development of bilateral and multilateral military contacts. Russian and Norwegian naval rescue services have now developed far-reaching practical

---

45 Various aspects of the Barents Initiative are addressed in the collective volume edited by Olav Schram Stokke and Ola Tunander (1994). My contribution to this book (Baev, 1994c) takes up the Russian perspectives of this enterprise.

46 The best source on these problems is the Bellona Report, which is based on extensive fact-finding. (See Nilsen & Bøhmer, 1994.) Harsh actions taken by Russian security services against Bellona activists (such as Alexandr Nikitin) in late 1995 and early 1996 have jeopardized further cooperation here. See Bathurst (1996).

47 This problem was discussed at a special meeting at the Defence Ministry in early November 1994; but as the Commander-in-Chief of the Russian Navy, Admiral Gromov, had to admit, the programme for disposing of decommissioned submarines remained on paper (INTERFAX, 1 November 1994 in FBIS-SOV-94-212).

cooperation, keeping in mind the tragic fate of the Soviet nuclear submarine *Komsomolets*, which sank with 42 people on board in April 1989 in international waters some 180 km south-east of Bear Island. The potential for such cooperation is linked to the prospects of the international 'opening' of the Northern Sea Route which goes from Murmansk to Vladivostok. Mention should be made of the 'Pomor' naval exercises in March 1994, where frigates from the Norwegian, Russian, US, British and Dutch Navies performed rescue and naval blockade operations.[48] Norway also helped to focus the NACC pilot study on the 'Cross-Border Environmental Problems Emanating from Defence-Related Installations and Activities' on the Kola Peninsula. Northern Fleet commanders especially appreciated the joint projects oriented towards improving the living conditions of naval officers.

Admiral Yerofeev, Commander of the Northern Fleet, and his subordinates are obviously much more positive towards the development of contacts with the former adversaries than are the naval authorities in Moscow. Thus, the Northern Fleet Headquarters preferred a low-profile reaction to the November 1994 incident involving violation of Russian territorial waters by a US submarine (referring in its official statement mostly to public concerns). By contrast, First Deputy C-in-C of the Russian Navy Admiral Kasatonov used this incident to justify a claim that NATO was developing only 'superficial contacts' with Russia while sticking to its doctrine of military superiority.[49] The Northern Fleet commanders have established an unprecedented direct link with the Foreign Minister, using the fact that in December 1993 Andrei Kozyrev was elected to the State Duma from Murmansk constituency. Kozyrev indeed has used every opportunity to expand the hidden military dimension of the Barents Initiative, even bringing his British counterpart Douglas Hurd to Severomorsk in May 1994 in hopes of eliciting his support for navy-to-navy contacts in the North.

The Barents Initiative is unique and can hardly be taken as a model for other regions, except perhaps Kaliningrad. The Initiative has brought tangible results to many families in Murmansk *oblast* – which might explain why Andrei Kozyrev decided to stand for election there and indeed why he was re-elected to the State Duma in December 1995.[50] At any rate, this is a case of really positive impact of economic and political reforms on the transformation of military structures. Even more important are the emerging new civil–military relations, though they are by no means free of the new Russian plague of corruption and criminality.[51] Certainly, the problems of the Northern Fleet, including the nuclear ones, are far from being solved. But it is the international cooperation

---

48 Admiral Yerofeev, on a more critical note, has complained to the Norwegian press about too penetrative activities of Norwegian intelligence vessels which, according to him, have violated the spirit of Barents cooperation. (See *The Military Balance in Northern Europe*, 1994–1995, p. 39.)

49 These statements could be found in ITAR-TASS, 3 November (FBIS-SOV-94-214) and INTERFAX, 8 December (FBIS-SOV-94-238) respectively.

50 This allowed Kozyrev to step down in January 1996 from the position of Foreign Minister, avoiding the humiliation of being sacked. See Kondrashev (1996).

51 The investigation of the 'uranium crime' committed by three naval officers who stole some 4 kilos of radioactive material from storage but failed to find a customer, hit the headlines in summer 1994. (See Litovkin, 1995a.)

that is seen as the most promising avenue for addressing the most burning issues. Seen in this perspective, today's Northern Fleet is perhaps the most 'Europeanized' component of Russia's Armed Forces.

4.5 Conclusion

It is too facile to declare that the 'Europeanization' of the Russian Army has essentially failed. The fundamental problem was that 'Europeanizing' efforts were not linked to the process of military reform; at best they were taken as the preliminary stage: first, re-educate generals and officers en masse, then reform the Army. But the inescapable fact was that the Western experience was becoming less and less relevant as the unreformed and shrinking Russian Army started to go down the drain.

It seems clear that for any armed forces in transition, options like 'Europeanization' and general degradation are incompatible. Instead of concentrating diminishing resources on the key future-oriented structures, weapon systems and technologies, the high command allowed for rapid decline in all basic components of Russia's defence posture. At the same time, the dramatic erosion of the social fabric of the Russian Army has essentially precluded the introduction of Western concepts of civil–military relations. What pushed the deterioration even further and brought a dramatic setback for 'Europeanizing' efforts was the war in Chechnya. In arms control, the West has been faced with rigid demands for revision of the CFE Treaty, even the readiness to violate its provisions unless 'flank limits' are lifted or suspended. Military-to-military contacts have inevitably been reduced, starting with the symbolic cancellation of General Grachev's invitation to the high-level security conference in Munich in January 1995. Even the Northern Fleet was not spared from the nightmare that the Chechen campaign had become: in February 1995 it had to send a composite marine regiment from its proud Kirkenes brigade to Grozny.

All in all, however, the situation should not be perceived as hopeless. As the disastrous Chechen campaign has brought back the issue of military reform to the forefront of security debates, new opportunities for 'Europeanization' could emerge. What now needs particular attention is the painful psychological trauma for thousands of Russian officers. Recovery and rehabilitation are becoming the key guidelines in returning the Army to its 'normal' relations with society and with the state. When a new Russian leadership makes a fresh effort in reforming the Army – and the second half of 1996 has good chances of seeing this – meaningful support should come from all Western partners (including also the East Central European states) to ensure that this reform proceeds smoothly. Reservations concerning helping a 'potential adversary' to beef up its strength should not stand in the way of this cooperation – only a modern and capable Russian Army could be a reliable and predictable partner for a new NATO.

PART III

THE DEVIL IS IN
THE DETAILS

In making use of war, policy evades all rigorous conclusions proceeding from the nature of war, bothers little about ultimate possibilities, and concerns itself only with immediate probabilities.

Carl von Clausewitz, *On War*, Book VIII, Chapter 6

5
Handling Conflicts in the Post-Soviet Space

5.1 Introduction

The scale and intensity of Russia's peace-keeping/peace-making activities in the Near Abroad could be compared only with those conducted worldwide under the auspices of the UN. Embodying various forms of interaction between foreign and military policies, they deserve closer examination than most of that available on the security studies market. The key issue here is the level of integration between Russia's increasingly self-assertive and offensive foreign policy, and its military policy which since early 1993 has been showing more and more restraint. (Chechnya, however absurd it may sound, is rather a continuation than a break with this trend.) A more general question is how to define the overall course – in which there is also an economic dimension. Is it neo-imperialist, i.e. aimed at restoring the Soviet empire in a new form? Or is it post-imperialist, i.e. primarily seeking to enhance internal security by preventing the numerous conflicts in the neighbourhood from spilling over? (See Chronology, pp. 123–126.)

5.2 Neo-Imperialism and Interventionism

A stream of official statements from the Russian leadership in 1995 – for which President Yeltsin's address to the CSCE summit in December 1994 provided a solid point of departure – if taken at face value, would seem to support the 'neo-imperialist' definition. References to Russia's 'special rights and responsibilities', claims to the role of security guarantor, attempts to monopolize conflict management – these now have become habitual diplomatic style. And many versions of the 'Monrovsky Doctrine' produced in Moscow's academic community have indeed introduced a discourse that deserves this designation.[1] However, several reservations should also be considered before attaching the label.

One thing is immediately clear about the new Russian policy: the desire to consolidate some 'Great Power' status and ensure a sphere of exclusive influence goes hand in hand with aggravation of the economic situation. Here we cannot

---

1 Andranik Migranyan (1994a), who claims the laurels for rediscovering Monroe, argues that any attempts from the USA and other 'third powers' to prevent the 'natural integration' of the post-Soviet space around Russia should be treated as encroachments on its exclusive sphere of vital interests.

examine in enough detail the depth of the economic crisis, but it stands to reason that inability to hold the depression in check can serve as a driving force for a more active pursuit of a nationalistic agenda.[2] Whether this ideology could compensate for growing social disorientation is, however, a different question. On the other hand, it could be argued that the economic situation in other newly independent states is even worse. Experts from the influential Council for Foreign and Defence Policy warned in summer 1994: 'As the neighbour-states are becoming weaker, in Russian public opinion and political circles along with general growth of nationalism there is a growing feeling of Russia's omnipotence, which is in fact illusory' (see 'Strategy for Russia – 2', 1994). But relative successes in economic reform – and Russia could claim very few of those by early 1996 – could ill compensate for the absolute decline in the basic components of national power. So we can start by assuming that the case for further analysis is definitely not one of traditional imperialism stemming from a position of strength, but of quasi-imperialism from a position of weakness.

The maximalist goal of rebuilding the former Soviet Empire within its 'inviolable' borders is obviously beyond the grasp of this quasi-imperialism, but even more moderate regional goals show a certain logical inconsistency. The focus on the 'Russians abroad' issue and on Solzhenitsyn's idea of a 'Slavic Union' should indicate that neo-imperialistic efforts would be concentrated on Belarus, Eastern Estonia, Eastern Ukraine and Crimea, and Northern Kazakhstan. But none of the three latter countries – though they have often reacted nervously to Russian rhetoric and accused Moscow of cherishing imperialistic ambitions – has evoked a convincing example of an attempt from Russia to provoke internal strife in order to swallow the Russian-populated territories.[3]

Actually, the single most important activity of Russian quasi-imperialism is conflict management, primarily in the southern rim of the geopolitical space of the former Soviet Union. This could be called 'opportunistic' in the sense that it often seeks to exploit the obvious lack of political organization across this space, where fledgling states are struggling with numerous challenges, seeking to prove their survivability. But these challenges show no respect for the new international borders which exist only on the maps, while various forms of spillover (refugees, arms smuggling, combatant training) are everyday facts of life. So the premise that Russia's internal security can best be achieved by controlling conflicts in the neighbourhood indeed looks convincing.[4] But only

2 Yegor Gajdar (1994), describing soon after his resignation 'the New Course' as 'cynical bureaucratic decadence', obviously underestimated this trend. He argued that the new policy-makers 'do not pursue state goals of a global scale that inspired Soviet bureaucrats. The current goals are of purely private character: strengthening of the state for the possibility of quick enrichment.'

3 Emil Pain (1994), one of the sober voices in the Presidential Council, has argued against imperialistic aspirations, warning that expansion towards Abkhazia, or Crimea, or Northern Kazakhstan would create 'a peculiar "hatred zone" on the parts of the independent states remaining after annexation'.

4 Russian Foreign Minister Kozyrev (1994b) has routinely exploited this premise: 'In regional conflicts, the intensity of which keeps mounting, there is simply no alternative to the use of force for the purposes of peacekeeping. For Russia this kind of "isolationism" would entail millions of refugees and chaos along the perimeter of southern borders.'

a thin line divides post-imperial security-building from neo-imperialist offence; as Yakov Krotov (1993) argued: 'Uniting for defence, it is easy to cross an invisible border, to fall into self-deception substituting what needs being defended with what is easy to defend.'

The final test of the neo-quasi-imperialist policy is its military dimension, and not so much the scale of military activities as the question of how well they serve political purposes. And looking back to the year 1992, one can hardly avoid concluding that at least several military operations were sharply at odds with what were the declared political goals. The first half of that year saw an uneven escalation of four violent conflicts, of which three were attempted secessions (Nagorno Karabakh from Azerbaijan, Transdniestria from Moldova, South Ossetia from Georgia) and Tadzhikistan was a case of civil war. The Russian Foreign Ministry adopted a strict non-interference approach, ignoring persistent appeals for support from Transdniestria and even the January 1992 referendum in South Ossetia, which brought an astonishing 99% vote in favour of joining the Russian Federation.

Russia's military leadership viewed the situation from a different perspective. In two of the four cases (Transdniestria and Tadzhikistan) Russian troops found themselves in the line of fire, rapidly becoming a party to the conflict despite their orders to remain 'neutral'. The most demanding pressure came from the south-western flank, where the 14th Army based in Moldova all but openly sided with the ethnic Russians who had initiated the secession and proclaimed the Transdniestrian Republic. As a third-category 'cadre' formation, this Army had most of its heavy weapons in storage and was essentially 'indigenous' (the majority of officers and warrant-officers were local residents) – so quick withdrawal was an impossible option. There was only one way to prevent the disintegration of several skeleton regiments that would have left huge stocks of arms to militant nationalists – to call them into a combat mission. Thus Moldova became a crucial watershed in framing the interventionist course of the Army.

The real possibility of losing either the 14th Army as such or control over the combat operations conducted by its units left only one option for newly appointed Defence Minister Grachev – to assume the command. Personal responsibility for combat orders was still politically too risky, so Grachev sent his trusted deputy General Lebed and then persuaded Yeltsin to appoint him commander of the 14th Army. In a matter of days Lebed had managed to work a miracle – troops became controllable and combat-ready; the clash around Bendery (20–25 June) proved his resoluteness; and since then the 14th Army has provided a firm deterrent against any efforts of the Moldova government to restore territorial integrity by force.[5]

This military action was immediately made into a political issue by fledgling Russian 'patriotic' forces. After all, it suited perfectly both the nationalists, who emphasized the 'Russians-against-the-others' aspect of the problem and the

---

5 On Lebed's role, see Simonsen (1995a). The most outspoken and well-informed critic of the 14th Army's political performance is Vladimir Socor (1992, 1993).

statists (or *derzhavniki*), who argued for 're-collecting lands' around Russia. Vice President Rutskoi openly joined the latter case, so for President Yeltsin it became urgent to find some legal framework for the military initiative.[6] He proposed making the 14th Army the guarantor of the ceasefire; the Moldova government – under strong pressure to fix the status quo – proposed instead bringing in a multi-national force with Romanian participation. A compromise deal, which had no analogies in the annals of peace-keeping, was struck between Yeltsin and Moldova's President Snegur on 21 July: it envisaged the creation of a peace-keeping force, to consist of five Russian battalions and three each from Moldova and Transdniestria.[7] The exclusion of the 14th Army from participation in this operation, as *The Economist* put it, 'means that one Russian army is keeping a peace that another has broken' (see 'Imperfect Peace', 1992).

Simultaneously, a similar trilateral political framework was set for the South Ossetian conflict and the CIS mechanism was created for managing the conflict in Tadzhikistan (both cases will be elaborated later in this chapter). That both 'trilateral' agreements as well as the CIS arrangement were just an umbrella for Russian actions was crystal clear for all parties involved, but they were also extremely interested in Russia taking the responsibility for cessation of violence. In autumn 1992 new demands for Russian peace-keepers came from Abkhazia and North Ossetia; while the former was temporarily put on ice, the latter was indeed urgent: this was the first time an armed conflict had erupted inside the Russian Federation. Without going into much detail, suffice to note here that by the end of 1992 Russia was involved in four open-ended peace-keeping operations (Moldova/Transdniestria, Georgia/South Ossetia, Tadzhikistan, North Ossetia/Ingushetia) and another one in Abkhazia looked pretty imminent. That this activity was ill-compatible with a 'non-interference' foreign policy was one thing; another was its shocking political translation: Russia was now backing two secessions (Transdniestria and South Ossetia), one case of ethnic cleansing (Ingush minority from North Ossetia) and was siding with tribal Communists in one civil war (Tadzhikistan).

From this moment both the foreign and the military policies entered a phase of rapid evolution, though in quite different directions. As for the military, they had reason to consider the operations as relatively successful – the ceasefires were observed in all cases except Tadzhikistan. But the continuing presence of Russian troops was a prerequisite, so the key factor seemed to be the shortage of battalions. In 1992, the military leadership appeared to be operating on the assumption that it could use in the 'hot spots' as many divisions (not to mention battalions) as necessary, while the scheduled withdrawal from Eastern Germany would provide more combat-ready troops. But already in early 1993, trying to set the pattern of rotation for 10 airborne battalions engaged in the above listed

---

6 As Migranyan (1994a) puts it: 'Rutskoi, by giving full support to the actions of the 14th Army in Transdniestria and by getting tough towards the Moldovan leadership, contributed substantially to stabilization in Transdniestria.'

7 As Suzanne Crow (1992a) has pointed out, Russia agreed to recognize Transdniestria as a part of Moldova, conditional on the pledge that in case of a change in Moldova's borders (meaning unification with Romania) this region would be permitted to determine its own future.

operations (plus another one contributed to UNPROFOR), the General Staff discovered that capabilities were stretched thin indeed. The status of the Mobile Forces will be analysed in the next chapter; what is relevant here is the general change of attitude to military interventions, in favour of a more cautious approach.[8]

This approach manifested itself in at least three cases, each of which looked sufficiently inviting from a neo-imperialistic perspective. Nagorno Karabakh and Abkhazia will be analysed later in this chapter. The most symptomatic yet often misinterpreted case concerned the three Baltic states that in 1993 and most of 1994 attracted a lot of political attention (see also Chapter 7.4). There are reasons to assume that in the autumn of 1992 the Russian Defence Ministry, seriously considering options aimed at preserving its military groupings in Latvia and Estonia, started to play on the most sensitive issue – the status of the Russian population.[9] In seeking to establish a direct link between the issues of troop withdrawal and alleged violations of the rights of Russian speakers, the top brass in Moscow were actually preparing the ground for a Moldova-type 'peace-keeping' intervention. But already in early 1993, the need to concentrate military efforts dictated the decision for a fast retreat from the Baltic area. As John Lough (1993a, p. 24) has pointed out, the military authorities had been 'negotiating with the governments of the Baltic states over the withdrawal of the North-Western Group of Forces without any political oversight'. What Lough failed to notice was that this was not necessarily that bad, since the withdrawal continued according to the established schedule despite increasingly hostile political rhetoric.

This brings us to the trajectory of Russia's foreign policy, which managed a breakthrough from its short-lived naive 'good-neighbourliness'. Paradoxically, the starting point was Yeltsin's declaration in his 1993 New Year Message that 'the imperial period in Russia's history has ended'. On 28 February 1993 addressing the Civic Union conference he made the first claim concerning Russia's 'vital interest in the cessation of all armed conflicts on the territory of the former USSR' and appealed to the UN 'to grant Russia special powers as guarantor of peace and stability in this region'.[10] Initially, this all looked more like attempts to borrow, post factum, some legitimacy for the ongoing peace-keeping

---

8 Only by early 1995 did this trend start to get recognized by some Western experts despite the gloomy shadow of Chechnya. Thus, Benjamin Lambeth (1995, pp. 86–87, 95) pointed out that 'The military nonetheless remains a responsible and stabilizing force in Russian society', adding also the observation that 'The high command genuinely seems to want Washington to perceive its "near abroad" peacekeeping activities as legitimate actions for the defense of Russian security and not as a pretext for rebuilding an empire.'

9 A mini-crisis erupted in late October when Defence Minister Grachev announced plans to suspend military withdrawals and one week later President Yeltsin issued a decree authorizing such a suspension and expressing 'profound concerns over numerous infringements of rights of the Russian-speaking population'. Many Western experts pointed to the similarity with Gorbachev's bending to military pressure (Hoagland, 1992), while George Kennan (1992) proposed to start a house-building programme in order to 'buy out the Russian Army'.

10 Among the numerous attempts to trace these developments, Suzanne Crow's penetrating analysis deserves special mention; both the above quotations are from Crow (1993c).

operations; then by summer 1993 the rhetoric progressed further, and seemed to be preparing the way for new interventions – and this, in turn, was intended, as Kozyrev put it in an interview to *Izvestia* (8 October), to prevent Russia from 'losing geopolitical positions that took centuries to conquer'.

The Baltic states were not excepted from this 'offensive defence'. Tensions with Estonia reached a critical level in June–July 1993, as approval by the Estonian Parliament of the controversial Law on Aliens provoked a referendum on autonomy in Estonia's easternmost city of Narva, which is populated almost exclusively by Russians. For policy-makers in Moscow this was a perfect opportunity to unleash a flurry of aggressive statements. They appeared not at all confused by the unconvincing results of the referendum, nor by the fact that most of the Russian speakers in Narva aspired to Estonian citizenship and not reunification with Russia. The military authorities, however, evinced no interest in exploiting this issue with the possible aim of 'peace intervention'. They continued to implement the political decision on complete withdrawal that had been taken a year earlier – though now policy-makers would have certainly accepted if not welcomed any disobedience. By the end of August 1993, troop withdrawal from Lithuania was completed, while the Foreign Ministry failed to prepare any official agreement on this major issue. Throughout the rest of 1993 and the spring and summer of 1994, the military echelons continued to leave Estonia and Latvia according to schedule, despite sporadic heated political exchanges which Defence Minister Grachev joined with few doubts.[11] This swift withdrawal allowed President Yeltsin to make a symbolic step of good-will, meeting the reiterated demands from the USA and Germany – by the end of August 1994, the 'Russians' were gone. The long-predicted military pressure never materialized, and without it the imperialist pose remained a mere bluff.[12]

On the other hand, this could be a dangerous bluff. It was instrumental in introducing a new political discourse which appeared far more comprehensible for many in the political elite than the previous liberal one. Since early 1994, mainstream politicians – panicking at the thought that Zhirinovsky was hot on their heels – had been vying with each other in empire-saving rhetoric. Foreign Minister Kozyrev was quick to trim his sails to the new winds, and his address to the Russian ambassadors in January 1994 set the tune for the campaign of the year.[13] More surprisingly, the military authorities, except for Defence Minister

---

11 Thus at a press conference marking the second anniversary of the new Russian Army, Grachev repeated the point that 'withdrawal of Russian troops is closely linked to guarantee of normal life for the Russian-speaking population', adding the explicit threat that 'it won't take long to send reinforcements'. (See Foye, 1994h.)

12 Russian military authorities showed remarkable restraint in such provocative incidents as the detention of two Russian generals in Latvia in January 1994; both soon were released with apologies from the Latvian Prime Minister. (See Bungs, 1994a.)

13 Kozyrev declared that Russia's vital interests were concentrated in the CIS and the Baltic states, and specified that raising the question about Russia's complete military withdrawal from the 'near abroad' came as close to being an 'extremist approach as the idea of sending tanks into all republics to establish some imperial order' (see Pushkov, 1994a). The prime ministers of Estonia, Latvia and Lithuania responded by issuing a joint communiqué condemning Kozyrev's statement as 'directed against the sovereignty' of the Baltic states (Bungs, 1994b).

Grachev (for whom it was perhaps more than just *noblesse oblige*), were not overly eager to subscribe to the pro-active discourse. Presumably, the generals had started to suspect that responsibility for implementing the 'Can-Do' approach would be placed on them while no one would bother about mobilizing the required resources.

Until autumn 1994, the only 'quasi-imperialistic' initiative that could be imputed to the military leadership was the presidential directive on military bases in the Near Abroad, issued in early April that year.[14] While creating disproportionate international resonance, in fact it merely provided some domestic legitimacy for what had been already settled bilaterally with a few neighbours – some of which (like Armenia) actually were interested in keeping Russian soldiers on their soil, whereas others (like Belarus) did not care much. More convincing evidence was the agreement on withdrawal of the 14th Army from Moldova within a three-year period, which was finalized by August and signed by both Russia's Prime Minister and Defence Minister in October. In fact, this agreement was more a declaration of intentions than a firm commitment,[15] but the readiness of the Russian military leadership to discontinue an operation that had been intended to serve as a model for conflict management was indeed symptomatic.

The intervention in Chechnya might seem to mark an abrupt departure from this cautious and self-restrained military course. But a closer look reveals that the military were by no means the instigators: rather to the contrary, they were forced to implement this variation of the 'Final Thrust to the South' as invented by Zhirinovsky[16]. It could be argued that some previous military 'successes' achieved by the Russian Army in the Caucasus had actually prepared the ground for such a massive use of force (see Galeotti, 1995). But on the other hand, the scale of the war effort in Chechnya and the unpreparedness of the Army for such an 'overload' could not but undermine the sustainability of other ongoing operations, making any new military enterprises practically impossible. The impact of Chechnya on foreign policy is more complicated: in public opinion and in most of the political elite support for any neo-imperialistic schemes has all but evaporated, but for Yeltsin and his entourage 'victory' has become a must. Thus, a scenario involving a new and successful intervention that could cover up the disaster in Chechnya is by no means unthinkable.

---

14 The directive gave formal approval to the Defence Ministry's intention to establish some 30 military bases in the neighbouring countries, including Latvia. After a formal protest from the latter, a clarification was given that the radar station at Skrunda could not be classified as a 'military base'; Russia's Foreign Ministry denied any responsibility for the directive and the 'technical errors' it contained. (See Foye, 1994e.)

15 General Lebed immediately responded with a statement that withdrawal would upset the 'fragile balance of military-political forces' and result in 'nationalization' and 'privatization' of the huge military stocks (Lebed, 1994b). Russia's Deputy Defence Minister Kondratyev visited the 14th Army Headquarters in late November 1994, and reassured the officers that no withdrawal mechanism or schedule was settled. (See FBIS-SOV-94-231, 1 December.)

16 That was the title of Zhirinovsky's book published in autumn 1993, in which he introduced a phantasmagoric plan for conquest of territories to the south of Russia, arguing also that 'New armed forces can be reborn only as a result of a combat operation' (as quoted by Klepikova & Solovyov, 1995, p. 156).

The only way to legitimize such a venture would be through the Commonwealth of Independent States (CIS). Indeed the Russian leadership explicitly invoked a 'threat' to increase military structures in this organization as a 'response' to possible NATO enlargement. While the Russian military leadership has unfailingly expressed profound scepticism towards the CIS, in Moscow's political circles this organization is increasingly seen as instrumental for the pro-active strategy.

5.3   The CIS as a Collective Cover for Unilateral Interventions

The Commonwealth of Independent States (CIS) is a peculiar institutional arrangement now embracing all possible spheres of relations between 12 of the post-Soviet states. Various and dynamic balances between centrifugal and centripetal forces within this organization result in an inconceivably 'variable geometry'. The focus here will be on the role of the CIS in conflict management, which remains one of the most controversial areas of its activities.

For the first time the issue of collective action in settling conflicts was discussed at the March 1992 CIS summit in Kiev, which also buried any remaining hopes of being able to preserve integrated military structures. The discussions resulted in the 'Agreement on Groups of Military Observers and Collective Peace-Keeping Forces', which actually provided only for traditional non-violent peace-keeping and envisaged the organization of multilateral forces on a case-by-case basis (for a detailed analysis see Crow, 1992a). This political compromise fell far short of the demands from the Russian military leadership to maintain stand-by forces for rapid deployment. Seeking to accommodate this position, President Yeltsin at the CIS summit in Moscow (6 July 1992) pressed for a decision to build joint peace-keeping forces; a few weeks later he sent to other leaders a special protocol for signature (see Greene, 1993).[17] The first victim of this pressure was consensus, since only seven signatures (minus Ukraine, Belarus, Azerbaijan and Turkmenistan; Georgia at the time remained outside CIS activities) validated this protocol as well as the agreement reached at the next summit in Bishkek (25 September 1992) on the responsibilities of the Joint Armed Forces (JAF) General Command in CIS peace-keeping operations. The second victim appeared to be implementability, since all forthcoming decisions related to conflict management remained on paper only.

It can be argued that Russia's political manoeuvres around the peace-keeping agenda in the CIS during 1992 remained half-hearted at best, aimed more at demonstrating to the top brass that their aspirations were taken seriously. Consequently, implementability was not a real problem. This started to change in early 1993, as Russia's foreign policy became set on the quasi-imperialist trajectory described above. At first, President Yeltsin tried to reassure the concerned neighbours that Russia was not seeking domination but looking for

---

17 This protocol 'On Temporary Procedures for Formation and Functioning of Collective Peace-Keeping Forces' was intended as an annex to the Tashkent Treaty on Collective Security signed two months earlier; it was never published in the official records.

collective security in which joint peace-keeping forces would be instrumental. His appeal to the CIS leaders on 17 March 1993 was obviously intended to set this organization on a new track compatible with Russia's more active course (Crow, 1993a).[18]

As Russian foreign policy began turning toward the CIS, seeking to make it instrumental, the Defence Ministry became increasingly sceptical. Experience from several unilateral interventions undertaken in the second half of 1992 had supplied convincing evidence that when and if legitimization was needed it could be better obtained by ad hoc arrangements. While Defence Minister Grachev and his Afghan team were inclined to follow a piece of advice from Napoleon – to plunge into a fight and then see how it would turn out – the General Staff arrived at the conclusion that political control over 'peace interventions', particularly if both were multilateral, was a recipe for disaster. The desire to keep a free hand brought the Russian military leadership on a collision course with the CIS Joint Command, which advocated NATO-style multilateralism. This ambivalent support for Russian control allowed Defence Minister Grachev to whisper in Yeltsin's ear that CIS Commander-in-Chief Air Marshal Shaposhnikov was taking sides with Ukraine and other 'allies', so in July 1993 the CIS defence ministers at their regular meeting in Moscow were stunned to learn that Russia had now decided to dissolve the JAF Command. This abrupt abolition buried not only the plans for standing joint peace-keeping forces but for military integration in the CIS framework as such.[19] There could be no better illustration of the latter than the Russian Military Doctrine approved in November 1993, which contains only one brief mention of the CIS.[20]

The only issue where Russian military and political views on the role of the CIS essentially coincided was the conflict in Tadzhikistan. As traditional inter-clan controversies in this country escalated to full-fledged civil war in the summer and autumn of 1992, the Russian military, although reluctant to get involved, found it impossible to withdraw from two key functions: protecting the 'external' border with Afghanistan, and maintaining security in the capital Dushanbe. While the former was justified by the Tashkent Treaty on Collective Security, the latter was never formally recognized but de facto performed by the

---

18 With this appeal Yeltsin tried to pacify Ukraine and several other neighbours who had been alarmed by his February address to the Civic Union which contained claims for 'special powers' as related to the self-proclaimed position of security guarantor. The previous reactions (described in Moscow as 'slightly emotional') indeed subsided but strong suspicions rendered Ukraine reluctant to settle its nuclear controversies with Russia in the CIS framework.

19 While personal animosity between Grachev and Shaposhnikov made an impact, more important were the prospects for the JAF General Command to become an independent decision-making centre if the plans developed by its Staff were to come anywhere close to implementation. By spring 1993, the Russian General Staff was perhaps more concerned about being dragged into some new resource-consuming operations than about being prevented from launching them. I have argued on this point in Baev (1994e). For a useful analysis, see Foye (1993b).

20 The contrast is sharp with the Draft Doctrine of May 1992, with its heavy emphasis on cooperative military efforts in the CIS framework. Up to late 1994, the Coordination Staff continued to produce and make public plans for enhanced military cooperation and integration, boldly ignoring the question of feasibility. For an elaborate proposal see the article by General Samsonov, Chief of the Coordination Staff (1994).

201st Motorized Rifle Division permanently based in Dushanbe.[21] We can hardly say that Moscow master-minded the return of former Communists to power, but it is undeniable that the direct involvement of the 201st Division on the side of the Hissar and Kulyab clans (due mostly to the indigenous roots of many officers) contributed to their victory by January 1993 (Neumann, 1994).

As the prospect of drowning in an Afghan-type quagmire became clear for the military strategists in Moscow, especially after border clashes in June–July 1993 had claimed heavy casualties among Russian troops, the General Staff began to press if not for withdrawal then for burden-sharing.[22] At that point the Foreign Ministry vigorously entered the game and developed a 'conceptual' background for the statement by President Yeltsin that Tadzhikistan's southern border was in effect Russia's southern border.[23] A natural corollary of this statement was the Agreement on Collective Peace-Keeping Forces signed on 24 September 1993 by Russia and four Central Asian states (Turkmenistan abstained from any binding commitments) inside the CIS framework. This Agreement formally established the Joint Command of the Collective Peace-keeping Forces and authorized it to implement the decisions taken by the heads of respective states regarding the use of these forces. What is particularly interesting about this Agreement are two last-minute editorial changes.

The first one was introduced on the initiative of Nursultan Nazarbaev, President of Kazakhstan, who insisted on using the term 'peace-keeping' instead of 'collective defence forces' though the latter definition actually gave a better idea of the real purpose of the operation. The second editorial change was made by Russian Foreign Ministry officials who, in preparing the final draft for signature, deleted all mention of Tadzhikistan from the text. Thus the Agreement, which to all intents and purposes was occasioned by one particular case of conflict, acquired a broader context and could be interpreted to apply to the CIS in general.[24]

As for the Russian military, their interests were focused on Appendix 2 to this Agreement, which specified that Russia would provide only 50% of the collective forces while Kazakhstan, Uzbekistan and Kyrgyzstan were expected to come with the other half. The Russian Defence Ministry immediately proposed to reorganize the 201st Division into a multi-national corps but this plan was effectively sabotaged by Russia's partners – the battalions from the Central Asian

---

21 At several CIS meetings during Autumn 1992 the possibility of collective action was discussed but all decisions were postponed until the internal situation had stabilized.

22 Deputy Defence Minister Gromov was particularly explicit against continuing involvement in Tadzhikistan, recalling his experience in leading the 40th Army out of Afghanistan. (See Gromov, 1993a, 1994; Umnov, 1994.)

23 The rationale for this statement as clarified by Deputy Foreign Minister Adamishin (1993) was remarkably simple: there was no other 'dam' to stop the tide of instability and terrorism fuelled by Islamic fundamentalism. It was not possible to apply the 'Russians abroad' issue since nearly the whole Russian community (which was as large as 400,000 in 1989) had fled from Tadzhikistan. The argument for stepping up Russia's involvement was supported also by many liberal experts in Moscow. (See, for example, Blagovolin, 1993.)

24 Andrei Zagorski has provided a valuable insight on the practical work on this Agreement; he insisted that the omission of Tadzhikistan was not intentional. (See Kreikemeyer & Zagorski, 1995, pp. 159–161.)

states simply never arrived. The situation was reviewed at the next CIS summit in Moscow (15 April 1994) and new decisions were taken on the mandate of the Collective Peace-Keeping Forces and on additional measures to stabilize the situation on the Tadzhik–Afghan border; however, Kazakhstan, Uzbekistan and Kyrgyzstan remained reluctant to provide any troops except for some border posts.

It may well be that in real terms political pressure from Russia on these states was not particularly strong, since it was their own security interests that were most affected by the ongoing conflict, and firm insistence from Moscow (perhaps supported by the threat to withdraw its troops) would have certainly produced the desired effect.[25] In fact, Tadzhikistan was to become instrumental to Moscow in securing the support of the Central Asian states in the CIS, thereby transforming this organization into a legal cover for Russia's activities in the Near Abroad. The deal behind the scenes was straightforward enough: Russia would continue to carry the burden in Tadzhikistan, and the Central Asian states would secure for Moscow carte blanche for any interventions in the Caucasus – which by then had become the prime target of Russia's aspirations.

The CIS summit held in Moscow in April 1994 revealed some contours of this deal, as the decisions related to Tadzhikistan were accompanied by the Statement on the Conflict in Abkhazia, which outlined a possibility of organizing a peace-keeping operation if the UN Security Council should prove unable to take any decision on this issue. This remarkably vague provision was interpreted by Moscow as a valid 'entry ticket'; a peace-keeping operation (described in greater detail in the next section) was launched in June 1994. Even more striking, the UN Security Council was officially informed that the CIS had provided a proper mandate for this operation, while in fact a mid-ranking official had been sent on a tour around the CIS capitals in order to collect the signatures of the various leaders on the decision issued by Russian President Yeltsin (Kreikemeyer & Zagorski, 1995, p. 164). After several postponements, a meeting of the Council of the CIS Heads of States – the only body which could authorize any action – finally took place in Moscow in October 1994, and duly issued the required mandate.

The end result of Moscow's diplomatic manoeuvres was a mixed blessing: on the one hand, the CIS was now transformed into a 'fig leaf' for Russia's neo-imperialist aspirations, but on the other hand, there remained only bleak prospects of any burden-sharing with neighbours in conducting peace-keeping – even operations in their best interests. In this situation, the Russian military leadership, particularly the General Staff, turned to the option of channelling real security cooperation through bilateral relations with a few key allies. Useful insight on this approach has been given by Dmitry Trenin (1994), who reduces the list of strategic allies to only three: Belarus, Georgia and Kazakhstan. He

---

25 The commanders of the Collective Forces and the CIS Coordination Staff were frustrated not so much about the failure in burden-sharing as about insufficient efforts by Russia to find a political settlement to the conflict in Tadzhikistan, which according to their judgement made the mission of this force impossible. See the comments by General Ivashov and General Pyankov in *Nezavisimaya Gazeta*, 3 June 1994 (Minasyan & Rotar, 1994).

argues convincingly that the concept of 'common military-strategic space', while seemingly meaningful if viewed from Moscow, actually made very little sense for other CIS member-states, since their security interests were miles apart (the example of Ukraine and Uzbekistan seems fairly convincing). His conclusion was to favour regional security structures in Central Asia and Transcaucasus which Russia could influence relying upon Kazakhstan and Georgia, giving them – and only them – reliable security guarantees.

A package of bilateral Russian–Kazakhstan military agreements signed during President Nazarbaev's visit to Moscow in January 1995 confirms that such an approach is in fact becoming practical policy. The declaration signed by two presidents envisages that 'from 1995, the parties will begin forming unified armed forces based on the principles of joint planning, training and use of troops (forces), and provision of weapons and military equipment for them . . .'.[26] But in practice, Kazakhstan has remained rather cautious in translating such ambitious declarations into practical steps; it carefully channelled the cooperation into the field of air defence, providing Russia with conditional access to some facilities that actually were of little use for the Kazakh Army. At the CIS summit at Alma-Ata in February, President Nazarbaev initiated the approval of the Memorandum on Peace and Stability, instead of discussing the practicalities of security cooperation – even though President Yeltsin had called the development of integrative ties in 1994 'unsatisfactory' exactly because of the lack of practical measures and had called for a 'breakthrough'.[27]

Russia's dominance in the CIS was strong enough to guarantee that both the organization and its member-states would remain silent about the war in Chechnya, avoiding any hints that could be interpreted as interference in the 'Big Brother's' internal affairs. But this war made Russia's promised investments in developing of any integrative military structures – even in such a well-prepared field as air defence – increasingly problematic. With the sustainability of the CIS operation in Tadzhikistan becoming more questionable than ever before, Russia's ability to instrumentalize the CIS for conflict management in the Caucasus by shaping the consensus of the Central Asian states eroded rapidly. For Moscow itself it is by no means clear how to adapt its 'managerial' approach to new realities; in the current debate the ambitious claims about reintegrating

---

26 The chief of Kazakhstan's General Staff clarified that the plans did not go as far as full merger of Armed Forces since that would 'deprive both Russia and Kazakhstan of part of their sovereignty'. (See INTERFAX, 1 February in FBIS-SOV-95–002. For the text of the Declaration see *Kazakhstanskaya Pravda*, 21 January in FBIS-SOV-95–016.)

27 The CIS Staff for Coordination of Military Cooperation presented at this summit its plan that elaborated the 'Basic Guidelines for the Integrated Development of the CIS' as approved at the previous summit in October 1994. The plan envisaged the creation of four regional security zones: Western (Belarus and Russia's Kaliningrad and Smolensk regions), Caucasian (Armenia, Azerbaijan, Georgia and Russia's North Caucasus), Central Asian (Kyrgyzstan, Tadzhikistan, Uzbekistan), and Eastern (Kazakhstan, Kyrgyzstan and Russia's neighbouring regions). The plan was duly shelved at the Alma-Ata CIS summit, but what is interesting about it is the intention to cut off Kazakhstan from Central Asia, which perhaps reflects concerns in Moscow about Nazarbaev's ambitions to become the regional leader. (See General Ivashov's interview with INTERFAX, 14 February in FBIS-SOV-95–031; General Samsonov's interview with *Rossiiskie Vesti*, 8 February 1995; and Nazarbaev, 1995b.)

the former empire around Russia often go hand in hand with selfish concerns about inviting free-riders and pulling chestnuts out of the fire for thankless clients. While warnings concerning the risks of Russia's 'somewhat reintegrationst policy' are quite common (see Zagorski, 1995, p. 270), the dangers of a neo-isolationist course with a strong nationalistic agenda are often overlooked. The CIS structures and dynamics, however fragile and uncertain, provide at least some resistance against Moscow's sharp turn in this direction – provoked first and foremost by Chechnya.

5.4   Russia in the Caucasus: Peace-Keeping and War-Making

Since the late 1980s, the Caucasus has become the most conflict-torn region across the post-Soviet space; the three newly born states (Armenia, Azerbaijan and Georgia) inherited such a load of ethnonational tensions and political instability that as of the mid-1990s none of them has firmly established its independence. Russia has assumed main responsibility for conflict management in this area; while jealously protecting its monopoly, it also has to face the fact that the burden is becoming too heavy (see Map 5.1).[28]

The pattern of use of military force in conflicts that were getting out of control was established during late perestroika, but none of those attempts (the list includes the dispersal of a rally in Tbilisi in April 1989, the assault aimed at restoring order in Baku in January 1990, and limited operations against Armenian paramilitary forces in Nagorno Karabakh in the spring and summer of 1991) was successful. Russia actually started its activities with yet another failure, sending some 500 troops to Chechnya in October 1991 to restore order and prevent the declared secession. The attempt was aborted before any bloodshed, and for the next eight months Russia remained more concerned about military withdrawal from the Transcaucasus.[29] Moscow's foreign policy also remained remarkably inattentive to the conflict developments in the Caucasian 'backyard' until a series of emergencies took it by surprise.

A new chapter in Russia's military involvement started in July 1992 with the launching of the first in a series of peace-keeping interventions. The target was South Ossetia, which since late 1989 had been attempting to increase its autonomy and then to secede from Georgia, with the inevitable consequence of an escalation in violent clashes. Russia certainly had its own political reasons for interference: in January 1992 the South Ossetians had voted by an overwhelming 99% for joining the Russian Federation and for reunification with North Ossetia.[30] There were also

---

28 The following analysis draws heavily on my chapter (Baev, 1995e) in the book *Peacekeeping in Europe* that resulted from the international conference organized by NUPI Peacekeeping and Multinational Operations Programme in November 1994. See also my article (Baev, 1995b) in PRIO series *Conflicts in the OSCE Area*.

29 In February 1992, the 366th Motor Rifle Regiment was withdrawn to Russia from Nagorno Karabakh. In May 1992, an agreement was reached on withdrawal of all Russian troops from Azerbaijan over a period of two years. (See Fuller, 1993.)

30 The drive for joining the Russian Federation remained strong in late 1994 despite growing tensions and competition with the North Ossetian leadership. (See Gorodetskaya, 1994.)

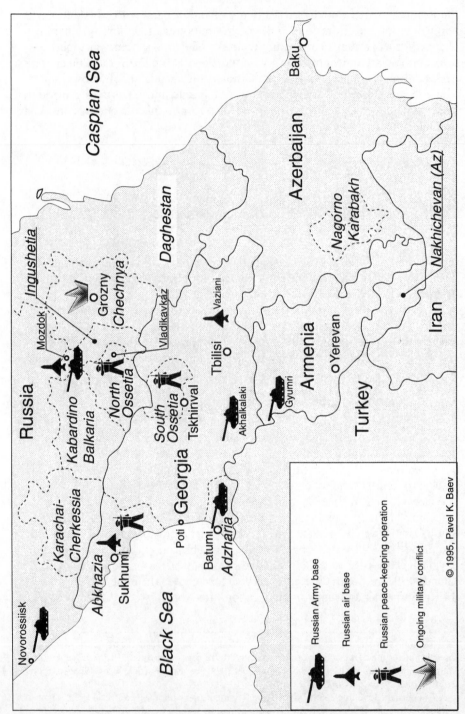

Map 5.1   *Conflicts, Peace-keeping Operations and Russian Troops in the Caucasus*

humanitarian reasons related to the some 70,000 refugees who had fled from the conflict-torn areas around the besieged South Ossetian capital of Tskhinval, mostly to North Ossetia. But most convincing were perhaps the military incentives for fixing a lever that would make it possible to apply pressure on Georgia in order to preserve key military facilities on its territory.[31]

The political setting for the intervention closely followed the example of Transdniestria (except that no attempts were made to bring it under the CIS umbrella, since Georgia had refused to join this organization), while both had no precedents in the annals of peace-keeping. The mandate was formalized in the agreement between the Russian government and the Georgian State Council (an interim body of highly questionable legitimacy created after the January 1991 coup against President Gamsakhurdia) with the consent of the South Ossetian Supreme Soviet which Georgia refused to recognize as a legitimate organ.[32] All three parties agreed to contribute one battalion each for the peace-keeping force, which would be answerable to the Joint Control Commission.[33] Deployment proceeded in a surprisingly smooth way, and the ceasefire has been observed ever since except for minor accidents.[34] The political price for this success was paid mainly by Tbilisi, since the peace-keeping operation effectively secures South Ossetian secession, with only occasional lip service paid to the territorial integrity of Georgia.

Perhaps the most striking feature about this operation is the strong impulse which it sent to conflict-pregnant Abkhazia. Just one week after Russian deployment in South Ossetia, the Abkhazian Parliament voted to re-establish the Constitution of 1925, which essentially meant independence from Georgia. Two weeks later, units of the Georgian National Guard stormed Sukhumi. The investigation of intricate plots behind the Abkhazian crisis is impossible within the limits of this chapter.[35] But one fact speaks strongly against any assumptions of coincidence. In May 1992, the Tashkent Accord on the distribution of the CFE Treaty limits among the newly independent states was signed; but only in July (i.e. after the quasi-settlement in South Ossetia) did Russia agree to transfer to Georgia its due: 220 tanks, 220 ACV, 285 artillery pieces, 100 combat aircraft and 50 combat helicopters. If there had ever been hopes that the stipulation on non-use of these arms in domestic conflicts would be taken seriously, the Abkhazian enterprise proved them false.

The official Russian position on the conflict in Abkhazia was one of strict neutrality, but for the military commanders whose troops were stationed in the

---

31 There was also a minor air base outside Tskhinval where a helicopter regiment was based, but this hardly figured high in the strategic calculations.

32 The agreement was finalized at a meeting between Yeltsin and Shevardnadze in Helsinki on 9 July 1992 during the CSCE summit.

33 In fact, the Russian reinforced airborne battalion had a strength of 950 (soon reduced to 700), the Ossetian militia battalion was 470 men strong, and the Georgian para-military troop had only 320 soldiers. (See Allison, 1994; Crow, 1992a.)

34 The Russian peace-keepers were attacked only once – immediately on arrival in Tskhinval, but lost several men during July due to sniper attacks and land mines. (See INTERFAX, 15 July 1992, 7 August 1992.)

35 For a precise and up-to-date analysis see Dale (1995); also useful is Baranovsky (1994).

very line of fire this idea was meaningless. The Russian military involvement in the fighting had various elements, some of which perhaps went far beyond any flexible definition of 'peace-keeping'. This refers first of all to the troops in Eshera (reinforced with an airborne battalion) which precluded Georgian forces from launching a further offensive and stabilized the front line along the River Gumista. Several operations aimed at evacuating holiday-makers and refugees, deliveries of humanitarian aid were also conducted, some of them with casualties.[36] But quite often these activities provided a cover for military support to the Abkhazian side. This could come in various forms – like the punitive air strikes on Sukhumi. Already in October 1992, Abkhazians (with hundreds of volunteers from the North Caucasus as well as Cossacks fighting on their side) defeated Georgians in Gagra, thus restoring control over the main line of communications with Russia. After this, trench warfare was to be the pattern of conflict for nearly a year.

But before the Abkhazian conflict entered its culminating phase in Autumn 1993 and immediately after the first Abkhazian counter-offensive, another conflict erupted in the North Caucasus, providing yet another Russian 'peace' operation. In late October 1992, ethnic clashes between Ossetians and Ingush spread in the Prigorodny district of North Ossetia, leaving some 500 people dead and some 40,000 Ingush expelled. The response from Moscow to this 'domestic' crisis was quick, and controversial. An airborne regiment plus some 2,000 interior troops were deployed to Prigorodny district to give a strong backing to the North Ossetian militia and press down Ingush resistance, while another armoured unit moved through Ingushetia to the border with Chechnya, to remind this mutinous autonomy that Russia was not going to let it be.[37] Order was restored in a matter of days, but the continuing presence of Russian troops has remained necessary to maintain stability – and this the Ingush side has good reasons to consider unacceptable.

In early 1993 the chain-reaction of conflicts in the Caucasian region continued with a new escalation of fighting around Nagorno Karabakh, but Russia definitely preferred to stay away from this imbroglio.[38] It was no longer possible to keep on providing spontaneous reactions to emergencies; the need for a more or less consistent strategy in the Caucasus was becoming too obvious. There were plenty of sentimental and 'civilizational' arguments, but in the context of

---

36 A helicopter with about 50 refugees on board was shot down by a surface-to-air missile on 14 December 1992; this incident led to further consolidation of an anti-Georgian line in Russian diplomacy. Catherine Dale (1995) is inclined to take it as the starting point for a series of self-assertive statements including Yeltsin's above-mentioned speech at the Civic Union conference in February 1993.

37 I am indebted to Valery Tishkov, former Chairman of the State Committee on Nationalities and now Director of the Institute of Ethnology, for insights on this conflict; see also 'Ethnic Cleansings Come to Russia' (1992) and Corley (1994). For unabashed praise of the operation see Raevsky & Vorob'ev (1994, especially pp. 34–35, 40.

38 Yeltsin and Nazarbaev tried a joint mediation initiative back in September 1991; its fruitlessness discouraged further Russian efforts, which remained limited to periodic meetings of foreign ministers that sometimes resulted in ceasefire agreements (as in September 1992) which were completely disregarded on the ground. In August 1992, Armenia concluded an agreement with Russia on basing of troops (7th Army Headquarters and one division) till the end of 1993.

practical policy they could be reduced to one basic geopolitical premise – strategic withdrawal from the Transcaucasus would inevitably lead to loss of control over the North Caucasus, and this in turn would start an uncontrollable disintegration of the Russian Federation. Although it may be an alarmist over-reaction to Chechnya's secession, this premise carries considerable political weight today, due to the clear trend toward erosion of the centre vis-a-vis new political forces in the periphery.

The conclusion to be drawn from this 'falling domino' hypothesis was clear and straightforward: the situation in the North Caucasus could be stabilized only if Russia could consolidate its political influence and military presence in Georgia. It was elaborated by quite a few academic experts,[39] and as early as Autumn 1992 the newly created Council for Foreign and Defence Policy in its Report 'Strategy for Russia' defined Georgia as a key strategic ally.[40] While this strategy was never properly formulated in any official documents, the military leadership eagerly contributed to its development. Looking at the military steps undertaken in late 1992 to early 1993, we may find evidence indicating that the General Staff arrived at the conclusion that the escalation of overlapping Caucasian conflicts – both horizontal and vertical – would pose a direct threat to Russia's 'soft underbelly' in Stavropol and Krasnodar *krai*. And it was the possible involvement of Turkey (perceived as a natural ally not only for Azerbaijan, but also for the Muslim highland peoples of the North Caucasus) that made those scenarios worrisome indeed. Hence Defence Minister Grachev's far-reaching statement that the Black Sea coast was of strategic importance for Russia, and that only permanent basing of military forces could secure Russia's interests (Dale, 1993). So the year 1993 saw a remarkable congruence between Russia's foreign and military policy in the Caucasus. Accordingly, Georgia became the main target of Russia's activities, and Abkhazia the key instrument.

The Abkhazian side was hardly an easy subject for manipulation. Vladislav Ardzinba, Chairman of the Abkhazian Supreme Soviet, played very skilfully on the desire of many among the Russian top brass to take vengeance on Shevardnadze for his 'anti-military' foreign policy – and not by directly ousting him from power but by making him weak and dependent. That made Russia a very questionable mediator, but Moscow invested considerable political effort in preserving its monopoly on managing this conflict. Georgia had to accept Russia's guarantees for the ceasefire negotiated in late July 1993 – only to see their worthlessness when the Abkhazians launched a surprise attack and captured Sukhumi two months later. At the time, all international attention was focused on Moscow, where the political crisis was reaching culmination.

This humiliating defeat did not make Shevardnadze a suitable partner for Moscow. The game continued in Western Georgia, where ex-President Zviad

---

39 See, for example, Kuvaldin (1992). For a more generalized approach see the chapters of Vitaly Naumkin and Tonya Putnam in Blackwill & Karaganov (1994). A useful overview can be found in Neumann (1993b).

40 The 'enlightened post-imperial course' as introduced in this Report included 'active (if possible, internationally legitimized) participation in conflict prevention and termination – if necessary with military forces' (Section 2.3).

Gamsakhurdia had a strong support base. He did not miss a chance to launch an offensive on the demoralized Georgian Army. The situation became desperate for the Tbilisi government when the rebels captured Poti, the main Georgian port on the Black Sea, and approached Kutaisi; Shevardnadze had no other choice than to appeal again to Russia. Moscow made its support highly conditional: Georgia would have to join the CIS and agree on the basing of Russian troops on its territory.[41] Consent was fixed at the summit in Moscow between President Yeltsin and the heads of three Transcaucasian states in October. In a matter of days a new Russian 'peace' intervention was launched. This included a marine battalion (from the Black Sea Fleet) landing in Poti, the deployment of another battalion for securing the main railway, and logistical support for Georgian troops which helped them to defeat the rebels in less than a week.[42] Unlike in other cases, these Russian troops were indeed withdrawn as soon as the mission was accomplished.

Moscow considered it necessary to consolidate its influence in Georgia and to keep a strong lever in the Georgian-Abkhazian conflict. As the first step in this direction, the bilateral Treaty on Friendship, Neighbourly Relations and Cooperation was signed in February 1994.[43] But it took months of political manoeuvring to fix the framework for a new peace-keeping operation which followed closely some previous tripartite arrangements but had more legitimacy due to implicit UN blessing[44] and the CIS umbrella (as analysed in the previous section). The operation, which started in June 1994, involved the deployment of some 3,000 Russian troops along the River Inguri, which acquired a status quite close to that of an international border. Abkhazians have not found it that difficult to interpret this deployment as a kind of security guarantee for its secession despite Russia's formal confirmation of the territorial integrity of Georgia. The Abkhazian government has moved very decisively to prevent the peace-keeping forces from taking any responsibility for the return of some 240,000 refugees, clearly intending to use the refugee issue as a bargaining chip to obtain international recognition.[45]

---

41 While the new agreement that later was incorporated in the bilateral Treaty allowed three Russian military bases in Georgia to be maintained until the end of 1995, it effectively annulled the agreement of May 1993 on complete withdrawal of all troops by the end of 1995. (See Fuller, 1994a.)

42 Reports of direct participation of Russian troops in clashes with Gamsakhurdia's forces were highly controversial. Perhaps a show of force was sufficient for destroying the fighting spirit of the rebels. As Baranovsky (1994, p. 195) pointed out, this civil war actually was 'closer to farce than to large-scale tragedy. "Landing units" arriving in a half dozen or so private Zhiguli automobiles were able to "conquer" whole towns.' He argued that both sides were 'contesting control of a system which had almost completely fallen apart'. (See also Mikadze, 1993.)

43 On the hidden agenda of this Treaty which 'gives Russia a strong political lever to influence the settlement of ethnic conflicts in Georgia' see Arbatov (1994a).

44 Certainly, UN Security Council Resolutions No. 849 and 858, which established the UN Observation Mission in Georgia, did not provide Russia with any authorization for conducting this operation, but the fact of UN acknowledgement gave it enough legitimacy. I am indebted to Shashi Tharoor for clarification on this point.

45 Thus, a sharp démarche from the Abkhazians in September, and some troop movement in support of it, forced Russian Deputy Defence Minister General Kondratyev to retreat in only a matter of days from his promise to start immediately the return of refugees. (See Mikadze, 1994.)

Russia's more active involvement in Abkhazia since autumn 1993 has indirectly supported its new diplomatic campaign aimed at conflict settlement in Nagorno Karabakh. Soon after Azerbaijan joined the CIS in September 1993, Moscow presented a plan for a permanent ceasefire that would be monitored by Russian observers. Elaborated by early 1994, this plan envisaged the creation of a security zone with 49 observation posts protected by some 2,000 Russian troops that could act as a 'separation force' (Allison, 1994, p. 8). Russian Defence Minister Grachev became the untiring advocate of this plan, while Yeltsin's plenipotentiary representative Kazimirov took several rounds of 'shuttle diplomacy' between Baku and Yerevan and smoothed the connections with the CSCE Minsk group (see Chapter 7.2). It was Grachev who negotiated the first more or less stable ceasefire agreement with his counterparts from Armenia, Azerbaijan and Nagorno Karabakh in February 1994 and a permanent one in May, but his expectations that troop deployment would follow suit were frustrated (see Fuller, 1994b). Azerbaijan kept on raising new objections against the participation of units from the 7th Army based in Armenia, against deployment of Russian border troops on its border with Iran, etc. These procrastination tactics were clearly aimed at getting the operation under the CSCE aegis and reducing Russia's contingent in the peace-keeping forces to some 30%. But up until December 1994, Moscow remained committed to its own plan, insisting that only Russian troops under Russian command could do the job, perhaps under some international monitoring.

By the end of 1994 Russia was conducting two open-ended peace-keeping operations in Georgia and another one on its own territory (North Ossetia/Ingushetia). It had secured the basing of the Transcaucasian Group of Forces (some 20,000 troops in Georgia and 10,000 in Armenia) at least for another year, and was beefing up the grouping in the North Caucasus MD. This impressive military activity had a strong impact on conflict developments in the region; from early 1994, all large-scale hostilities were 'frozen' and ceasefires were indeed observed. This permitted relative political stabilization; the only coup attempt in Azerbaijan in October 1994 was defeated without any bloodshed. Certainly, this 'pacification' remained fragile; none of the conflicts was actually resolved, while most negotiations were deadlocked. Perhaps it took no less than a miracle to ensure that none of Russia's military operations ran into serious trouble. Moscow was eager to build on this success, however uncertain. Despite the growing bills for peace-keeping, planning was under way for a new operation in Nagorno Karabakh.

The one remaining problem was Chechnya, which had defied all attempts to bring it back under Moscow's control and refused to yield to increasing military pressure. A 'forceful solution' of this crisis was expected to consolidate Russia's political gains and military positions in the Caucasus – but obviously Moscow was running low on miracles. A humiliating military defeat in Chechnya could well lead to a political disaster on even a larger scale. While in strategic terms the issues are the sustainability of Russia's peace-keeping operations and the durability of its military presence in Transcaucasus; in political terms, a dramatic erosion of Russian influence in the Caucasus has become the dominant trend. One Georgian expert has stated the widely held perception: 'In the end it will be

122 PART III: THE DEVIL IS IN THE DETAILS

Russia that will make the final decisions and enforce them. This belief is itself a self-fulfilling prophecy and an important factor encouraging active Russian involvement in the region' (Nodia, 1995, p. 39). But after the disastrous assault on Grozny, that is no longer the case. Perhaps Azerbaijan now demonstrates most clearly this new disregard for Russia's opinions, particularly in striking its oil deals with the West (see Holoboff, 1995).[46] With very few available economic instruments, unimpressive and diminishing military capabilities, and eroded political prestige, Moscow will have to be satisfied with a much smaller role in the Caucasus than it used to have.

5.5 Conclusion

The dynamics of conflicts in the geopolitical space of the former Soviet Union have been remarkably uneven. Making a general calculation, we may note that the year 1992 saw seven serious conflicts (Nagorno Karabakh, coup in Georgia, South Ossetia, Transdniestria, Tadzhikistan, Abkhazia, North Ossetia), and the year 1993, six (Nagorno Karabakh, Tadzhikistan, Abkhazia, Western Georgia, coup in Azerbaijan and violent confrontation in Moscow). Some of these conflicts lasted for only a few days (all the coups, and also the conflict in North Ossetia) or a few weeks (like the rebellion in Western Georgia), while others had several peaks and troughs (like Abkhazia and Nagorno Karabakh). The de-escalation trend has been clear since November 1993; and it is undeniable that Russia's interference has substantially contributed to its development. Since summer 1992, the deployment of Russian troops resulted in the cessation of violence in five 'hot spots' (Transdniestria, South Ossetia, North Ossetia, Abkhazia, Western Georgia); the conflict in Tadzhikistan became controllable and even the chain of coup attempts after autumn 1993 was discontinued. After the Russian Defence Minister brokered a firm ceasefire in Nagorno Karabakh in May 1994, for the first time after the breakup of the USSR there was relative stability over its vast territory (except for some minor skirmishes in Tadzhikistan and periodic clashes between Dudaev's forces and opposition in Chechnya). Russia's intervention in Chechnya in December 1994 not only added one more conflict to the list and dramatically raised the threshold of violence: it quite possibly marked the breaking point for the stabilization trend.

True enough, most Russian interventions did not follow international standards of peace-keeping; their legal basis was shaky, and they did not bring political solutions to the conflicts any closer. There is also enough evidence for the conclusion that Russia never acted as an impartial and neutral 'third party', but always pursued its own military and political interests. Indeed, careful and limited use of military instruments allowed Moscow to restore its political influence in many of the newly independent states (Georgia being the most obvious

---

46 Another example is Abkhazia's stiff resistance to the pressure from Moscow to find a compromise with Georgia and allow the return of the refugees. Russia's new line in Abkhazia is influenced by the unreserved support that Shevardnadze has given to the 'forceful solution' in Chechnya. (See Rotar, 1995a.)

example). And the CIS was certainly made instrumental in legalizing at least some of Russia's interventions and in consolidating Russia's influence in the Near Abroad.

But none of these developments has come anywhere near to restoring the empire; after four years of economic depression, Moscow itself has few illusions about re-establishing the pattern of territorial expansion. Perhaps bold ideas about 'overcoming the situation of unbearable contraction' sometimes spelled out by politicians from the democratic camp (Lukin, 1995, p. 11) could be taken as contradicting evidence, but no one in Moscow is ready to invest one rouble in any expansion. Actually, as Russia's foreign and military policies are gradually becoming better integrated, the latter has become one of the main sources of restraint. The post-imperial course, especially as far as conflict management is concerned, has been aimed primarily at reducing the risks and minimizing the costs of political influence – and that by no means could qualify as dominance. It would also be an overstatement to explain all developments in the CIS as enforced by Russia – the integrative trend certainly has its own potential for development. But even the 'keep-it-cheap' course gradually got Russia involved in a number of open-ended and resource-consuming commitments. So the key question has concerned the sustainability of Russia's post-imperial course. And here the war in Chechnya is making a negative answer seem increasingly plausible.

Chronology of Post-Soviet Conflicts

1991

19–21 August	Military coup in Moscow. Mikhail Gorbachev, President of the USSR, detained in Crimea; Boris Yeltsin, President of Russia, leads the mass resistance in Moscow.
6 September	Coup in Chechnya. General Dudaev comes to power. Next month he is elected President by a highly questionable vote.
5–11 November	President Yeltsin declares emergency situation in Chechnya; Interior Troops sent to Grozny. The decree annulled and the troops withdrawn without any bloodshed.
1 December	Transdniestria declares independence from Moldova after a referendum. Armed clashes start to escalate.
7 December	Leaders of Belarus, Russia and Ukraine meet in Belovezhskaya Puscha (Belarus) and declare the dissolution of the USSR and creation of the Commonwealth of Independent States (CIS).
22 December	Military coup begins in Tbilisi against President Gamsakhurdia.
31 December	Official end to the USSR.

1992

6 January	Georgian President Gamsakhurdia declared deposed, flees to Chechnya.
19 January	South Ossetia votes overwhelmingly for joining the Russian Federation; escalation of fighting between Georgian troops and Ossetian militia.
25 February	Escalation of fighting around Nagorno Karabakh. Massacre of some 400 Azeris near Khodzhaly; Azerbaijanian offensive on Askeran.
3–6 May	Armed clashes between pro-Communist and opposition demonstrations in Dushanbe mark beginning of civil war in Tadzhikistan.
15 May	President Mutalibov overthrown by a coup in Baku; next month Abulfaz Elchibey elected new President of Azerbaijan. The city of Lachin captured by Nagorno Karabakh forces; the first corridor to Armenia opened.
21–22 June	Intensive clashes between Moldovan troops and Transdniestrian militia around the city of Bendery; Russian 14th Army interfere on the side of Transdniestria.
14 July	Agreement between Russia, Georgia and South Ossetia on cessation of violence; trilateral peace-keeping force begins to patrol the established security zone.
21 July	Agreement between Russia, Moldova and Transdniestria on cessation of violence; trilateral peace-keeping force begins to patrol the established security zone.
14 August	Georgian troops invade Abkhazia, capturing the capital Sukhumi and landing in Gagra to block the border with Russia.
7 September	Opposition forces seize control of Dushanbe, forcing President Nabiyev to resign. Escalation of civil war in Tadzhikistan.
3 October	Abkhazian forces re-capture Gagra.
31 October – 3 November	Armed clashes in Prigorodny district of North Ossetia; Russian troops deployed to enforce the state of emergency.
10 December	Pro-Communist forces re-capture Dushanbe; widespread atrocities against opposition.

1993

22 January	CIS mandates a peace-keeping operation in Tadzhikistan aimed at securing the border with Afghanistan.

27 March	Large-scale offensive by Nagorno Karabakh forces; some 40,000 sq km of Azerbaijan territory captured; second corridor to Armenia opened at Kalbacar.
24 May	Withdrawal of Russian troops from Azerbaijan completed.
30 May – 4 June	Demonstrations in Grozny against President Dudaev; pro-presidential forces open fire and expel the opposition from Grozny to the southern regions of Chechnya.
4–28 June	Rebellion in the city of Gyandzha led by Colonel Husseinov leads to a military march on Baku and coup against President Elchibey. Heidar Aliev becomes new President of Azerbaijan.
13 July	Escalation of armed clashes on Tadzhik–Afghan border; a border post captured, 25 Russian soldiers killed.
23 July	New offensive by Nagorno Karabakh forces results in capture of Agdam.
July–August	Russia brokers a ceasefire in Abkhazia; UN mandates an observer mission to monitor it (UNOMIG).
31 August	Withdrawal of Russian troops from Lithuania completed.
16 September	Surprise attack by Abkhazian forces on Sukhumi; all Abkhazian territory cleared from Georgian troops.
October	Fighting in Western Georgia between government troops and forces loyal to former President Gamsakhurdia. Russia launches a peace-keeping operation.
3–4 October	Street riots in Moscow. Troops loyal to President Yeltsin launch an assault on the Parliament building (the White House).
10–26 October	New offensive of Nagorno Karabakh forces in Fizuli and Cabraiyl areas.
19 December	Unsuccessful Azerbaijan counter-offensive in northern part of Nagorno Karabakh.

1994

3 February	Russian–Georgian Treaty on Cooperation and Friendship signed in Tbilisi.
18 February	Ceasefire agreement on Nagorno Karabakh signed in Moscow by Defence Ministers of Russia, Armenia, Azerbaijan and a representative from Nagorno Karabakh.
16 May	Second ceasefire agreement on Nagorno Karabakh signed in Moscow by the same officials.

12–13 June	Armed clashes in Grozny between forces loyal to Chechen President Dudaev and the opposition.
15 June	Russia launches a peace-keeping operation to monitor ceasefire in Abkhazia.
15–20 August	Armed clashes in Nadterechny district of Chechnya controlled by the opposition to President Dudaev.
31 August	Withdrawal of Russian troops from Estonia and Latvia completed.
15 October	Joint armed groups of the Chechen opposition attempt an assault on Grozny.
20 October	An agreement on ceasefire between the government of Tadzhikistan and the opposition enters into effect; border clashes continue.
26 November	Chechen opposition forces reinforced with Russian tanks attempt another assault on Grozny; repelled with heavy casualties.
11 December	Russian troops invade Chechnya from three directions; beginning of the Chechen war.
31 December	Russian troops attempt a decisive assault on Grozny; repelled with heavy casualties.

1995

20–21 February	Most of Grozny captured by Russian troops after indiscriminate bombing and shelling.
March–May	Argun, Gudermes, Shali, Vedeno and most other Chechen strongholds captured by Russian troops; Chechen forces retreat to mountain areas.
14–20 June	A group of Chechen fighters led by Shamil Basaev seizes hundreds of hostages in Russian city of Budennovsk. After an unsuccessful attempt to rescue hostages, the terrorists are allowed to return safely to Chechnya.
20 June	Russian–Chechen peace talks open in Grozny as demanded by the terrorists in Budennovsk.
30 July	Military agreement on partial withdrawal of Russian troops and disarming of Chechen armed formations is signed in Grozny. Political negotiations continue.
31 August	Russian troops withdrawn from Vedeno and a few other strongholds in southern Chechnya. Disarmament of the Chechen formations has barely started. Minor clashes continue daily.

6

The Russian Army as Peace-Keeper

6.1 Introduction

The Russian Army was not particularly well prepared for the extensive tasks and responsibilities in conflict management which it undertook from mid-1992. The rich and increasing UN experience was not considered very relevant, whereas the main source of its own experience was actually Afghanistan. That war saw surprisingly few attempts on the part of Soviet military leadership to re-structure and modernize the Army – quite in line with the way that the political leaders in the Kremlin had tried to minimize its impact on Soviet society. With the beginning of the 1990s – as the Afghan-hardened generals rose to the top – came increasing efforts to transform the Army into an efficient instrument for 'small wars'. However, the shrinking resource base, drastic cuts in the defence budget and squabbles among the top brass all undermined this course. The Chechen war revealed dramatically how wide was the gap between high ambitions fuelled by the impressive 'paper strength' of the Army, and its real capabilities.

6.2 Small Wars, Big Battalions

Low-intensity conflicts never were a priority in Soviet military thinking. The USSR's mighty and combat-ready air-mobile forces were built rather to act as a spearhead for offensives in the main strategic directions. In the new strategic environment of the 1990s, the value and usefulness of such forces increased dramatically but the split of the Soviet military structures proved highly destructive. By late 1991, the Airborne Forces (VDV) consisted of seven airborne divisions (ABD) and nine airborne brigades (ABB); the Naval Infantry had one marine division and four marine brigades; besides that, twelve elite *Spetsnaz* brigades were subordinate to the Main Intelligence Directorate (GRU). All these units were based inside the borders of the USSR but – unfortunately for Moscow – less than half of them on Russian soil.

When General Grachev was appointed Defence Minister in May 1992, he immediately announced that the concept of Mobile Forces would be central to the reform of the Russian Army. The first plans elaborating this concept, which appeared already in late 1992, were indeed grandiose (Vladykin, 1992). The intention was to reshuffle the whole structure of the Armed Forces, since the Mobile Forces Command was planned as a joint command having under its control 10–12 independent regiments of transport aviation, bombers and fighters, as well as air assault (helicopter) regiments/brigades, artillery brigades, engineers,

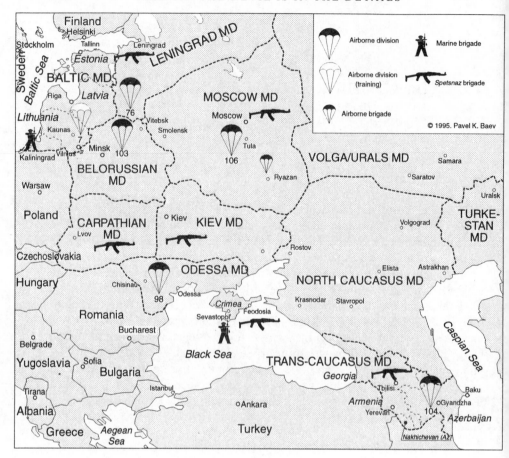

Map 6.1   *Soviet Airborne, Marine and* Spetsnaz *Forces in the Western Part of the USSR in 1991*

means of satellite communications, etc. (For a complete scheme see Woff, 1993.) The 'striking fist' of the Mobile Forces was to be five airborne divisions, eight airborne brigades, six mechanized infantry brigades, six naval infantry battalions and six *Spetsnaz* brigades. The second echelon for the Mobile Forces were the Rapid Reaction Forces, subordinated to the General Staff and comprising three army corps (three to four mechanized infantry brigades each), one tank and one mechanized infantry division supported by five missile brigades, three helicopter brigades, and one air army. In fact, this strategic reserve would include all remaining combat-ready units in the Army and the Air Force (Hall, 1993; Raevsky & Vorob'ev, 1994).

Detailed as it was, this plan was to remain a memorable piece of wishful thinking. Even forming the Mobile Forces Command on the basis of the VDV Command proved impossible, since the other branches of the Armed Forces were scarcely enthusiastic about ceding control over their units. The Transport Aviation Command was particularly reluctant, as it was already leasing out its valuable assets for all sorts of commercial activities in the CIS and abroad;

GRU firmly insisted on retaining control over *Spetsnaz*. Moreover, Defence Minister Grachev and his 'paratrooperized' Ministry had to face the fact that the number of available combat units was three to four times less than envisaged. The 98th ABD and the 103rd ABD were 'nationalized' by respectively Ukraine and Belarus, the 104th ABD was blocked in its garrisons in Gyandzha (Azerbaijan), the 7th ABD had just started redeployment from Kaunas (Lithuania) to North Caucasus.[1] Reorganization of the 'heavy' units withdrawn from Germany into new 'light' brigades was complicated by poor planning and lack of facilities at the new bases.[2]

In principle, the 76th (Pskov) and the 106th (Tula) ABDs plus four available ABBs could have constituted a solid enough backbone for the Mobile Forces as far as the European part of Russia's territory was concerned. However, any reorganization was prevented by the intensive engagement of these troops in peace-keeping operations elsewhere. According to my estimates, by late 1992, the VDV Command had contributed one battalion to UNPROFOR, two regiments to Moldova, one reinforced battalion to South Ossetia, one regiment to North Ossetia, and some elements to Abkhazia and Tadzhikistan (Table 6.1). Trying to settle a six-month rotation pattern, this Headquarters discovered a sharp deficit of combat-ready units.

On the other hand, these initial peace-keeping operations showed a trend towards engaging regular Army units and other 'non-elite' troops that had neither special training nor equipment. The most blatant examples were the 201st Motor Rifle Division in Tadzhikistan and the 14th Army in Transdniestria, but there were also Interior Troops in North Ossetia and Border Troops in Tadzhikistan. While figures of between 10,000 and 15,000 were often given officially as the number of Russian troops involved in peace-keeping operations, my estimates indicate an overall total for the end of 1992 (which includes not only 'mandated' units but also those used without any mandate – like the 14th Army or the troops in Abkhazia) as high as 27,500.

These problems caused considerable readjustments in plans for the Mobile Forces. In spring 1993, Defence Minister Grachev stopped arguing about grandiose Rapid Reaction Forces as well as about including in the Mobile Forces elements from the Air Force. Instead he now preferred to speak about the Immediate Reaction Forces based in the vicinity of conflict areas and able to jump into the 'hot spot' in a matter of hours (Ovsienko, 1993). But his most serious new point concerned including in the Mobile Forces several Army divisions reorganized and retrained for peace-keeping operations. The 27th Motor Rifle Division redeployed from Germany to Totskoye (Volga MD) in mid-1993 became the pilot unit for peace-keeping missions. Several special courses were organized at its base and two battalions were sent to

---

1 One regiment of the 98th ABD which had been based on the territory of Moldova was withdrawn by early 1993 and redeployed to Ivanovo, Moscow MD. Another airborne regiment was brought to Naro-Fominsk, Moscow MD from the 7th ABD while the headquarters of this division is now in Novorossiisk, North Caucasus MD. (See Woff, 1995a, p. B15–12.)

2 For my earlier analysis of the problems involved in implementing the Mobile Forces concept, see Baev (1993).

Table 6.1   *Russian Troops Involved in 'Peace' Operations by the End of 1992*

	VDV	Army	Border	MVD	Total
Transdniestria	2,500	9,000	—	—	11,500
S. Ossetia	1,000	—	—	—	1,000
Tadzhikistan	200	8,000	2,000	—	10,200
N. Ossetia	1,000	—	—	2,000	3,000
Abkhazia	500	500	—	—	1,000
UNPROFOR	800	—	—	—	800
Total	6,000	17,500	2,000	2,000	27,500

Columns:
VDV, The strength of the Airborne Troops deployed.
Army, The strength of the Ground Forces deployed, including the 14th Army in Transdniestria and the 201st Division in Tadzhikistan.
Border, The strength of the Border Troops deployed.
MVD, The strength of the Interior Troops and OMON detachments deployed.
Navy, The strength of the Marine Infantry deployed.

Rows:
Transdniestria, The strength of both the 14th Army and the peace-keeping battalions deployed in this area.
N. Ossetia, The strength of Army and MVD troops deployed in North Ossetia.
S. Ossetia, The strength of the peace-keeping battalion deployed in South Ossetia (Georgia).
Tadzhikistan, The strength of the 201st Motorized Infantry Division and Russian Border Troops deployed in this state.
West Georgia, The strength of the peace-keeping forces deployed in this area in Autumn 1993.
Abkhazia, The strength of both the regular Russian troops and the peace-keeping battalions deployed in this region (Air Force is included in the Army).
UNPROFOR, The strength of the Russian troops provided for the UN peace-keeping operation in the former Yugoslavia.

Sources: The Military Balance, 1993–1994, 1994–1995; *SIPRI Yearbook* 1993, 1994; 'Post-Soviet Armies', *RFE/RL Research Report*, 18 June 1993; Roy Allison, *Peacekeeping in the Soviet Successor States*, 1994; Suzanne Crow, 'The Theory and Practice of Peacekeeping in the Former USSR', *RFE/RL Research Report*, 18 September 1992; Michael Orr, 'Peacekeeping – A New Task for Russian Military Doctrine', *Jane's Intelligence Review*, July 1994; A. Raevsky & I.N. Vorob'ev, *Russian Approaches to Peacekeeping Operations*, 1994; Richard Woff, *The Armed Forces of the Former Soviet Union*, 1995

Transdniestria and South Ossetia to replace the paratroopers there (Gordon, 1993). The 201st MRD in Tadzhikistan was also reorganized, reinforced to a level of 15,000 (50% over strength) and converted into an all-professional unit where most of the soldiers had enlisted for two-year contracts (Erlanger, 1993). At the same time, the 104th ABD was finally evacuated from Azerbaijan, but its redeployment to absolutely unprepared facilities in the Volga MD resulted in complete disorganization.[3]

The idea of the Immediate Reaction Forces found its implementation in beefing up the military grouping in the North Caucasus MD. Early in 1993,

---

3 Stephen Foye (1993d, p. 53) has described this odyssey in detail, concluding that 'The plight of the 104th Airborne Division suggests that even Russia's most elite military forces face daunting problems under the current circumstances and many may be virtually incapable of combat.'

Grachev started to argue that this was indeed a 'frontline' Military District; in March 1993 President Yeltsin issued a special decree 'On Reorganization of Military Structures in the North Caucasus'. During 1993, besides the 7th ABD redeployed to this area from Lithuania, two ABBs and two MRBs were formed here from various elements withdrawn from Transcaucasus and Germany (see Woff, 1995a, p. B15–9). In addition, the 345th Airborne Regiment (which in the late 1980s had been under Grachev's command in Afghanistan) was deployed to Gudauta, Abkhazia, to form the backbone for Russia's military presence in this conflict zone. Another noteworthy precedent was the engagement of naval infantry: one marine battalion from the Black Sea Fleet was involved in the peace-making operation in Georgia despite the endless quarrels between Russia and Ukraine on the status of this Fleet.[4] These reorganizations and redeployments allowed the General Staff to build a substantial reserve for possible new peace-keeping operations despite the absolute increase in the number of troops involved in ongoing operations to some 36,000 by the end of 1993 (Table 6.2).

Table 6.2   *Russian Troops Involved in 'Peace' Operations by the End of 1993*

	VDV	Army	Border	Navy	MVD	Total
Transdniestria	1,500	10,000	—	—	—	11,500
S. Ossetia	—	1,000	—	—	—	1,000
Tadzhikistan	500	15,000	2,500	—	—	18,000
N. Ossetia	—	500	—	—	2,000	2,500
West Georgia	—	500	—	500	—	1,000
Abkhazia	1,000	500	—	—	—	1,500
UNPROFOR	800	—	—	—	—	800
Total	3,800	27,500	2,500	500	2,000	36,300

For notes and sources see Table 6.1

Efforts to increase this reserve continued in the first half of 1994. The 45th MRD based in Leningrad MD was made another 'peace-keeping' division and sent one of its battalions to Transdniestria. This allowed the Russian Defence Ministry to spare another airborne battalion to UNPROFOR in February 1994 without any overstretch. But the burden of extensive 'policing' in the Near Abroad was becoming heavier. In March 1994, Deputy Defence Minister Kondratyev admitted that during the previous 18 months, 105 Russian servicemen had been killed in action and more than 200 wounded (presumably, these figures did not include Border Troops and Interior Troops).[5] Despite the net increase in 'professional' contracts in the Army, it was growing more difficult to find men willing to enlist to serve in the hot spots. So in order to beef up the 201st MRD in Tadzhikistan to some 18,000

---

4 This battalion landed at Poti (the main port in Western Georgia) and took control without any clashes with rebel forces, which simply evaporated in hasty retreat. (See Chapter 5.4.)

5 He also made the point that only 9,000 troops were currently deployed for peace-keeping operations in the Near Abroad. (See Foye, 1994c.)

(nearly double the normal strength) it became necessary to send draftees, abandoning plans to make this a 'professional' unit. Even the two first-line airborne divisions (76th Pskov and 106th Tula) had only about 75% of the authorized strength and were unable to fill the ranks of junior officers and warrant officers (Map 6.2).[6]

These shortages still allowed the Russian military authorities to pursue their long-cherished idea of a peace-keeping operation in Abkhazia. While the proposal made by Defence Minister Grachev in September 1993 to deploy two airborne divisions there was most probably a bluff, new plans for a 3,000-strong separation force looked realistic enough. Georgia agreed to include in this operation the 345th ABR based in Gudauta (and known to be pro-Abkhazian) on condition that two battalions from the 145th MRD based in Batumi (and considered to be more Georgian-friendly) would also be involved. Besides, two battalions – from the 27th and the 45th 'peace-keeping' divisions – were brought in (see Orr, 1994b).

Table 6.3   *Russian Troops Involved in 'Peace' Operations as of August 1994*

	VDV	Army	Border	MVD	Total
Transdniestria	500	9,000	—	—	9,500
S. Ossetia	—	1,000	—	—	1,000
Tadzhikistan	500	18,000	2,500	—	21,000
N. Ossetia	500	2,500	—	2,500	5,500
Abkhazia	1,500	2,000	—	—	3,500
UNPROFOR	1,500	—	—	—	1,500
Total	4,500	32,500	2,500	2,500	42,000

For notes and sources see Table 6.1

This operation, launched in June 1994, increased the total number of Russian troops involved in 'peace' activities to some 42,000 (Table 6.3). The command structure for these operations remained strikingly underdeveloped; actually they were run primarily from the office of Deputy Defence Minster Kondratyev.[7] This led to lack of coordination between peace-keepers per se and other troops involved in supporting roles, and at times even to tensions – for example between the commander of the 201st MRD and the commander of the CIS peace-keeping forces in Tadzhikistan. An even more unexpected and undesirable

---

6 In July 1994 Defence Minister Grachev publicly speculated about a forthcoming presidential decree that would authorize him to recruit some 200,000 soldiers for the units of the Mobile Forces (Foye, 1994k). It was not only budget realities that undermined these expectations; in fact experienced paratroopers had begun to look for salaries and career opportunities in various private security companies. (See Freeland, 1995.)

7 In the Ministry, there was a small Directorate for Supervising Peace-Keeping Forces under General Arinakhin (Woff, 1995a, p. B16–7). But Kondratyev relied primarily on the Airborne Troops Command where a special position of Deputy Commander for Peace-Keeping was established in late 1992. General Staskov, appointed to this position in October 1993, maintained direct command and control lines to all hot spots, except Tadzhikistan, since the latter remained under CIS auspices. (See Woff, 1995d.)

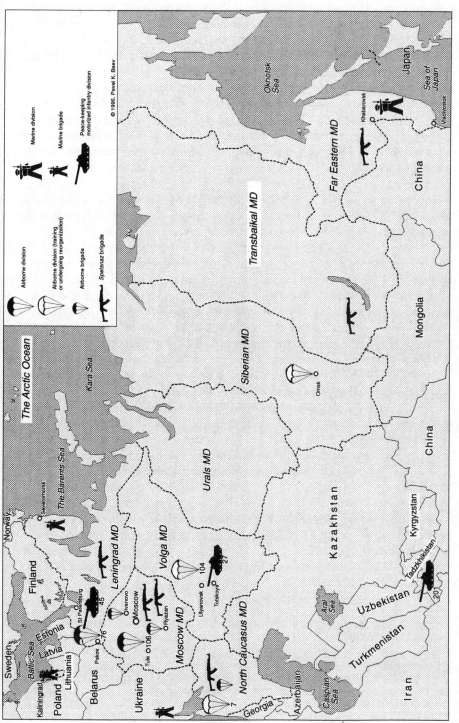

Map 6.2 Russia's Mobile Forces

consequence was the emergence of tight links between Army units and Interior Troops that started in North Ossetia and gradually spread to the North Caucasus MD, where the commanders became more willing to follow recommendations from the Ministry of Interior than orders from the Defence Ministry. Looking for reductions, the Russian Defence Ministry agreed to withdraw the 14th Army from Transdniestria in the course of three years, and issued a directive on disbanding its headquarters; but General Lebed quickly mobilized political support in Moscow and the directive was withdrawn (Zhilin, 1994d).[8] In fact, a new directive with the same content was issued half a year later, when Lebed submitted his resignation. As for the blueprints for the Mobile Forces Command, they were left to gather dust in the archives of the General Staff.

The attempts to build a strike grouping of Mobile Forces in the North Caucasus MD were not particularly fruitful, despite reiterated pledges from the military leadership.[9] One motor rifle division was redeployed to this area from Germany in 1994, and two new-type motor rifle brigades were formed on the basis of another MRD, but the level of combat readiness continued to decline. By mid-1994 the number of tanks in the three divisions and six brigades based in this MD had decreased to 250 (from 300 the previous year), and only 815 armoured combat vehicles were left of 1,200 (some of those were transferred to the Interior Troops). There were only two helicopter regiments with some 70 Mi-24 attack helicopters. The main instrument for power projection was actually the Air Force grouping, which included three divisions equipped with modern aircraft (90 Su-24, 90 Su-25, 90 MiG-29), but poor maintenance and training drastically reduced the real capabilities of this force.[10]

The failure to build combat-worthy Mobile Forces was revealed dramatically by the war in Chechnya. This will be described in greater detail later in this chapter, here let us simply note that the consequences of this campaign for the integrity of the Russian Army were devastating. There were no reserves to compensate for the losses in the 'frontline' grouping that had been intended to deter the spill-over of the conflicts in the Caucasus into Russia.[11] The prestige of the Mobile Forces and therefore the credibility of conflict deterrence were severely undermined. As General William Odom, former director of the US National Security Agency, put it: 'There's been five or six years of deterioration, virtually no training, massive draft resistance. They have physically unhardened soldiers commanded by officers who have had to sell off most of their equipment just to keep the troops fed' (quoted in Nelan, 1995, p. 22).

---

8 Deputy Defence Minister Kondratyev, visiting the 14th Army in late November, told the officers: 'Forget about the agreement. It was signed but there is no mechanism of withdrawal.' Negotiating with Moldova's leadership, he also raised the issue of giving this army the status of a peace-keeping force. (See INFOTAG 28 November 1994 in FBIS-SOV-94-231.)

9 Visiting this MD in June 1994, Defence Minister Grachev spoke about plans to build there a powerful army group capable of waging several small-scale conflicts simultaneously, or even a regional conflict. (See Foye, 1994j.)

10 All figures are from *The Military Balance*, 1994–1995.

11 By late March 1995, in the Airborne Troops alone over 400 paratroopers had been killed, including some 50 officers, and over 1,000 wounded (Woff, 1995d).

The Airborne Troops became one of the main sources of discontent in the Army, its command alienated from Defence Minister Grachev, and the elite divisions and brigades barely controllable by the centre (Zhilin, 1995).[12] General Kondratyev – after refusing to take responsibility for the Chechen campaign – was fired in February 1995. General Podkolzin has had to swallow his criticism of the conduct of the war in order to keep his position and has only asked to spare the Airborne Troops further experiments with creating the Mobile Forces (see Podkolzin, 1995). In the summer of 1995, paratroopers who had just returned from Chechnya were brought to patrol Moscow's streets in anticipation of possible Chechen terrorist attacks – that hardly made any improvement in their morale or combat readiness, but proved once again that the policy-makers in the Kremlin remained eager to exploit to the maximum their 'elite' units.

6.3 Peace-Keeping: Doctrine and 'Knowhow'

Russian military views on conducting peace-keeping operations differ strikingly from thinking in the West. The Soviet Union refrained from participating in any peace-keeping activities during the Cold War; accordingly the Soviet military never gave these operations the benefit of any consistent analysis. As both the UN and Russia have more or less simultaneously entered the period of extensive use of military instruments in conflict management, conceptualization has proceeded along different avenues. In the West, numerous security experts who rushed into this new market have by and large taken the previous UN experience as the point of departure for developing bold ideas about 'second-generation peace-keeping' (or 'muscular peace-keeping', or 'peace-keeping with teeth', etc.).[13] The main difference with new thinking in Russia has apparently come from the fact that in the latter peace-keeping remains part and parcel of the concept of low-intensity conflicts. The natural point of departure for Russian strategists was the war in Afghanistan; so the concept of peace-keeping was to go full circle, to arrive at another war – in Chechnya. But the experience accumulated in the course of numerous operations in 1991–95 is indeed a unique one, so the operational and tactical principles developed on this basis make a useful and valuable subject for analysis.

For the Russian military, the initial requirement concerning 'peace interventions' was that the political arrangements were expected to be clear, non-ideological and implementable. Here the Afghan experience is highly relevant, since military operations were completely at odds with vague political goals which failed to provide a comprehensible rationale for waging the war,

---

12 Another particular element of the new military disarray was the semi-independent status of the *Spetsnaz* forces controlled by the Main Intelligence Directorate (GRU). Thus, the *Spetsnaz* brigade in the North Caucasus MD was withdrawn before the invasion in Chechnya, since GRU as a part of the General Staff raised strong objections against this adventure. Mark Galeotti has been quoted with a similar point by Bruce Clark (1995).

13 Useful overviews can be found in Berdal (1993, 1994) and Roberts (1994).

except for some 'international duty'.[14] In a sense, the insistence of the Russian military on a clear political arrangement is similar to the basic peace-keeping requirement of a strict political mandate.[15]

The main difference concerns the issue of political control on the military implementation of the mandate – indeed, a Russian general would consider as absurd a chain of command which required authorization of every air strike by a civilian 'commissioner'. Russian military authorities much prefer to take an active part in negotiating the political arrangement for every operation in order to secure a free hand in the field.[16] This is not only a product of Clausewitzian military mentality but also a lesson learned from carrying out 'political' missions (as in Tbilisi in April 1989 or in Vilnius in January 1991) and thereafter having to take the blame for bloodshed.

While there is an understanding that every peace-keeping operation in all phases remains a complex action in which the military part is just one element, there is also a strong desire to make other elements subordinate to the military goals. That is why putting an end to the violence has become the central goal of all Russian peace-keeping operations. A direct consequence is lack of political progress in settling respective conflicts which makes – perhaps against the best intentions of the Russian military – nearly every deployment an open-ended one. From this perspective, the only really successful peace-keeping operation in the former USSR was securing the key lines of communication in Western Georgia in October–November 1993. One marine battalion from the Black Sea Fleet and several units from the Trans-Caucasus Group of Forces were engaged in this operation, which was completed in the course of a month.

The problem of political arrangements for peace-keeping operations involves three key interlinked issues: neutrality/impartiality, consent and credibility/minimal force. Russia could not even pretend to be neutral in any of the conflicts in the former USSR in the sense of absence of its own interests: actually, many official declarations about the extent of Russia's vital interests make what is nearly a commitment to provide leadership in management of every conflict. Political leaders in Moscow still insist on their neutrality in the sense that Russia's interests centre on termination of conflicts as such, not on enforcing 'imperial' solutions. However, this claim too obviously comes into contradiction with

---

14 It was Deputy Defence Minister Gromov who insisted most on the pre-eminence of the political side of peace-keeping over military operations as such, referring to his Afghan experience. See, for example, his interview with *Krasnaya Zvezda* (Gromov, 1993b).

15 Thus, Brian Urquhart (1990), defining conditions for success of peace-keeping, pointed to a viable political context and feasibility of the mandate. Not that these conditions were always met, and as Fetherston (1994, p. 37) correctly observed: 'Forced ambiguities, which reflect the lowest common denominator of agreement, leave peacekeepers caught in the middle of varying interpretations of equivocal documents.'

16 Deputy Defence Minister Kondratyev, who was in charge of several operations in 1992–94, in a number of interviews made the point that in certain situations the military could take on the essentially political task of negotiating the mandate for an operation. This approach was adopted particularly for the operation in Abkhazia launched in June 1994. See his article in *Krasnaya Zvezda* (Kondratyev, 1993).

many of Russia's specific interests in the Near Abroad: economic (especially oil), national (such as 'Russians abroad'), strategic (including forward military basing), etc.[17]

A way around these inconsistencies was found: by making the parties to the conflict full partners and participants in the peace-keeping operation. In this 'untraditional' approach, the issue of consent becomes inextricably linked to the issue of Russia's impartiality. The hidden agenda here is that in secession-type conflicts, providing equal status to the 'second' party comes quite close to recognition of secession, and the operation as such inevitably turns into one of securing the quasi-independence of a rebellious province. Accordingly, the main problem is to obtain the consent of the 'first' party, i.e. the state which is the victim of secession. It took serious political efforts on the part of Russia to press Moldova into consent in summer 1992 (for the peace-keeping operation in Transdniestria) and Georgia in summer 1992 (South Ossetia) as well as in Summer 1994 (Abkhazia). On the contrary, since Russia's efforts were not particularly consistent in the case of Nagorno Karabakh, Azerbaijan remained reserved against the operation. Part of the explanation is that one of Russia's main methods of arm-twisting was to emphasize that no one else would come with troops for the operation, whereas in Nagorno Karabakh the option of the first-ever CSCE intervention remained open through 1992–94.

The issue of impartiality becomes even less convincing if we recall that in at least two cases Russia decided that granting recognition to the 'second' party was against its interests, and went on to launch peace-keeping or rather 'order-restoring' operations in support of the existing governments. One of these cases is Tadzhikistan, where Moscow has been paying lip-service to the issues of 'national reconciliation' and 'dialogue with the opposition', while in fact the aims of the operation are to cut off supplies from Afghanistan and to isolate the Gorny Badakhshan area, which is controlled by the opposition.[18] Another case was the already mentioned operation in Western Georgia in autumn 1993, aimed at securing lines of communications which actually provided strong backing to the government forces and helped to suppress the rebellion in a matter of weeks.

In both 'models' – pressing a government into consent, or giving it support against the opposition – the success of an operation hinges crucially upon the

---

17 Suzanne Crow (1993c, p. 5) pointing out that since late 1993 Russian officials have openly described peace-keeping as a method of influence, adds: 'Russia's ceasing to hide its great power ambitions behind the rhetorically more palatable guise of humanitarian assistance is a direct result of the implicit acceptance of these ambitions by the West.' Roy Allison (1994, p. 51) confirms this with the point that while Russia was certainly pursuing its own interests in dealing with local conflicts, 'in itself this behaviour is only natural and not reprehensible (even if it does not conform with the principle of impartiality in peacekeeping efforts)'.

18 The incompatibility between the declared goal of 'national reconciliation' and the real conduct of the operation became especially obvious in late 1994 to early 1995, when Russian Border Troops refused to take into account the Tehran Agreement between the Tadzhik government and opposition that had established a ceasefire from 20 October. This led to escalation of clashes on the border, particularly from April 1995 (see Strugovets, 1994). The Tadzhik government interpreted Russia's position as an invitation to sabotage further negotiations with the opposition (see Shermatova, 1995a).

credibility of Russia's military commitment. Even in dealing with 'frozen' conflicts, Russia has never limited its role to observing/monitoring the ceasefire – it has insisted on securing it by providing a sort of 'deterrence by punishment'. Therefore, even if the agreement envisaged deployment of only a token peace-keeping force (with Russia's contribution of 30–50% and the rest provided by the parties to the conflict), it was implicitly acknowledged that a powerful grouping of Russian forces based nearby would be ready to interfere in case of any serious violation. The 14th Army played this role of a superior force-in-waiting for Moldova, and the Mobile Forces' grouping in the North Caucasus MD was intended to do the same for Georgia. As far as Nagorno Karabakh is concerned, we may assume that the Russian military grouping in Armenia (currently the 7th Army has only one MRD) could have been reinforced – first of all with a sufficient air component – so as to provide a credible deterrent. And it was the lack of such capabilities in Tadzhikistan – a lack all too obvious when compared with the Afghan war – that from the very beginning made the operation vulnerable, indeed destined to failure (see Neumann & Solodovnik, 1995).

These political-military arrangements for peace-keeping operations have a direct impact on the operational principles of their conduct. The most striking difference here with the traditional UN peace-keeping 'code of conduct' is the basic approach to the use of force. While in the 'classical' UN operations arms may be used only in self-defence, in the type of peace-keeping commonly described as 'second generation' (see Gow, 1995) the range of military options is certainly wider but the main guideline is still avoiding breaching the consent – the absolutely central element of any operation. Thus, Charles Dobbie (1994, p. 137), the author of the British Army Field Manual *Wider Peacekeeping*, proposes 'a helpful rule of thumb' – use of the minimum necessary force, specified as 'the measured application of violence or coercion, sufficient only to achieve a specific end, demonstrably reasonable, proportionate and appropriate; and confined in effect to the specific and legitimate target intended'.[19]

This way of thinking remains absolutely foreign to the Russian operational planning related to peace-keeping. Notably, the term 'rules of engagement' – certainly a key notion in the Western concept – is absent from the Russian military vocabulary.[20] This is highly characteristic and testifies to the desire to keep the hands of the military free from any political interference in all high-risk situations of loosely controlled conflicts. While agreeing that a peace-keeping force as such could be kept on the minimal level, Russian strategists take it rather as a 'trip-wire' connected to the readily available prevailing force. And when an operation is launched before a ceasefire is established, Russian planners certainly

---

19 Giving a seminar at the Norwegian Defence College on 8 June 1994, Lt Col. Dobbie went into such details as warning against the use of force and escape routes – the latter meaning that lethal force should not be used against belligerents who are in a position from which they cannot escape. From a Russian perspective, such requirements are simply incomprehensible.

20 I pointed out this symptomatic linguistic deficiency in Baev (1994e). Useful analysis of the evolving operational principles can be found in Greene (1993). A Russian participant in the first US–Russian peace-keeping exercises in August 1994 became famous with the remark: 'They used the same tactics as we do, but I think they shot too late and they made too much noise' (*Newsweek*, 19 September 1994).

prefer to bring in as much force as possible, considering 'over-kill' much less of a danger than a 'position of weakness'.[21] The main limitation involved in such an approach is actually shortage of Russian forces, and this is often taken as a transitional phenomenon linked to unsatisfactory funding for building the Mobile Forces.

The Military Doctrine approved in November 1993 offers few guidelines on conducting peace-keeping operations, though local conflicts 'engendered by aggressive nationalism' are recognized as one of the main sources of military threat. Two aims that are identified – to localize the seat of tensions and put an end to hostilities at the earliest possible stage – both point to a pro-active strategy which envisages employment of maximum rather than minimum force. In reality, the pattern of peace-keeping that can be discerned from a number of Russian operations is more cautious and reactive. In at least several cases (including South Ossetia, Transdniestria and Abkhazia) Russian military planners tended to wait until the conflict reached a 'natural' stalemate which would allow a stable ceasefire to be established. And it was the relative stability on the front lines around Nagorno Karabakh from early 1994 that allowed the Russian General Staff to consider a possible peace-keeping operation in practical terms.

Looking at these cases, we may conclude that from a Russian military perspective, 'linear' peace-keeping (securing a ceasefire between two parties to the conflict along a specific dividing line) is an option much preferable to 'territorial' peace-keeping (securing order on a specific territory). The former could include full control over a specially defined demilitarized zone, but leaving the territories on both sides of it by and large in the hands of the parties to the conflict. Abkhazia provides the best example of such an operation (Map 6.3); but even the 14th Army in Transdniestria refrained from taking any territorial control, and its commander General Lebed in fact became involved in bitter controversies with the leadership of this self-proclaimed republic.[22]

The 'territorial' option is recognized as unavoidable in conflicts that occur inside the Russian Federation, or that affect compact settlements of ethnic Russians in the Near Abroad, or threaten regimes seen as important allies for Moscow. Two key principles for reducing the risks involved in such operations are: close cooperation with local authorities (and accordingly local military/ paramilitary forces), and joint efforts with Interior Forces, Border Troops, etc. The operations in North Ossetia and Tadzhikistan (the latter in fact combines linear and territorial options) illustrate how the Russian military leadership, while keeping overall control, seeks to limit the tasks of the deployed Army units to those which go beyond policing but do not require special anti-terrorist techniques.

---

21 A discussion of alternative models of 'coming symbolically' vs. 'coming in force' in the pages of *Voenny Vestnik* between several officers involved in the training programme in the Volga MD has been keenly analysed by Allison (1994, pp. 26–30).

22 According to the Russian press, in early August 1994 the leaders of Transdniestria came to Moscow in order to lobby in the Defence Ministry for the removal of General Lebed. The result was the plan for restructuring the 14th Army and disbanding the 'redundant' Army Headquarters, which in turn was abandoned when Lebed mobilized his support base in Moscow. (See Socor, 1994.)

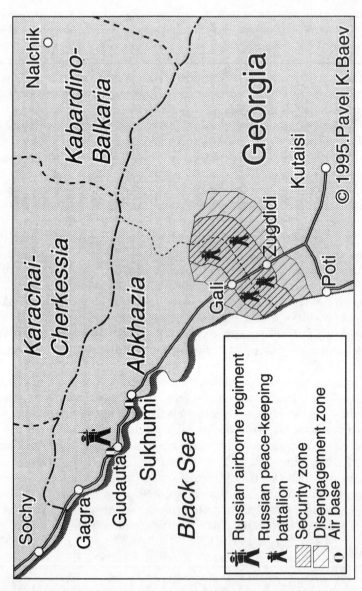

Map 6.3   *The Peace-keeping Operation in Abkhazia*

Among the few sources that can shed light on Russian military thinking related to such operations, the writings of General Ivan Vorobyev, Head of Tactics Department, Frunze Military Academy, are perhaps most consistent. In several publications (Vorobyev 1993, 1994) he has drawn useful generalizations from recent experience combined with the lessons from Afghanistan.[23] His main point is that peace-keeping is always conducted in a highly uncertain environment where a fragile ceasefire may at any time be violated by actions of 'illegal armed groupings', leading to the resumption of high-intensity hostilities. Russian troops, while conducting peace-time functions (observation, monitoring, etc.) should be prepared to act decisively against armed groups and to engage in various combat operations. Accordingly, peace-keeping techniques will include all sorts of counter-insurgency tactics (combing, blocking, ambush, etc.) and even elements of manoeuvre warfare, such as combined air–ground strikes.

From this perspective, the distinction between peace-keeping and peace-enforcement – which is one of the main issues in contemporary Western security studies – looks utterly academic.[24] Russian strategists definitely place 'peace operations' in the continuum of low-intensity conflicts;[25] accordingly, peace-keeping forces are taken as the first echelon which can provide operational intelligence and deal with small-scale threats, but which should be reinforced in a matter of days if not hours with more powerful second-echelon forces to provide effective 'escalation dominance'. The watershed on which the pernicious fallacy of such a perspective was fully revealed was the war in Chechnya.

6.4 The Chechen Campaign

The war in Chechnya has acquired such a scale and become so devastating for the Russian Army that analysis of the campaign as such should be preceded with a brief survey of its unique setting. After proclaiming its independence in October 1991, the Chechen Republic had effectively functioned outside Russia's control, refusing to participate in any federal initiatives.[26] This did not provide for internal stability, and by mid-1993 tensions had turned into violent confrontation. On the surface, it looked like a typical post-Soviet competition between branches of power, and President Dudaev had few doubts about using his troops to dissolve

---

23 An elaborate description of peace-keeping tactics can also be found in a UNIDIR publication (Raevski & Vorob'ev, 1994) which unfortunately contains few references. For the analysis in the Frunze Academy of the Afghan experience, see Grau (1994).

24 According to Charles Dobbie (1994, p. 145), the British Army Field Manual *Wider Peacekeeping* postulates that there is no 'middle ground' between peace-keeping and peace-enforcement, and that these two types of operations are guided by radically different principles.

25 Roy Allison (1994) and Michael Orr (1994a) have arrived at similar conclusions, while Mark Galeotti (1994d, p. 33) insists on the distinction between peace-keeping and peace-enforcing operations, referring to two different Russian terms (*Operatsii po podderzhaniyu mira* – literally 'operations in support of peace' and *Mirotvorcheskie operatsii* – literally 'peace-creating operations'). Actually, the terms are often used interchangeably; for example, the joint Russian-US exercises in August 1994 were called *mirotvorcheskie* though nothing else but traditional peace-keeping skills were trained.

26 The following analysis draws on my paper (Baev, 1995c) which I presented at a seminar in the Royal Institute of International Affairs, London in February 1995 and later published as an FSS Briefing Paper. I am indebted to Edmund Herzig for valuable comments.

the Chechen Parliament in June 1993. What lay behind this quasi-democratic facade was the age-old competition between several major *teips* (clans). Dudaev secured support from the highlanders against more prosperous lowlanders, so the leaders of the latter retreated to Nadterechny district, which borders on Russia's Stavropol *krai*.[27] What made this power struggle particularly destructive was the highly controversial agreement on Russian military withdrawal from Chechnya from early 1992, according to which large arsenals were left behind. This enabled Dudaev to build a considerable military force (with several dozen tanks and ACV) and to arm nearly the entire male population of the republic. Dudaev also kept firm control over flourishing 'shadow' businesses, turning Chechnya into a 'free criminal zone' which, in turn, meant that he could mobilize substantial financial resources for his political agenda.

In 1993, President Yeltsin issued several decrees, supplemented by government orders, for tightening control on the borders of Chechnya. These had little practical effect, however, since Daghestan was not particularly interested in implementing them, while the border between Chechnya and Ingushetia was not even demarcated after the split in 1991. It seemed as impossible to let Chechnya go, as it was to keep it in. The first half of 1994 saw increasing demands in Russia to seal off Chechnya due to several incidents of hostage taking and hijacking in Stavropol and Krasnodar *krai*, all involving Chechens. In Moscow, the official propaganda campaign was intensified, depicting Dudaev's regime as criminal, illegitimate and losing popular support.

By summer 1994, the internal clashes in Chechnya had escalated into full-scale civil war. Several opposition groupings consolidated their control over Nadterechny district and established bases in other areas, threatening to reduce Dudaev's control to merely the capital Grozny. For Moscow it became increasingly tempting to extend its support for the 'healthy forces' (as Yeltsin called them) in order to bring into power a more controllable regime. This support initially included financial aid and some arms and military equipment; but Dudaev played rather skilfully on discord among the opposition leaders and defeated their several uncoordinated attacks. In early November, policy-makers in Moscow decided to secure clear military superiority for the opposition. Some 70 tanks plus several attack helicopters and combat aircraft were 'leased' to the newly formed Provisional Council. But the decisive assault on Grozny on 26 November was repelled, with heavy casualties. The Russian Defence Ministry tried to deny any involvement and referred to 'some mercenaries', but several dozen Russian officers captured by Chechen government forces (and set free after various parliamentary delegations visited Grozny) confirmed that they had been hired by the Federal Counterintelligence Service.[28]

From this point, the nature of the conflict changed irreversibly. The opposition

27 One of the best descriptions of this regional setting can be found in the analytical review *The Chechen Crisis*, prepared under the auspices of the Centre for Social Studies and Marketing, Moscow (Tishkov et al., 1995).

28 These official 'deny responsibility' tactics – so familiar from the Soviet era – made a fiasco of the whole propaganda effort in preparing the 'forceful solution' (see Shevelyov, 1994). Neglect of POWs also affected attitudes in the officer corps – even those who turned pro-victory remained definitely anti-Grachev (see 'The Military Mess in Russia', *The Economist*, 17 December 1994).

forces were utterly demoralized due not only to the military failure but especially to the unmasked connections with Moscow. And Dudaev was able to turn his case from fighting with compatriots into standing firm against external intervention (see his December 1994 interview with *Moscow News*); the 'anonymous' air raids in early December only added new evidence (Yemelyanenko, 1994). Thousands of new volunteers were attracted to his side, starting a real *Gazavat* (holy war) in the tradition of Sheikh Mansur, the Chechen national hero, while Russian policy-makers clung to the perception that the enemy numbered but a few hundred supporters of Dudaev.

At its special meeting on 29 November Russia's Security Council gave Defence Minister Grachev one week to ready his forces; the presidential edict issued on the next day made Grachev the leader of a special inter-departmental group to be responsible for the 'restoration of constitutional order' in Chechnya.[29] The original plan, developed by the commanders of the North Caucasus MD and approved by Grachev, envisaged that the 'active phase' of the operation would take about one week (7–13 December) and result in capturing Grozny and establishing effective control of the whole southern (lowland) part of Chechnya.[30] The grouping of 23,800 men (of which 4,800 were Interior Troops) with 80 tanks and some 200 ACVs was indeed assembled by 5 December. It consisted primarily of units of the North Caucasus MD (such as the 131st Maikop Motorized Infantry (MI) Brigade, the 19th MI Division, the 33rd 'Don Cossack' MI Regiment, and the 21st and 56th AB brigades), while the divisions of the 8th Army Corps (recently redeployed from Germany to Volgograd *oblast*) provided only composite regiments/battalions. The main reinforcements were the composite regiments of the 'elite' airborne divisions (76th Pskov and 106th Tula).[31] Intensive last-minute training was organized in order to boost the combat-worthiness of the composite units, hence the delay in beginning the actual operation.[32]

The invasion commenced in the morning hours of 11 December, and immediately the whole *blitzkrieg* plan started to fall apart.[33] Only the 'Northern'

---

29 A group of Russian parliamentarians presented a case to the Constitutional Court, questioning the legal basis of the decision to invade Chechnya. It was revealed during the hearings that the presidential edict of 30 November was annulled by the President himself on 11 December and the real basis for the operation was the governmental decision taken on 9 December. Still, the Constitutional Court on 31 July 1995 ruled that no constitutional provisions were violated. (See Nikitinsky, 1995).

30 In the following analysis the unattributed quotations are from the lengthy presentations of Grachev and General Kvashnin at the Assembly of Russian Military Leadership on 28 February, as published in *Krasnaya Zvezda*, 2 March 1995 (see Grachev, 1995; Kvashnin, 1995).

31 General Podkolzin, Commander of the Airborne Forces, later concluded that deployment of composite units was one of the grave mistakes in planning, while one fully manned airborne division could have done the job (Podkolzin, 1995).

32 General Golovnev (1995), Deputy Commander of the Ground Forces, claimed that he had spent a month in Mozdok before the operation, training the arriving 'paper' units at shooting-ranges and testing grounds. Admitting that his crash-course was a poor substitute for normal drill, he concluded: 'The last thing to do is to train your troops under fire. And we were forced to do just this.'

33 While Grachev later denied that *blitzkrieg* had been planned and claimed that a slow manoeuvre was ordered to avoid any civilian casualties, his original plan to capture key strongholds in Grozny by the seventh day of the operation had few points to support the latter claim but plenty of 'Can-Do' assessments.

column was able to advance more or less smoothly through the areas controlled by 'friendly' opposition, while the 'Western' column was delayed by mostly 'passive' resistance in Ingushetia and the 'Eastern' column was stopped in Daghestan and had to shift its direction more to the north (Map 6.4). Grachev later argued that these routes were chosen deliberately in order 'to convince the population yet again that a peaceful settlement was essential', but the miscalculations in planning were undeniable. Not until 26 December did all three columns reach the northern outskirts of Grozny; nothing close to a tight blockade could be established, due perhaps to the already sharp deficit of forces. Grachev, who was controlling the whole operation from Mozdok, North Ossetia, started to demand reinforcements from all possible sources; by early January, composite regiments from the Moscow, Leningrad, Volga and even Siberian MDs plus the Marine battalions from the Northern, Baltic and Pacific fleets had increased the total strength of the grouping to some 38,000 men with 230 tanks and 450 ACVs. But the decisive assault on Grozny was attempted before these fresh forces arrived.

The order to attack on New Year's Eve was later justified by the 'surprise factor', but it was the commanders of the various Russian units that were most taken by surprise. Some commanders (including airborne units) never received the combat order at all, others discontinued their proceedings after the first sign of resistance. So instead of a coordinated advance of four assault groupings on a converging salient, it was only the columns of the 81st MI Regiment and the 131st MI Brigade that were able to move along several north–south streets with relative success. Occasional sniper-fire made the unhardened infantry reluctant to leave their APCs, so it was only small and isolated armour units that reached the railroad station and even the square in front of the presidential palace. In both places they came under heavy fire, found their retreat routes blocked and suffered heavy losses.[34] Not until the evening of 1 January did two assault airborne battalions break their way to the railroad station – only to find out that there was nobody to 'deblockade' there. The lesson from this defeat was duly learned, and Grozny was taken slowly, street by street, assault units moving in only after heavy artillery barrages.[35] The presidential palace was captured on 19 January and President Yeltsin announced that 'the military phase of the operation is over', but battles in Grozny continued up to the end of February.

Several features of this first phase of the campaign look strikingly controversial but remain unexplained. The first is the absence of any 'decapitative' action directed against Dudaev's headquarters, which would have been necessary to make the *blitzkrieg* plan work. The Airborne Troops command proposed a plan for such a 'special operation' (very much along the lines of the assault on Kabul

---

34 As General Lebed (1995a) has put it: 'The Russian troops crawled into Grozny, having neither battle-plans nor maps nor even a clear-cut mission. The stress was laid on armoured hardware which without due cover from motorized infantry turned into slow-moving targets in the city conditions.'

35 Lester Grau (1995, p. 4) has concluded from his well-informed analysis of these urban tactics: 'The Russians were faced with the dilemma of having to destroy Grozny (which they considered to be one of their cities) in order to save it.'

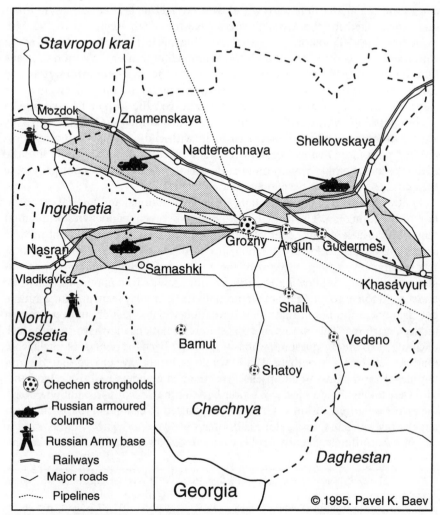

Map 6.4   *The Chechen Campaign*

in December 1979) and later blamed Grachev for choosing the ineffective 'go-slow' strategy (Zhilin, 1995). The Defence Minister in turn claimed that 'to uncover and isolate the leading officials' in Chechnya was a task reserved for the Federal Counterintelligence Service (FSK), but the latter failed to deploy any of its 'elite' units, sending inside the 'enemy's territory' only a hastily assembled team of 17 'operation officers'.[36]

Even more of a puzzle is the complete absence from the operation of the highly professional *Spetsnaz* brigades subordinated to the Main Intelligence Directorate (GRU). The elite airborne divisions were also represented only by

---

36 Colonel Bezugly (1995) stated in an interview that the FSK team provided valuable information on the 'enemy's defences', actually performing the task of the Military Intelligence, but never had any 'action capabilities'.

composite regiments that were withdrawn already in February.[37] Some other units earmarked for the Mobile Forces (like the 506th Regiment of the 27th 'peace-keeping' Division or several Marine battalions) were deployed to Chechnya for a short time but withdrawn immediately after the period of heavy fighting was over. Military sources pointed to the lack of coordination and combat support between the paratroopers and 'regular' infantry units – in many cases, the dismal performance of the latter forced the former to take on the assault missions without due support. Defence Minister Grachev, perhaps anticipating direct disobedience, rushed in with cadre reshuffling, often pro-moting 'paras' and dismissing Army officers.[38] But throwing decisively into the battle the most combat-worthy units of the Army, he was cautious not to overuse them and to avoid their permanent entanglement.

Another unexplained question concerns the operational and tactical organiza-tion of the campaign. The lack of coordination between manoeuvres of different units and the lack of direct combat support during the first weeks of fighting were as obvious as the lack of any general concept for the operation.[39] While the latter was presumably centred on Grozny, the aim of encirclement and blockade was never implemented, allowing first the reinforcements to come in and then the undefeated forces to retreat to other strongholds. This may seem an exaggeration, but the conclusion is still that the intervention violated just about every rule of modern warfare.[40] The bottom line for all miscalculations may have been the lack of clarity as to the key question: who is the enemy? Even the poorest of intelligence (and this is hardly a hypothetical case) would probably have proved that 'disarm-ing illegal formations' was nonsense, but the commanders had to pretend that they were taking this political aim seriously. After the disastrous assault on Grozny the picture changed abruptly: Grachev now started to claim that 'the enemy' was a real army which in Grozny alone had some 15,000 fighters with 50 tanks and 100 ACVs.[41] Accordingly, massive artillery and air strikes were called to 'soften' this

---

37 General Ivan Babichev, Commander of the 76th Pskov ABD, on several occasions stopped the advances of his column, seeking to avoid civilian casualties. During the battle of Grozny, he was made the commander of the Western grouping. As Richard Woff (1995a, Update 1, p. 1–9) has observed: 'Of all commanders in the field Babichev has continued to receive the most glowing praise from a wide range of participants in the war in Chechnya for his leadership, professional ability, and compassionate concern for the welfare of those "in his care"...' In April 1995, Babichev was promoted to command the Krasnodar Army Corps in the North Caucasus MD.

38 Unofficial sources gave the figure of 557 Army officers who were dismissed from the ranks for refusing to carry out combat orders. (See FBIS-SOV-95-068, 10 April.)

39 The exclusion of the General Staff from planning the campaign and conducting its initial phase has already been discussed (see Chapter 3.3); there is certain evidence behind the guess that the Headquarters of the North Caucasus MD drafted the original plans very much under the guidance of 'colleagues' from the Interior Ministry and the FSK. In early January, the commander of the North Caucasus MD, his deputies and Chief of Staff were all dismissed. (See Galeotti, 1995; Woff, 1995c.)

40 Deputy Defence Minister Gromov (1995a) gave a clear answer to the question about strategy and tactics of the Chechen operation: 'In this case there is nothing to assess since neither strategy nor tactics has been observed. It would seem that the experience in Afghanistan had to teach us some-thing.'

41 Referring to the Great Patriotic War experience, General Kvashnin concluded that a grouping of 50,000–60,000 men would have been necessary to storm Grozny.

'deeply echeloned' defence, all 'collateral damage' notwithstanding. As for the politicians in Moscow, to them the price of the 'victory' became unimportant, and the Army started to destroy systematically the entire social infrastructure of the Chechen Republic – apparently forgetting that it was supposed to be fighting on 'home' territory to restore the 'constitutional order'.

Yet another feature which calls for attention is the interaction between the Army and the Interior Troops. Grachev and other military authorities persistently referred to the 'joint' character of the operation, in which the non-military forces were expected to secure the 'rear' and then take over the main burden once key strongholds had been captured. The appointment of General Colonel Kulikov, Commander of the Internal Troops, as the Commander of the Federal Forces in Chechnya – to replace Grachev – on 1 February was intended to symbolize this re-allocation of tasks. But the level of real coordination between military units and interior forces remained dramatically low through the whole campaign. The military commanders complained bitterly that their troops were ill-equipped, poorly supplied and had to fight without enough food, whereas the interior forces and OMON were provided with modern communication equipment, bullet-proof vests and abundant supplies. When the Interior Troops indeed conducted their first combat operation storming Samashki, they showed such indiscriminate brutality that the name of this village became yet another symbol of genocide (Felgengauer, 1995b; Kovalev, 1995a).

Five months after the invasion, most towns and villages in lowland Chechnya were occupied by the federal forces, but the highlands remained unsubdued. The demands from Moscow to 'finish off' the campaign before the expected Russian–US summit and the arrival of European leaders to celebrate the 50th anniversary of the victory in World War II led only to a temporary ceasefire. And the sheer impossibility of establishing any semblance of 'normal' political control over the 'liberated' territories – to say nothing about rebuilding the social infrastructure – testified to the senselessness of all military efforts, losses and atrocities. It took a terrorist attack, unprecedented in scale and brutality, on the small Russian town of Budennovsk to convince politicians in Moscow, and first of all Prime Minister Chernomyrdin, to open negotiations with Dudaev. And in the course of these uneasy negotiations, it was the military commanders on both sides – General Anatoly Romanov, Commander of the Joint Grouping of the Federal Forces (he succeeded Kulikov after the latter was promoted to the Minister of Interior in July), and General Aslan Maskhadov, Chief of Staff of the Chechen Forces – who most strongly resisted the political pressure for continuing the war and managed to produce a meaningful military agreement (see Zamyatina, 1995). This agreement did not provide for a real peace. Skirmishes and terrorist attacks made an uneasy environment for further negotiations, and even those were discontinued when an assassination attempt on General Romanov nearly succeeded: on 6 October he was badly wounded when his car was blasted in the centre of Grozny.[42] Heavy fighting in Gudermes

---

42 Some comments speculated that General Romanov was targeted not only due to his key role in the peace process but also in retribution for earlier operations, particularly since Romanov had been in charge of the assault on Samashki in April. See Starostina, 1995.

in mid-December 1995 claimed hundreds of civilian casualties and confirmed once again that even overwhelming military might could not deter the defiant fighters and that Moscow had no political solution for its Chechen war.

6.5   Conclusion

As Yury Afanasyev, one of those in Russia who truly deserves the name of liberal-democrat, has put it, 'The arm-twisting "peace-keeping" policy quite logically led to the first bloody war on Russia's territory – in Chechnya' (Afanasyev & Karpinsky, 1995). Perhaps an overstatement, this still points to an important connection. The Chechen war indeed came as a natural product of Russia's self-assertive political course which had converted conflict management into a tool for applying pressure. Quite characteristically, the whole intervention which soon escalated into a full-scale war was presented as merely yet another 'peace operation' aimed at disarming 'illegal formations' and restoring constitutional order. Sergei Kovalev (1995a, p. 22) has torn down this cheap disguise: 'We have been overtaken by a dirty wave of national patriotism.'

What is less obvious about this connection is that the Chechen war was not that much a consequence of the military pattern of peace-keeping, as a result of the inability to maintain this pattern. By the end of 1994, it had become clear what the main problem was with Russian peace-keeping in the Near Abroad: resources. The pattern as such, although controversial and more offensive than the 'second-generation' UN peace-keeping model, proved remarkably efficient. Despite a high level of risk involved in every operation, it was only in Tadzhikistan that a Russian/CIS operation ran into serious trouble, but even there the level of combat casualties remained acceptable. Political demands for new 'peace operations' were growing both in Moscow (as a materialization of the pro-active nationalist course) and in some conflict areas, first of all in Nagorno Karabakh.

But the problem was resources. The direct and indirect costs of maintaining several open-ended operations simultaneously were becoming prohibitive. It was not the financing of the 'forward deployment' as such, but the expense involved in building combat-worthy Mobile Forces, manpower shortages, lack of training and logistics that resulted in a 'peace-keeping overstretch' (Orr, 1994b). The only real solution to this could be a substantial reduction of military involvement in the Near Abroad, but political pressure precluded any steps in this direction. While to many Western analysts the unsustainability of Russia's interventionist course was all too obvious (Galeotti, 1994d), scant consideration was given to this in Moscow.

Faced with an impossible situation, the Russian military leadership was compelled to abandon its more cautious approach to peace-keeping (based more on deterrence than on waging combat operations) and attempted to solve the overstretch problem with a 'small-and-successful-war' gamble. The Army found itself pushed into a hopeless adventure; failure in Chechnya was absolutely predictable – and was indeed predicted by many in the military leadership, including General Gromov.

The outcome of the Chechen war will inevitably affect Russia's other interventions. Perhaps politicians in Moscow remain reluctant to draw far-reaching conclusions from the simple fact that they have to make a compromise with Dudaev. But the military cannot postpone the disastrous consequences of this campaign, and will also have to do something about other ongoing operations. The first symptom was, perhaps, the decision to halve the Russian peace-keeping force in Transdniestria, a decision taken unilaterally in mid-November 1994 despite valid objections from Moldova (Prihodko, 1994) and elaborated to include the 14th Army in summer 1995 (Yemelyanenko, 1995). But the sheer amount of military effort wasted in Chechnya and the prospect of prolonged guerrilla warfare – which is by no means removed by the negotiations in Grozny – directly undermine Russia's ability to maintain the peace-keeping operation in Abkhazia or to continue the military presence in Transcaucasus. Another withdrawal, conceivable at least since mid-1993 and now apparently all but inevitable, is from Tadzhikistan.[43] The consequences for stability in Central Asia may not necessarily be dramatic in the short term, but Russian retreat from Tadzhikistan could have serious repercussions for internal conflict in Uzbekistan and the very survivability of Kazakhstan over the next decades.

---

43 Rajan Menon (1995, p. 150) has taken 'the irreducible reality of preponderant Russian power' as the basis for his scenarios of possible developments in Central Asia. This assumption perhaps needs certain correction after the Chechen war, which has contributed to drastic reductions of the military component of this power.

7
Russian Peace-Keeping and European Security

7.1 Introduction

Russia's experiments in conflict management on the territory of the former USSR have made a strong impact on many key developments in European security. With the problem of 'new generation' or 'wider' peace-keeping advancing to the forefront of international security debates, the task of establishing a broad European common ground has become recognized as crucial. This has involved two key elements: providing international legitimization for the 'peace interventions' in the CIS area, and promoting Russia's participation in conflict management and peace-keeping in Europe and elsewhere. As for the latter, developing cooperation in the Balkans could, with certain reservations, be called a success, though the conflict management itself certainly was not. In the Baltic area, multilateral preventive diplomacy helped to defuse the conflict-pregnant relations between Russia and Estonia, Latvia and Lithuania. But only minor achievements could be registered in transforming the Russian 'peace-creating' (*mirotvorcheskie*) operations in the CIS area into legitimate international peace-keeping enterprises. And the war in Chechnya has not only undermined this uncertain progress but also jeopardized the capacity of European security institutions to deal with regional conflicts.

7.2 Involving International Institutions

Ambiguity is perhaps the term that best can characterize Russia's attitude towards giving various international organizations and partners any role in conflict management on the territory of the former Soviet Union. However, a certain consistency can be traced in the records of praising and downplaying, inviting and rejecting. And the main criterion – however simple this assumption may seem – has been whether the international partners were perceived as able to serve Russia's interests. Here, of course, different groups among the political elite had quite different understandings.

The second half of 1992 saw an obvious discrepancy between the military leadership and the Foreign Ministry (as described in Chapter 2); while the latter came under attack from the rising conservative opposition and also from the Supreme Soviet, President Yeltsin prudently refrained from taking sides. The position of the military was fairly straightforward – they had initiated several 'peace interventions' and were now determined to keep a free hand in dealing with them while also considering new ones. A penetrating external observation or even more so direct participation was considered as highly undesirable. Foreign Minister Kozyrev, however, was seriously concerned that this interventionist course could damage his policy of accelerated rapprochement with the West and sought to transform the open-ended operations into more legitimate international enterprises.

In fact, the two sides were arguing about interaction with different international structures. The military made a strong point against any possible NATO involvement in 'domestic' post-Soviet conflict management.[1] Kozyrev advanced arguments in favour of inviting the UN and the CSCE, making a special point that this would help to make the latter into a real institution for European security.[2] This idea found support in the Report 'Strategy for Russia' (which was otherwise rather critical of Kozyrev's performance) prepared by the newly born Council for Foreign and Defence Policy.[3] Less obvious were the expectations of Kozyrev and other liberal experts that criticism from the West would place strict limits on further interventionism, while the arrival of observers and – it was hoped – peace-keepers from other European countries would make it possible to restore some political control over the Russian Army.[4]

But instead of the expected (and perhaps hoped-for) criticism, the Russian Foreign Ministry saw what could be called 'benign neglect' and in some cases even semi-official 'Go-Ahead' signals. This gave the military grounds for arguing that what the West was actually interested in was to make Russia the 'guarantor of stability' in the former USSR.[5] So when President Yeltsin finally took a stand in his speech to the Civic Union on 28 February 1993, it was centred on a declaration that

> Russia continues to have a vital interest in the cessation of all armed conflicts on the territory of the former USSR. Moreover, the world community is increasingly coming to realize our country's special responsibility in this difficult matter. I believe the time has come for authoritative international organizations, including the United Nations, to grant Russia special powers as guarantor of peace and stability in this region.[6]

---

1 CIS Commander-in-Chief Air Marshal Shaposhnikov on several occasions argued against giving NATO any role in peace-keeping in Europe, while General Kolesnikov, (then) Deputy Chief of General Staff, issued a warning that NATO was planning direct interventions under the pretext of guaranteeing control over nuclear arsenals. For a precise description see Crow (1992b).

2 President Yeltsin expressed support for this idea during the CSCE summit in Helsinki in July 1992.

3 Sergei Karaganov (1992b), the initiator of this Report, went even further, writing on his own: 'Russia's special role in settlement of conflicts will be approved by the CSCE and the UN, and will be controlled by them.'

4 I have elaborated this argument in Baev (1994e).

5 Thus Air Marshal Shapshnikov in an interview ('Radio Rossii', 11 December 1992) claimed that conflict escalation is 'leading Western politicians to conclude that it would be much more profitable for them to do business with a single, qualitatively reinvigorated, democratized state or union of states than with a large number of states that lack a certain degree of stability either within or between them'.

6 ITAR-TASS, 1 March 1993. For a penetrating analysis see Crow (1993a).

This statement marked a drastic change in Russia's foreign policy. On the surface, it was mostly a shift of emphasis towards the UN – from inviting real contribution to (if not control) over the peace-keeping operations to demanding formal recognition of the ongoing ones and carte blanche for possible new interventions. But behind this, it meant a radical departure from the West-oriented perception of Russia's interests (where regional conflict management was a peripheral issue) to one focusing on the Near Abroad, where conflict management became the central problem but its international legitimization came under the category of 'nice but not necessary'.

The only aspect of the peace-keeping problem that allowed Kozyrev to retain it as a high-profile foreign policy issue was financing. He managed to persuade the top brass – who were by now becoming increasingly aware of the burden of conflict management – that the UN 'blessing' could involve serious benefits since substantial funds were available in its peace-keeping budget. It is rather unlikely that such experienced diplomats as Adamishin, Lavrov or Vorontsov harboured any illusions that the UN indeed would rush to pour its meagre resources into the bottomless barrel of Russian peace-keeping even if its legitimacy were somehow recognized. Most probably, this diplomatic game was intended to confirm Kozyrev's new 'patriotic' credentials and give some weight to his conceptualizing, the best example of which was his speech at the UN General Assembly on 28 September 1993. On this occasion, he bluntly dismissed doubts about Russia's 'untraditional methods' of peace-keeping (such as involving the belligerents in the operation) and emphasized that 'no international organization or group of states can replace our peace-making efforts in this specific post-Soviet space'.[7]

The UN indeed remained unconvinced by this self-serving campaign but in Moscow Kozyrev managed to secure himself a place in the same boat with the military 'peace-makers'. This was clearly illustrated by the joint statement issued by the Foreign and Defence Ministers after the UN Secretary General visited Moscow in early April 1994, in which they blamed the UN for failing to provide tangible support for Russia's efforts and also indicated that the CIS mandates for the latter made any 'permission' from New York redundant. And Kozyrev cunningly reserved as his weapon of last resort the option of diverting some funds to his military colleagues from Russia's contribution to the UN peace-keeping budget.[8]

In late 1993, Kozyrev shifted the priorities of his international intrigue around Russia's peace-keeping more in the direction of the CSCE. One reason for this was the unfolding crisis of UN peace-keeping which Russia was all too willing to exploit (Lavrov, 1994). Perhaps one of the fruits of these weakness-exploiting tactics came with the UN acknowledgement of the Russian peace-keeping operation in Abkhazia in June 1994. But a more immediate reason for greater attention toward the CSCE was the first NATO enlargement crisis, detonated by Yeltsin's careless 'Go-Ahead' remark in Warsaw in August. Kozyrev's genuinely

---

7 As quoted by Crow (1993c). See also Kozyrev's article in *Rossiiskaya Gazeta* (1993c). Useful analysis can be found in Shashenkov (1994).

8 Roy Allison (1994) has drawn particular attention to this option.

Byzantine strategy was centred on the proposal to raise the peace-keeping potential of the CSCE, making it the main framework for European security; this in time would then serve to make NATO enlargement a non-issue. But the hidden agenda of this pan-European campaign was the conviction that it would never be possible to make of the CSCE a real security institution with peace-keeping capabilities, although its political prerogatives could be somewhat consolidated.[9] Thus, in some cases the CSCE would be able to provide a legitimate mandate for Russia/CIS operations; but more important: Russia would have the right to deny any mandate for possible NATO 'out-of-area' operations. This was the intention. However, what seemed to be a 'win–win' game was soon to backfire, leaving Russia isolated.

Kozyrev launched his campaign with a kick-start at the CSCE Council meeting in Rome in December 1993. Despite hard lobbying and some lukewarm support from the West (British Foreign Minister Douglas Hurd went perhaps the longest mile towards meeting Kozyrev), the proposal was blocked by firm opposition from the East European bloc, including the three Baltic states and Ukraine. But in the course of the year which separated this meeting from the CSCE summit in Budapest, European diplomats managed to pick two bargaining-chips from the Russian 'package' and use them as levers to re-orient Moscow's whole offensive.[10]

The first issue concerned setting clear criteria for peace-keeping operations which would provide legal grounds for CSCE recognition of certain CIS/Russian interventions. While initially Kozyrev expressed a quite positive attitude,[11] Russian diplomats effectively obstructed the efforts of several working groups to define such criteria. The issue was not settled before the summit; last-minute efforts in Budapest produced no miracles; and soon after, Russia's Chechen War made further discussions basically meaningless. From the Russian perspective, this outcome could be taken as a draw: while its own operations remained unrecognized, Moscow would still have the possibility to deny legitimacy to any NATO action.

The second issue was the peace-keeping operation in Nagorno Karabakh. By early 1994, painstaking efforts in the CSCE Minsk Group started to bring some results, building the political framework for a possible separation/ceasefire-monitoring operation. Vociferously advocating a strengthening of all-European capabilities for conflict management, Moscow found it indeed difficult to object to the first-ever peace-keeping operation under CSCE auspices. Several attempts to seize the initiative and launch the CIS operation before CSCE mediation could come anywhere close to agreement were undertaken during the first half of 1994. Interestingly enough, it was Defence Minister Grachev who delivered

---

9 Sergei Karaganov (1994d), speaking about a deep crisis of European security, has pointed out that Russia alone tried to strengthen the CSCE but there was no real chance for success.

10 I am indebted to Piotr Switalsky, Assistant to General Secretary, CSCE, for the valuable insight which he gave during the conference on 'Peacekeeping and the Role of Russia in Eurasia' organized by the Swedish Institute of International Affairs, Stockholm, 14–15 October, 1994.

11 This was clear from the article which he authored together with Douglas Hurd, published in *Izvestia* and *Financial Times* (Hurd & Kozyrev, 1993).

hard pressure for securing the consent of the parties, while Russian special envoy Vladimir Kazimirov worked hand in hand with Jan Eliasson, Chairman of the Minsk Group.[12]

It was Azerbaijan that frustrated all Russia's manoeuvres, so at the end of the day Moscow was left with a choice between two evils in Budapest. The drama of that moment was that the litmus test for Russia's support for the CSCE was set before any real decisions on NATO enlargement had been drafted: that meant that Moscow had to agree on creating a precedent of genuinely international peace-keeping on the territory of the former USSR without any clear prospects for instrumentalizing of all-European structures against Atlantic ones. The only escape from this self-made trap seemed to lie in procrastination – which was in fact not so difficult, given the procedural constraints in the CSCE (by no means reduced after its re-naming as 'Organization') as well as numerous obstacles in the 'field'.[13]

In this context, the ups and downs of the peace-keeping dimension of Russia–NATO relations look only natural. The paranoid fears of 1992 (especially among the Russian military) that the Atlantic Alliance could seize a chance provided by some local conflict and jump into the former USSR in order to defeat Russia soon gave way to more realistic assessments of NATO capabilities. One illustration of the latter was Moscow's self-confident reaction (in August 1993) to the leaked draft of a US Presidential Directive which envisaged direct US involvement in conflict management in the former USSR.[14] Still, the desire to weaken the former enemy by making him into just another loose European institution was present; indeed it may well have been the real incentive for Kozyrev's attempt to play the NACC card (North Atlantic Cooperation Council). During 1993 he sent up quite a few trial balloons proposing that this institution should be made a 'peace-keeping laboratory', that a 'vertical line of responsibility' be established from the UN to the CSCE and NACC, etc.[15] Little enthusiasm was registered; actually Moscow seemed quite content with the NACC status as low-budget talk-shop.

By contrast, NATO's Partnership for Peace (PfP) programme was an entirely different matter. Though Russia loudly demanded special status in

---

12 As Elizabeth Fuller (1994b, p. 17) has acknowledged, 'it is not clear whether the Russian leadership was playing a double game – that is, whether Kozyrev and Kazimirov deliberately misled or lied to Eliasson when they assured him earlier in May that there was no competition between Russia and the CSCE to mediate a settlement – or whether, as appeared to be the case in Abkhazia in September 1993, the Russian Foreign Ministry and the military are pursuing separate and contradictory policies.'

13 As one Russian comment concluded, 'You need a lively imagination to regard this document as agreed, given the present differences between the sides.' (See Vinogradov, 1994.)

14 The Russian Foreign Ministry bluntly dismissed this option. For a good review of the issue see Allison (1994, pp. 35–36). When the Presidential Directive (PDD-25) was finally issued in May 1994, it limited the American role in this area to a purely symbolic one.

15 See, for example, his article in *Segodnya* (Kozyrev, 1993a). Dmitry Trenin (1993) elaborated this approach further, proposing to make NACC an independent organization and the main headquarters for peace-keeping in Europe. Indeed, the papers of the Ad Hoc Group on Cooperation in Peacekeeping could remain one of the most impressive paper results of the NACC activities. See, in particular, Progress Report in *NATO Review*, no. 6, December 1993.

this programme – and peace-keeping was among the key issues in the proposed 'expanded' agenda – its willingness to increase bilateral cooperation was questionable from the very beginning. Defence Minister Grachev, speaking in Brussels in late May 1994, proposed that the PfP programme be moved under NACC auspices, aiming to make the latter the military component of the CSCE. Signing the framework agreement one month later did not alleviate doubts, but perhaps even increased suspicions that PfP was more important for NATO than for Russia (Clarke, 1995a). It was perceived as not only helping NATO to establish its role as the central pillar of European security, but more specifically as acknowledging NATO's right to conduct 'peace interventions' outside its traditional area of responsibility. The symbolic consolation prize for this would be participation in various joint peace-keeping military exercises – at own expense. These doubts, more than controversies around the enlargement issue, would seem to explain Kozyrev's theatrical refusal to sign the special programme for partnership during his special appearance at the North Atlantic Council in December 1994.

The resolution of this rather overplayed crisis came after the Yeltsin–Clinton summit in Moscow that was a part of the celebration of the 50th anniversary of the victory in World War II. A few encouraging words from the US President persuaded the Russian Security Council on 24 May to approve a remarkable compromise. In the best tradition of Soviet planning, the Security Council decided that the European security system should be based on the framework of the OSCE and that NATO should be one element of it. With this in mind, Russia could then enter into a partnership with the Alliance, provided the latter did not expand to the east (Baev, 1995f, p. 31). While this decision reads like a distinguished piece of wishful thinking, it at least opened the way for signing the partnership programme with NATO – which was done in Brussels on 31 May without much fanfare. But the experience from this crisis, together with growing disappointment from isolation in the OSCE and a lukewarm welcome in the G7, led many Russian experts to the conclusion that Moscow should limit or even reduce its interaction with international organizations. They argued that on the political side, an intensive involvement would only consolidate Russia's current position of weakness (Karaganov, 1995), while on the economic side, it would hardly contribute to and might even hamper the rebuilding of industrial power (Goncharov, 1995). Such assumptions recognized that no amount of rigid rhetoric could reverse the decline of Russia's international influence – the trend determined by internal weakness and aggravated by blunders in foreign policy.

One issue with a strong impact on Russia's international profile in general and on Russia–NATO relations in particular, including the prospects for cooperation in peace-keeping, has been the wars in the Balkans. To this we now turn.

7.3   Russia, NATO and Peace-Keeping in the Balkans

Russia's participation in multi-national efforts to keep the conflicts in the Balkans under control has been one of the recurrent issues in its relations with key Western partners, and also has had some 'reflective' influence on its own peace-keeping policy in the Near Abroad.[16] This influence was certainly more on the political than on the military side, since the Russian Defence Ministry stuck to the opinion that participation in UNPROFOR could add scant new experience to that gained from Russia's endeavours in the post-Soviet space. Still, the interaction in the Balkans created a link between conflict management in the former USSR and macro-level developments in European security.

Russia joined international peace-building efforts in the former Yugoslavia in early 1992, well before the priorities of its own foreign policy had been formulated. Driven by the desire to make Russia into a 'normal' European power, the Foreign Ministry saw no better way to do this than by supplying one battalion for the UN peace-keeping operation in Croatia (the Defence Ministry was not yet formed). But even then it was fairly predictable that the cooperation with the West would inevitably be limited by the necessity to protect Russia's own national interests. While during 1992 Foreign Minister Kozyrev had few doubts about leaving the initiative and the responsibility for making peace in the Balkans primarily to the EC, early in 1993 he started to refer to Russia's 'special' role in the region.

Russia's gradual departure from a policy of unashamedly sailing in the wake of the EC flagship in Yugoslav waters involved three main issues: lifting economic sanctions against Serbia and Montenegro, preventing the arms embargo on Bosnia from being lifted, and the introduction of economic sanctions against Croatia (after fighting resumed briefly in Krajina in January 1993). With the wisdom of hindsight, one can argue that any historical sympathies towards Serbs, 'pan-Slavic' and religious feelings actually were of very little relevance to the framing of Russia's pro-Serbian political drift: this was influenced more by the desire to preserve some influence in the Balkans and to secure a prominent position in the new European security architecture (Lynch & Lukic, 1993). In other words, it was not ethnic nationalism so much as state nationalism that prompted Russia to side with the Serbs.

What placed strict limits on Russia's ambitions to plot out an independent political course in the Balkans was the deficit of resources – not only economic, but political and military as well. When Kozyrev in early 1993 presented a proposal to double the Russian component of the UNPROFOR, it was rebuffed by the General Staff, who were deeply concerned about the lack of 'elite' forces for their own peace-keeping (Lough, 1993c). The same reaction met the bold ideas for launching a joint Russian–NATO intervention in support of the Vance–Owen plan that were put forward by several experts and found some support in the Foreign Ministry (Sharp & Baranovsky, 1993). Kozyrev's space for manoeuvre was limited to sheer diplomacy: actually the aim of his sporadic manoeuvres was to acquire some more bargaining chips without any intentions

---

16 The following analysis draws on my chapter in the five-author Chaillot Paper (see Baev, 1994b). It also has had the benefit of being discussed at the Wilton Park seminar on 'Europe's Balkan Wars: Lessons for the International Community' (23–26 May 1994) and the international conference on 'Peacekeeping and the Role of Russia in Eurasia' organized by the Swedish Institute of International Affairs, Stockholm (14–15 October 1994) which led to a chapter in the book edited by Lena Jonson and Clive Archer (Baev, 1995i).

of seriously altering the cooperative arrangement with the Western partners. Western benevolence or at least indifference to Russia's 'domestic' peace-making enterprises was also a stake in this game. But certainly Kozyrev would never have dared a straightforward attempt to strike a bargain with NATO, asking for carte blanche in the Near Abroad in exchange for carte blanche in Bosnia (which would be tantamount to defining it as NATO's 'Near Abroad').

By mid-1993, Kozyrev had also discovered that the Balkan experience actually allowed Moscow to claim legitimacy for its own interventions, by providing two key arguments: first, no one else is able to shoulder the burden; second, Russia is not violating any international norms. Backing secessions in Transdniestria, South Ossetia and Abkhazia made the second argument rather unconvincing, but Russia indeed could point to the precedents created by UN peace-keeping operations in Croatia, where the 'blue helmets' up to spring 1995 acted to secure Serbian control over Krajina, and in Bosnia, where partition as a principle was accepted and incorporated in various peace plans. And the failure of international efforts which enjoyed absolutely legitimate mandates to stop the violence in Bosnia made it perfectly possible for Moscow to pretend that enough had been done to justify its chosen course – which had at least brought a cessation to violence in several hot spots.

The further drift of Russia's foreign policy towards self-assertive nationalism in early 1994 called for somewhat more active steps. Indeed, the Balkans were one of the few places where it seemed possible to put some substance into 'Great Power' declarations, and the obvious point of departure was the new political consensus that NATO air strikes against the Bosnian Serbs were unacceptable. This consensus involved not only the mainstream groupings of the political elite, but indeed a broad spectrum from Gorbachev (1994) to Zhirinovsky, although they arrived at the 'No-Bombing' conclusion from very different starting points. The Foreign Ministry was eager to embrace this guideline, which still allowed a certain distance to a clear-cut pro-Serbian line (Lavrov, 1994). Meanwhile, many politicians in Moscow shared the judgement that the USA, France and the UK obviously outmanoeuvred Russia in the UN, leaving it no chance to use its veto in the Security Council. As the option for air strikes moved to the forefront in early 1994, Moscow started to insist on two mutually incompatible points: that it should be consulted with; and that the air strikes were unacceptable as such. The legal basis for both claims looked rather shaky, and the ultimatum of 10 February left little doubt that NATO intended to go its own way, sticking to UN Security Council Resolution 836 and disregarding any second thoughts from Moscow.[17]

It was the NATO ultimatum on Sarajevo in February 1994 that created for Russia a chance to step in and restore its role as a major actor in the Balkans. One meaningful contribution to this was the readiness of the Russian military

---

17 Misha Glenny (1994) has accurately pointed out: 'Russia and NATO were on a collision course, with both sides having maneuvered themselves into a corner. NATO was certainly in no position to back down, while President Yeltsin (under increasing pressure from the nationalists and the military) evidently believed that he could not accommodate the Americans on this issue. A real danger arose that the Bosnian conflict might develop into a proxy dispute between Russia and the US.'

leaders to send additional troops to Bosnia – and indeed it was a unique situation when the arrival of a few hundred Russian peace-keepers could make such a huge difference. The diplomatic victory at Sarajevo was heralded as re-establishing Russia's 'Great Power' status in global affairs despite its economic dislocation, political muddle and military decline. Amidst celebration, Moscow also took pains to point out that actually it had saved NATO's prestige since the Alliance had been applying pressure without policy, recalling some arguments from the deadlocked 'pro–contra' intervention debates in the West.[18]

But it was indeed premature of Moscow to bask in this one-off political triumph. Several rounds of escalation around Gorazde already in April revealed the deficit of resources and political will behind Russia's initiative. Bitter reactions across the spectrum of Russia's political elite concerned more than offence at not being consulted. While for extremists it was a perfect cause for another hysterical attack on Foreign Minister Kozyrev, for many moderate politicians it was a testimony to obstructiveness from the West and NATO in particular (Ambartsumov, 1994). The escalation of NATO's intervention seemed to correspond with the views expressed by some Western experts that resolution of the February crisis only consolidated Russia's sphere of influence in the Balkans and prevented the Alliance from proving its own relevance (Eyal, 1994). There were reasons to suspect that, failing to agree on its own consistent policy, a jealous NATO decided to trip Russia up.

Whatever the rationale for bombing Serbian positions, it certainly undermined both the prospects of Russian–Western burden-sharing and the narrow basis of Russian mediation. The Foreign Ministry found its conceptual approach to the Balkans shattered, since it was able to persuade the Serbs to make certain concessions only so far as 'punishment' could be prevented. Another signal of diminishing Western interest in cooperation with Russia was the lukewarm reaction to President Yeltsin's face-saving proposal for a special summit on Bosnia, which was quietly buried. Angry and disappointed, Russian policy-makers were able to deny that they never had the stomach to carry the weight – and to justify a low-profile participation in the new Contact Group created in late April. This allowed for a non-committed attitude towards the new map for the partition of Bosnia, which this group produced in May. And when the Bosnian Serbs rejected the plan in August, Russia was able to pretend that some space for manoeuvre still existed and to push for rewarding Belgrade's cooperative attitude.[19]

As for relations with NATO, although developments in Bosnia periodically did cause some strain, they certainly were not the decisive factor in Russia's policy.[20] Thus, NATO air strikes in late November caused by escalation of

---

18 As Dan Smith (1993, p. 20) pointed out, 'There is something rather eerie about the intervention debate. Since the London conference six months ago, the issue has moved on, but the arguments have not changed – they have just got louder.' This observation remained relevant some two years later.

19 William Pfaff (1994) argued with insight: 'The Russian government finds the Serbs today a nuisance and embarrassment . . . However, Moscow has also been able to make use of Serbia in its own rehabilitation as a world power, at Serbia's expense.'

20 As one analyst commented on the Gorazde crisis: 'While NATO's failure to consult the Russians had derailed the movement toward Russia signing Partnership for Peace, the Bosnian Serbs' intransigence put it back on track.' (See Mihalka, 1994b, p. 43.)

fighting around Bihac heard only minor objections from Moscow; the main 'threat' was in fact to withdraw Russian battalions from UNPROFOR.[21] Some Western experts, speculating on circumstantial evidence and overlooking the real trends in Russia's peace-making activities, assumed that Moscow was interested in continuation of the Balkan wars so as to keep NATO attention diverted from Russia's imperialistic grasp of the CIS (Bonnart, 1994). Such a perception is hardly any more realistic than the suspicion of some Russian traditionalists of a master-plot behind the cataclysms in the former SFRY and the former USSR, so the blockades and the air strikes in Bosnia are a sort of 'simulation exercises' for future NATO intervention against Russia. But as William Pfaff (1994) put it, 'Here we enter the clouded zone of European, and particularly East European and Russian, political paranoia.'

Potentially, the current Russian course could prove profitable, since Serbia would seem the key to any settlement in the Balkans. But any claims for a major role that may issue from Moscow are doomed to remain hollow. As Marten van Heuven (1994, p. 46) argues, 'Ultimately, Russia will probably be content with a lesser role, as long as Moscow is seen to be part of the process.' But this lesser role could well centre on preventing NATO from assuming the lead. Little foresight is needed to predict that Moscow will use all available channels to deny the legitimacy of any new NATO initiative, thus making sure that peace-keeping will not become a new business for the Alliance.[22]

These efforts proved futile during the dramatic escalation of the Balkan wars in the summer of 1995. Croatian *blitzkrieg* in Krajina took Moscow by surprise and President Yeltsin rushed with an initiative to organize a special Serbo-Croatian summit in Moscow, supported by vague threats to take the issue to the UN Security Council. The blunt 'No' from Zagreb forced the Russian Foreign Ministry to modify the initiative and to combine it with new US mediation efforts (Eggert & Yusin, 1995), but obviously these hectic activities failed to take into consideration the damage inflicted on Russia's international prestige by the Chechen War (Sabov, 1995). Hence the scant enthusiasm concerning the proposal to send another Russian peace-keeping battalion to Gorazde. Moscow tried to play its only trump card – cordial relations with Serbian President Milosevic and General Mladic, Commander of Bosnian Serb Forces; but the former was disappointed by Russia's inability to lift the economic sanctions, and the latter, by its inability to prevent or even condemn in a meaningful way the massive NATO air strikes in late August.

The only thing Russia can possibly bank on is the ineffectiveness of Western involvement in the Balkans; indeed it was primarily quarrels between the USA and the three European members of the Contact Group that allowed Moscow to

---

21 Vitaly Churkin (1994), newly appointed Russian Ambassador to Brussels, mentioned in an interview that 'picking bones with NATO does not work today since the UN Security Council did give authorization'. Commenting on the rift between the USA and European allies on lifting the arms embargo against Bosnia, he emphasized that the plan to discontinue the Russian contribution to UNPROFOR was supported by both the Foreign and the Defence Ministries.

22 Christoph Bertram (1995a, p. 70), arguing that Bosnia has shown that the role of 'subcontractor' to the UN or the CSCE is a blind alley, concludes: 'To regenerate its own credibility as a serious actor in serious international conflicts, NATO will also have to be able to operate on its own.'

secure a better position in the political manoeuvring than it could really have claimed. Kozyrev even hoped for further improvement since the chances that the massive bombings would make the Serbs more compliant at the negotiating table were problematic at best. Even when Richard Holbrooke started to press vigorously for a new initiative in early autumn, Moscow calculated that the envisaged large-scale NATO involvement would bring the Alliance into deep trouble and further undermine its cohesion.[23] So when it became clear that the US leadership could indeed deliver an implementable agreement, Kozyrev had no possibility to block it. After some diplomatic twists and turns, Yeltsin agreed on joining the operation with some 2,000 new troops.[24] But the formula of Russian participation, as finalized by Defence Minister Grachev in late October, provided for more than just face-saving. It has also provided a possibility for Russia to distance itself from NATO's quite possible failure in its largest ever operation; and if things should go really wrong, Russian airborne battalions could contribute to making a disaster out of a failure.

It is fairly obvious that in 1993–94, the failure of both the EU and NATO to consolidate a new security role in the Balkans had increased Russia's inclination to go its own way with conflict management in its own Near Abroad. And when Russia so dramatically raised the threshold of violence in Chechnya in early 1995 – and failed so miserably to get any 'solution' – both Croatia and NATO found it quite possible to experiment with their own peace-enforcement, disregarding Moscow's opinions. Even if they succeed, Russia will have very little incentive for keeping to the international standards of peace-keeping – whatever this term will now mean.

7.4   Conflict Prevention: Russia and the Baltic States

In the four-year period of their new independence, Estonia, Latvia and Lithuania have not only established it in a quite solid way, but also have gone a long way towards Europe. If in 1992 or 1993 it was still possible to consider the three Baltic states as parts of Russia's Near Abroad (Baev, 1994d), today it is necessary to analyse regional developments there primarily in a European context.[25] Many of the problems that continue to bedevil bilateral or rather 'one-to-three' relations between Moscow and Tallinn, Riga and Vilnius are rooted in their common Soviet past, but the involvement of international political and security institutions has become the main avenue of solving those.

In early 1991, the Russian leadership came out decisively on the side of the

---

23 One commentary pointed to the risk of NATO's 'wading deeper into the war with Bosnian Serbs. As Russia's condemnation of Nato's latest raids indicates, there would probably come a point at which Moscow would feel obliged to take a stand against increasing Western military action in the Balkans.' (See Barber, 1995.)

24 One simple fact makes a convincing evidence of links between various kinds of 'peace operations': in the Russian airborne brigade sent to Bosnia, 60% of officers have combat experience from Chechnya. (See Parish, 1995.)

25 For a useful comparison of the 'quiet and little-noticed success' in the Baltic and the 'momentous failure' in the Balkans, see Bertram (1995b, p. 68).

Baltic independence movements and was actually their main ally in the struggle against the Soviet centre – where Gorbachev vacillated under pressure from his generals and party *apparatchiks*. But when in early 1992 Russia was internationally recognized as the main successor-state of the USSR, two main problems immediately manifested themselves in relations with newly independent Estonia, Latvia and Lithuania. The first one concerned the basing of some 120,000 former Soviet troops that now came under Russian command (Clarke, 1992). The second problem was the fate of some 1.7 million ethnic Russians who had settled in the three Baltic republics mostly after 1945.[26] Both of those problems contained the seeds of serious trouble, but it was the link between the two that threatened to trigger a violent conflict. Therefore, the strategy for conflict-prevention as collectively designed and carefully implemented by the Western countries focused primarily on de-linking.

Russian leadership was quick to pledge to withdraw all troops from the Baltic states, but rather slow in translating this into schedules and real redeployment – and inexcusably slow in recognizing the explosive nature of the 'Russians Abroad' issue.[27] On their side, the leaders of Estonia and Latvia rather short-sightedly contributed to aggravating this issue by introducing draft legislation that effectively denied the right to citizenship for the ethnic Russians and other Russian speakers (there were some 300,000 Ukrainians and Belorussians in the three Baltic states). In this delicate situation it was the Russian military leadership that invented the strategy of 'linking', seeing the growing ethnic tensions as the best possible justification for prolonging the military presence in the Baltic region. President Yeltsin showed willingness to subscribe to this strategy already in October 1992, when he confirmed the order given by the Defence Ministry two weeks earlier to suspend the withdrawals, referring to his 'deep concerns at numerous violations of the rights of the Russian-speaking minorities' (Hoagland, 1992).[28]

An underlying rationale for this strategy was the geopolitical assessment that once the independence problem was solved, Western interests and involvement in Estonia, Latvia and Lithuania would gradually diminish, resulting in a marginalized status for the three on the broader European security agenda (Portnikov, 1991). But these expectations never came true; as Ole Wæver (1992, p. 37) has correctly pointed out, 'The Baltic republics constitute symbolically and emotionally the apex of the Baltic Sea Region.'

The leaders of the three newly born states made the best of this situation – campaigning for their cause with remarkable success, downplaying the national question and placing in the centre the issue of military withdrawals. From late

---

26 For thoughtful analyses of the 'Russians Abroad' problem as related to the three Baltic states see Kirch & Kirch (1995), Mlechin (1995), Tishkov (1993).

27 At the CSCE summit in Helsinki in July 1992, Russia agreed to include in the Concluding Document the notion of 'early, orderly and complete withdrawal of foreign troops from the territories of the Baltic states'. The following month, Moscow proposed the deadline for withdrawal by the end of 1994.

28 The issue was brought to the UN General Assembly which in November 1992 approved a resolution calling for the complete withdrawal of foreign troops from the Baltic states, and another one in December expressing concern about the status of the Russian-speaking population there.

1992, the Russian leadership faced coordinated pressure in all major international fora (and directly from such key partners as the USA and Germany)
which accentuated two key points: that the linkage between the military and ethnic issues was unacceptable, and that the troop withdrawals must be completed
in the course of the next two years. President Yeltsin stubbornly pursued his
course, which justified a comment by Christopher Donnelly: 'The Baltics will be
the single most important symbol of East–West confrontation after Berlin' (as
quoted in Nagorski, 1992, p. 14).

The most striking (though not immediately obvious) contradiction in the
Russian conflict-instigating course was that by early 1993 the military leadership
had most probably concluded that rapid withdrawal from the Baltic was
inevitable. Perhaps the deficit of combat-ready units, which became apparent
after several 'peace interventions' in 1992, was the most convincing reason, but
there were certainly regional factors as well. One of them was the geographic discrepancy between the main military bases and the areas of compact settlement
of ethnic Russians. In strategic terms, it was the military presence in Lithuania
that was of key importance since it secured access to Kaliningrad and consolidated the Western bridgehead (Map 7.1).[29] But Lithuania had only about 9.5%
ethnic Russians among its whole population and quickly approved quite liberal
laws on citizenship.

Another strategic consideration concerned the bases for the Baltic Fleet.
The most valuable were the submarine bases at Paldiski (Estonia) and Liepaja
(Latvia), but the Russian Defence Ministry – which had been invaded by paratroopers – ranked the Navy rather low on its list of priorities. And when the
costs of maintaining major garrisons in the Baltic states were roughly calculated, the net assessment was that it was perhaps only the strategic
reconnaissance facilities at Skrunda (Latvia) that were worth paying for.
Accordingly, the military echelons continued to leave Estonia, Latvia and
Lithuania, heated political exchanges notwithstanding. By mid-1993 the total
strength of the North-Western Group of Forces was reduced to some 40,000
troops (Galeotti, 1993a).

The culmination of Moscow's political offensive came in Summer 1993,
focused on the most vulnerable point: the Narva region in North-Eastern
Estonia, populated almost exclusively by ethnic Russians. The question that
triggered political escalation was the Law on Aliens approved by the Estonian
Parliament in late June which was taken by many Russians as discriminatory.[30]
President Yeltsin and Foreign Minister Kozyrev condemned this Law as
'apartheid' and 'ethnic cleansing', using every opportunity (including the G-7
summit in Tokyo) to press the case. Implicit political and quite probably financial support was given to the referendum in Narva on the question of autonomy

---

29 Lithuania hosted three Russian divisions: the 7th Airborne, the 107th Motor Rifle and the 3rd
Coastal Defence; the latter was converted from a motor rifle division in 1990 in order to take its 270
tanks and other equipment out of the CFE Treaty limits. Estonia and Latvia had on their territory
one cadre division each.

30 Of Narva's 85,000 adult population, only some 6,000 at that time were Estonian citizens. (See
Hanson, 1993.)

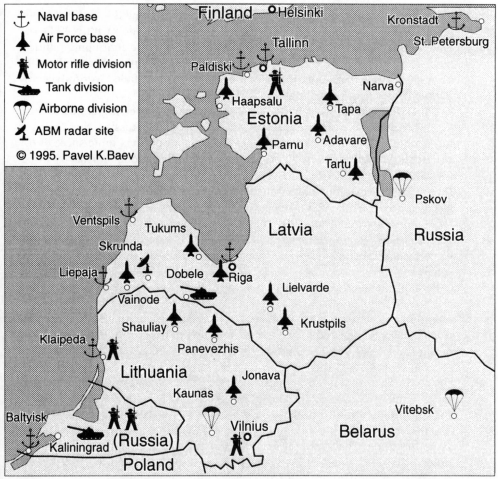

Map 7.1   *Soviet Military Presence in Estonia, Latvia and Lithuania in 1990–91*

conducted in July.[31] It would not be an exaggeration to say that on the political level everything was made ready for a Russian 'peace intervention' in support of the 'popular demand' in Narva (which was not that difficult to organize) for reunification with Russia.

Yet, the military leadership showed no interest in launching such an operation. No Russian troops were based in the Narva area; indeed, in the whole of Estonia there were only some 6,000 troops left, mainly in the rear services, so any intervention would necessarily involve cross-border deployment. In the Leningrad Military District, there were more than enough forces for a *blitzkrieg* intervention (including the 76th Airborne Division in Pskov), but the strategic value of the Narva area was insignificant. Certainly the prize was not worth the

---

31 The outcome was not particularly convincing: the turnout was just about 50%, but 90% of the votes were in favour of autonomous status. Compare the diametrically opposed opinions of Carl Bildt (1993) and Andrei Kozyrev (1993b).

price the military would have been forced to pay for taking it – and that could quite possibly have included resumption of the confrontation with NATO, but now from a position of weakness. In sharp contrast to the continuing political tensions around Narva, military withdrawal from Lithuania was completed by 31 August 1993, even though bilateral negotiations had failed to produce any political agreement by that date.

While the year 1994 saw periodic escalation of controversies related to both key problems, the overall impression was that on the Russian side this was more a political 'show' than real policy. Estonia and Latvia quite successfully countered Moscow's claims about violations of 'international norms' by working carefully with the CSCE High Commissioner for National Minorities and showing willingness to incorporate most of the recommendations of the expert groups of the Council of Europe into their respective legislation. This enabled them to mobilize additional international pressure (first of all from the USA) on the issue of troop withdrawal, and Russia was forced to abandon many of its pledges and claims.[32] By 31 August 1994 all Russian troops had left Baltic soil.

Perhaps there were certain expectations in the Russian Foreign Ministry that resolution of the military question would make it possible to concentrate more attention on the issue of the rights of the Russian population. But the international partners appeared to be inclined to keep this a low-profile question. The declaration on the Baltic states adopted at the CSCE Budapest summit in December welcomed the withdrawal of Russian troops but only briefly mentioned the issue of human rights; in February 1995, Latvia was welcomed into the Council of Europe as a full member.[33] Accordingly, both Estonia and Latvia showed no intention to promote compromises with Russia, especially on the controversial question of granting citizenship to retired military officers. At the same time, some balanced steps were continued in their internal policies in order to ease tensions with the Russian-speaking communities and prevent smouldering political protests from becoming radicalized.[34]

One remaining stumbling-block in normalizing Russian–Estonian and Russian–Latvian relations concerns the delimitation of borders. Both Estonia and Latvia insist on the legal continuity between their present states and those that existed in the inter-war period, thus implying the validity of the treaties signed with Russia in 1920. Moscow categorically declares these treaties invalid and refuses even to discuss any possibility of changes of present borders that

---

32 Sweden also provided crucial political support for Estonia and Latvia, supplementing it with substantial economic aid. As *The Economist* pointed out, the reasons were more pragmatic than altruistic: 'If the Baltic states are well governed and well defended, they are less likely to fall victim to bullying, or to more subtle attempts to turn them into the docile autocracies being established to Russia's south' ('Sweden's Baltic Bulwark', 1994).

33 For a bitter warning against the latter see the 'open letter' from Ramazan Abdulatipov, Deputy Chairman of the Federation Council, to Max van der Stoel, CSCE High Commissioner for National Minorities, published in *Nezavisimaya Gazeta*, 14 October 1994.

34 Several minor amendments to the Law on Aliens extending the deadline and simplifying the procedure of applying for residence permits, approved by the Estonian Parliament (albeit after heated debates) in July 1995, could provide an example. (See Gukasov, 1995.)

were established between 1944 and 1954.[35] This position was confirmed in the most demonstrative way during President Yeltsin's visit to the Pechory district bordering Estonia in November 1994.[36]

This is a problem that will have to be defused. Latvia has been patiently seeking a legal compromise that could be acceptable to its public opinion but without involving any serious redrawing of the present border. Estonia, on the contrary, seems determined to maintain its territorial claims, though this course may well prove extremely counter-productive. Denying the legitimacy of the existing border in the area where, within Estonia, there lives a compact community of Russian population could pave the way for interstate territorial conflict (Nesvizhsky, 1995). That it was averted in summer 1993 does not in itself provide guarantees against new confrontations. Many in Estonia have been arguing against using this charged issue in the internal political struggle.[37]

The accelerated Russian military withdrawal from the three Baltic states had one highly undesirable consequence: excessive militarization of Kaliningrad *oblast*. Earlier plans to create in this exclave a free economic zone and, perhaps, to resettle there ethnic Germans from Kazakhstan were postponed in the face of more urgent needs to host the many military units withdrawn from Lithuania and Latvia (as well as from Germany and Poland) and to store enormous amounts of military hardware. This indeed made Kaliningrad a 'garrison state' (Petersen & Petersen, 1993), but initiatives from the Baltic neighbours to promote its demilitarization were rebuffed by Russia as interference in internal affairs.[38]

In general, intensive controversies between Russia and Estonia, Latvia and Lithuania during 1992–94 may even have helped the latter three to establish their places in key European institutions. They reached several agreements with the EU and were granted the status of 'associate partners' in the WEU; individual programmes in the framework of Partnership for Peace were signed with NATO and implementation is well under way. Certainly, some of the projects would seem to aim too high; the much-advertised plan for a Baltic peace-keeping battalion provides a good example of a politically meaningful initiative that makes very little military sense (Meri, 1994). But the main result has been a substantial reduction in conflict potential in the area. Russia has now accepted that its influence in the Baltic states will be counter-balanced by the impact of

---

35 Estonia lost some 2,300 square kilometres (about 5% of its territory) to Leningrad and Pskov *oblast*, Latvia lost some 1,400 square kilometres (about 2% of its territory) to Pskov *oblast*. (See Bungs, 1994c.)

36 'This border was, is and will be Russian and we shall not cede a single centimetre of land no matter who claims it' – these were Yeltsin's words that hardly made an agreement any more feasible. (See ITAR-TASS 23 November, in FBIS-SOV-94-226.)

37 Toivo Kuldsepp, Director of the Estonian Institute for Foreign Affairs, pointed out that the border problem was a major obstacle for Estonian desire for integration in the 'democratic structures of Europe', speaking at the seminar on 'New Security and New Risks in the Nordic Area' organized by the Nordic Journalist Centre, Helsinki, 27 October 1994.

38 The resolution on this issue approved by the Baltic Assembly in mid-November 1994 was met with strong criticism from the Russian Foreign Ministry and provoked a flurry of 'patriotic' comments in the mass media.

international involvement. There are now new opportunities to develop military-to-military contacts in the Baltic region – if the Balts can manage to overcome their quite understandable allergy and recognize that such contacts could contribute to regional stability and have nothing to do with returning to Russia's 'sphere of influence' (Baev, 1995h). Indeed, regional stability remains a legitimate concern – particularly since the combination of ethnic tensions and border problems in the Narva area makes a powder keg that will require permanent international attention and careful defusing efforts on the part of the Estonian leadership.

7.5 Conclusion

On New Year's Eve 1994 Russian tanks moved inside Grozny, only to be burned by defiant Chechen fighters. Since that point, the whole international agenda of Russian peace-keeping has changed dramatically. The indiscriminate bombardments soon approved by Moscow as the only possible tactics led to the systematic massacre of the civilian population. The military rule established on lowland Chechnya produced massive violations of human rights. While official international reactions were moderately critical and certainly stopped short of calling the operation by its true name – a 'crime against humanity' – the damage to Russia's prestige in key international organizations was serious, quite possibly irreparable.

The international institution that has sought most persistently to influence the settlement of this conflict has been the Organization for Security and Cooperation in Europe, with appeals to its newly approved Code of Conduct. Istvan Gyarmati, OSCE special envoy, led a fact-finding mission to Chechnya and tried to propose mediation, but Russia remained unwilling to allow any real internationalization of the conflict (Baev, 1995f). In practical terms, the OSCE role was reduced to hosting the laboured Russian–Chechen talks that started after the Budennovsk hostage crisis of June 1995.

But already during spring 1995 the Russian Foreign Ministry undertook a number of 'face-saving' manoeuvres on the European arena, including granting unexpected approval to the OSCE resolution which stressed massive violation of human rights. Sergei Kovalev, the most impassioned critic of the 'military solution' in the Russian Parliament, was allowed to speak at the session of the Council of Europe, which duly postponed Russia's application (Smithers, 1995). But Kovalev (1995b, p. 43) also warned strongly against isolating Russia and emphasized that:

> Only a selective and targeted combination of support and pressure can assist the transformation of the Russian state from its historical role as the bane of the Russian people into a guarantor of their prosperity and security, from a continual threat to neighbouring countries into a reliable and equal partner.

That Russia's voice was becoming less important and generally less welcome on many problems of European security – including the issue of NATO enlargement – was only part of the problem. Russia's role in the Balkans was inevitably weakened; the escalation of hostilities in August 1995 proved that Moscow in fact had nothing to contribute to the necessary settlement and its new rapprochement with the Serbian leadership hardly changed anything in this respect. Moreover, the prospects for cooperation in peace-keeping between Russia and its key Western partners (if indeed we may use that term) have been jeopardized. The Partnership for Peace agenda – even finalized and duly signed – would hardly be implementable.

Before Chechnya, the chances for international recognition and legitimization of Russia's 'peace interventions' did not look particularly strong. Today they are close to zero. In this situation, Russia's cooperativeness in launching the OSCE peace-keeping operation in Nagorno Karabakh is becoming more problematic than ever, and failure in the Transcaucasus could seriously damage the credibility of this organization which hardly increased much in Chechnya. Neither would it be realistic to expect from Russia any flexibility in allowing NATO to take on a role in peace enforcement in possible local conflicts in Europe – and again the loud (albeit rather hollow) protests from Moscow to the air strikes in Bosnia in late August to early September 1995 provide convincing evidence. Thus the Chechen war could well create another deadlock in international peace-keeping similar to that of the late 1970s and early 1980s – when the Cold War was at its peak and the UN Security Council remained unable to take any meaningful decision.

OUTLOOK

From the Taiga to the British Seas
The Red Army is the Strongest.

Popular Soviet song

8

Through the Fog of War

The whole story of transition of the Army that used to be Soviet and was forced to become Russian is now intersected by the watershed of war: before and during. While the 'after' remains clouded, it is already clear that the impact of the Chechen campaign will go beyond that of the Afghan War, and could be justly compared with such military disasters as the Crimean War of 1854–55 and the Russo-Japanese War of 1905. The military leadership, while admitting that the Army carried the main burden in Chechnya, has strongly denied any responsibility for unleashing it.[1] And Russia's Security Council, gathering on 30 August 1995 to discuss the situation in Chechnya for the first time since its meeting on 29 November 1994 – with many new faces around the table – found no better way to boost the fragile peace process than to issue a series of new ultimatums (Vinogradov, 1995a, 1995b). By then, in Chechnya itself, the routinely violated ceasefire was still holding, and even the 6 October assassination attempt on General Romanov which left him badly injured saw no punishment. This was due not so much to the military agreement signed on 30 July as to the fact that neither side felt able to resume large-scale hostilities. However, neither side was ready for meaningful political concessions (Zamyatina, 1995). The Russian leadership had expected that the elections for a new leader of the republic would permit stabilization of the internal situation (and the elections to the State Duma were to confirm that Chechnya would remain a part of the Russian Federation), but the heavy fighting around Gudermes in mid-December proved otherwise.[2] In this highly unstable situation – and indeed throughout the whole ignominious military campaign – the most painful strains in Russia, and the most serious consequences, have come in the field of civil–military and military–political relations.

By the end of 1994, the progressive weakening of Yeltsin's grasp of power had opened the way for any grouping of determined officers and politicians dreaming about a strong-hand solution to consider a coup d'etat in practical terms – even more so as the tragic events of October 1993 had set new standards for the acceptability of violence in political struggle. The charged atmosphere of imminent coup hovered over the Kremlin during the first months of 1995, but gradually Moscow returned to its normal hectic life, with financial scandals and bureaucratic reshuffling dominating the agenda and the parliamentary

---

1 General Kvashnin (1995) made a classical neo-Clausewitzian point in his speech at the Assembly of High Command which examined the lessons of the Chechen campaign: 'Wars are started and ended by politicians. The Army is merely a means of waging them. This war is no exception.'

2 Vladimir Rubanov, Deputy Secretary of the Russian Security Council, argued at the seminar organized by PRIO in mid-October 1995 that the aim of the internal Chechen dialogue was to marginalize the 'irreconcilable opposition' and isolate Dudaev. Personal records.

elections looming ever closer. Perhaps a coup was averted not so much by the dismissal of quite a few top military officials, including three Deputy Defence Ministers (Generals Gromov, Kondratyev and Mironov), as by the very fact that the Army by then found itself involved in a protracted and bloody war – and had to concentrate on waging it successfully. Thus, even more bitter was the frustration of the victory-obsessed generals when in late July they were ordered to halt their advances into the mountains and to let the desperate Chechen fighters go down into the lowlands.[3] The temporarily silenced 'military opposition' became a sort of political force hovering in the wings – and the resignation of General Lebed in May confirmed that the generals had begun considering their stakes in the increasingly uncertain political game.

The war in Afghanistan produced the 'Afghan' cohort in the officer corps, but the war in Chechnya has effectively split it into two: 'the refuseniks', who took a stance against it and have been dismissed from the ranks; and 'the warriors', who went through all the bloodshed and have often been promoted. While the latter harbour now deep irritation, both against the political leaders who unleashed the war but denied the army the right to get its victory and the Defence Minister who personally contributed to making it a real disaster, the former have started looking for new allies in the political elite. Obviously neither the 'old democrats' with their loose coalition headed by Yegor Gajdar, nor the 'new democrats' with emerging potential leaders like Grigory Yavlinsky, are promising partners – not that they have been making any efforts to build bridges to the Army.[4] Their opposition to the war (Gajdar attempted to mobilize anti-war sentiments but failed to build a real platform) seemed suspiciously reminiscent of an anti-Army campaign. Perhaps more attractive could be the 'right-centrist' grouping around Prime Minister Viktor Chernomyrdin. Defence Minister Grachev strongly encouraged officers to enter the election campaign under the banner of the pro-governmental bloc 'Our House is Russia'. But for many in the frustrated officer corps this 'party of power' carries responsibility for severe cuts in the military budget and for neglect of reforms in the Army.[5]

---

3 General Kvashnin – with the December 1995 wisdom of hindsight – argued in an interview that Dudaev's army had been completely destroyed and another week of offensive operations could have entirely eliminated the organized resistance. See Kolpakov, 1995.

4 On Gajdar's electoral strategy see his article in *Izvestia* (Gajdar, 1995a). Yavlinsky presented his approach in the same periodical some three months later (Yavlinsky, 1995). Neither contained any ideas concerning the military electorate. Gajdar's decision to put on his party's list General Vorobyev, former Deputy Commander of the Army, who resigned in protest against the Chechen War, has changed nothing in this respect. My own analysis of the political battles in Moscow in the shadow of Chechnya can be found in Baev (1995g).

5 Chernomyrdin enticed into his electoral bloc – 'Our House is Russia' – General Lev Rokhlin, one of the 'heroes' of the battle for Grozny, but the latter looks pretty theatrical in the party of governors and 'generals' of oil and gas. General Mironov, who after his expulsion from the Defence Ministry was given a post of Military Adviser to Prime Minister Chernomyrdin, prefers to keep a low profile in politics. As for General Gromov, he initially decided to join the list of Ivan Rybkin, Chairman of the State Duma, who was attempting to build a 'left-centrist' coalition, but then Gromov preferred to start his own party, 'My Fatherland'. Like many other newborn groupings, this party failed to cross the 5% threshold in the December elections, but Gromov was elected to the State Duma as a single-constituency representative. See Simonsen, 1995b.

In this massive call-up of general officers into politics, some new links between the radicalized military and the 'irreconcilable' opposition to the Yeltsin regime have started to be forged. Back in 1993, the opposition could count quite a few retired senior officers under its banners (General Makashov and General Achalov were particularly active), and after the October events so prominent an anti-Yeltsinist as Alexandr Sterligov (a retired KGB General himself) persistently reiterated the message that 'the next leader of Russia will come from the ranks of the military'.[6] While Zhirinovsky failed to transform the strong military vote for his party in December 1993 into reliable ties, other nationalist forces have had more success. The Communist Party mobilized some old-timers like Generals Makashov and Varennikov. A little-known party called 'For the Motherland!' enlisted General Podkolzin, Commander of the Airborne Troops, and Admiral Baltin, Commander of the Black Sea Fleet. But what captured most attention was the Congress of Russian Communities (KRO) which held its meeting in early April 1995 with two new political stars: Yuri Skokov and General Alexandr Lebed (Balburov, 1995). The former had, in the course of his work in the Security Council back in early 1993, established good personal contacts with the political establishment and the military high command, including Gromov and Kolesnikov. The latter clearly aspires to build on his popularity in the officer corps and to rally support around the image of the victorious warrior with clean hands (Gostev, 1995). The next meeting of the Congress, held in early September after intensive summer campaigning, gave the impression that this political platform had a potential for mobilizing remarkably wide support. The party received considerable coverage during the election campaign, and many predicted that KRO could indeed achieve what the anti-reform opposition has been seeking in vain ever since the August 1991 coup – to deprive Yeltsin's regime of the support of the Army. Such expectations were disappointed by the election results (KRO failed to cross the 5% barrier), but General Lebed, who was elected to the State Duma from a single constituency, remains a strong presidential candidate for the June 1996 elections.

The high political aspirations and ambitions of the military made a sharp contrast with the unbelievably poor state of the Army which, as Paul Goble (1995b) has observed, acquired two faces: one of power and one of poverty. The latter has been strongly accentuated by the fact that it is the Army itself that has borne most of the brunt of the Chechen War. Debilitating undermanning, unbelievably poor training and severe logistical problems were all revealed during the first weeks of the campaign, and with such clarity that the necessity of emergency measures was politically recognized. Defence Minister Grachev was quick to propose several palliative measures and orchestrated a new round of demands for funds and resources.[7] But despite some dramatic statements – for example, that the Air Force needed some 300 new aircraft in 1995 but would not get a

---

6 As quoted in the editorial in *Moskovskie Novosti*, no. 40, 1994. Alexandr Rutskoi, presumably, was not on the 'short list'; besides General Alexandr Lebed, General Andrei Nikolaev, Commander of the Border Troops, was mentioned as a potential leader.

7 Thus, he introduced a plan to beef up at least one division or several brigades in every military district to 'near normal' strength so that they would be able to act on short notice.

single one[8] – both the Finance Ministry and the Parliament agreed to keep military expenditures approximately on the level of the 1994 budget. Grachev made this austerity his main defensive line against new pressures for military reform, particularly against transforming the Defence Ministry into a civilian structure (Lobov, 1995).

Launching a counter-offensive, Grachev aggressively pushed a proposal to amend the Law on Military Service. Yielding to this pressure, the State Duma passed in early April 1995 an amendment that extended the duration of compulsory military service from 1.5 to 2 years and allowed all graduate students to be drafted.[9] While the social consequences of this legislation were postponed until the autumnal draft period, it was immediately clear to many experts that the envisaged increase in available manpower would make it possible to postpone further or bury altogether many long-overdue reforms in the military structures (Latsis, 1995). Chief of General Staff Kolesnikov confirmed that even with the new draft, the authorized strength of the Russian Armed Forces would be reduced by 217,000 troops by the end of 1995, compared with the 385,000 reduction in 1994.[10] Continuing reductions are forced primarily by the necessity to maintain supply and salary levels, though the 'frozen' budget would inevitably make this problematic, opening the floodgates to further dissatisfaction within the officer corps.[11] The delays in paying officers' salaries in July–August were directly related to the fact that the Defence Ministry had spent about 1.9 trillion roubles on the Chechen campaign in the first half of 1995. This sum (about USD 450,000,000, or up to 15% of the total Army spending during that period) had not been envisaged by the military budget.[12] And shortly after the Russian government sent the 1996 state budget to the Duma in late August 1995, Defence Minister Grachev announced that the planned outlays for defence 'unquestionably cannot entirely satisfy the country's armed forces'.[13] Arguing against Grachev's ideas on priorities in resource allocation, Alexei Arbatov and Gennady Batanov (1995) predicted: 'Russia will get a combat-unable, poorly equipped and poorly trained, impoverished and alienated Army which will not be able to defend the country from an external threat and will itself become an internal threat.'

The huge waste of resources in the Chechen war has deeply undermined the combat readiness of the Army, particularly its ability to maintain peace-keeping

---

8 General Soroka, Deputy Commander of the Air Force, made this point at hearings in the State Duma. (See FBIS-SOV-95-069, 11 April.)

9 The legislation was approved immediately after the presentation of General Kolesnikov, Chief of the General Staff, without any preliminary hearings and even without the text of proposed amendments. (See Arbatov, 1995b.)

10 Addressing the State Duma again on 11 April. (See FBIS-SOV-95-070, 12 April 1995.)

11 General Gromov explained why the support for reforms was rather weak in the Army itself: 'Reforming requires a psychological, moral readiness among officers for sudden and drastic changes. To my mind, such readiness was and is absent. When an officer has no place to live, when he is unable to use his professional qualifications, he does not care about reforms' (Gromov, 1995b).

12 The figure was provided by General Osadchy, Head of Department of the Main Directorate for Budget and Financing of the Ministry of Defence. (See *Izvestia*, 25 August.)

13 He was backed by Deputy Defence Minister Kokoshin, who demanded more funding for the military industries. (See *Broadcast Monitor*, vol. 1, no. 85, 30 August [e-mail].)

activities in Russia's Near Abroad. As far as the Mobile Forces are concerned, the rebuilding of the 104th (Volga MD) and 7th (North Caucasus MD) Airborne Divisions will be seriously hampered by logistic shortages and also by the increasing departure of junior officers, 'contract' warrant officers and sergeants attracted by higher salaries and better conditions in other 'elite' forces and private security services.[14] The 27th and 45th 'peace-keeping' divisions will remain seriously overstreched particularly due to their participation in the Implementation Force in Bosnia-Herzegovina – even if no new deployment to Chechnya is ordered. Many units assigned to the 58th Army in the North Caucasus MD have suffered such losses in the Chechen campaign that their combat-worthiness even after 'emergency repair' would be quite low. In general, it is Russia's progressive military weakening that has determined the pattern of strategic retreat.

The operation in Transdniestria has brought the first evidence of this trend. Russia unilaterally decided to halve its peace-keeping forces there even before the Chechen campaign, and the decision to reduce the strength and the status of the 14th Army came as a follow-up. The resignation of General Lebed could pave the way to 'nationalization' of the armaments and stocks of the 14th Army by the Transdniestrian government – and this would certainly make any political settlement much more difficult. Another possible military withdrawal is Tadzhikistan, where the opposition is methodically increasing pressure on the besieged Russian border posts, while the 'peace-keeping' 201st Division is becoming increasingly reluctant to engage in any combat operations. The CIS summit in Minsk in May 1995 saw new evidence of Russia's decreasing political influence in this area as the neighbour-states (Kazakhstan and Uzbekistan and even Afghanistan) assumed mediatory roles between the Dushanbe government and the opposition.[15]

But the region where Russia's positions have been damaged most by the war in Chechnya is certainly the Caucasus. Moscow's unpredictability and lack of any consistent strategy for the region have been revealed as clearly as its military weakness. In this situation, Azerbaijan could feel quite free to settle its oil deals with Western partners paying scant heed to the 'legitimate' interests of the northern neighbour.[16] Russian Defence Minister Grachev, seeking to confirm

---

14 In spring 1995, the Russian Defence Ministry launched a wide-ranging campaign for signing short-term contracts (three to six months) with privates and sergeants for serving in Chechnya. But the lack of funds for this programme pushed the so-called 'contractniks' to earn their money through all sorts of extortions from the civilian population. This semi-criminal reputation of contract service has spread to involve plans for 'professionalization' of the Army. (See Zhilin & Ukhlin, 1995.)

15 The mandate for the CIS peace-keeping forces was formally extended for another half year, but Uzbekistan and even Kazakhstan have started to express doubts concerning the future of Russia's military presence in Central Asia. (See Shermatova, 1995b.)

16 The 'oil' interests in the Chechen war – emphasized strongly by some experts (Afanasyev, 1994) – were never explicitly stated. Moscow's massive investment in rebuilding the oil industry in Chechnya in Summer 1995 (Yakov, 1995) could be taken as an evidence that those interests were indeed at least one of the key factors in decision-making. But as Elaine Holoboff (1995, p. 257) has pointed out, 'Like everything else that went wrong with this conflict, Moscow's original goal of securing economic and strategic advantages for the Russian oil industry, probably now lies in the grim ashes of Grozny's rubble.'

that Russia's 'forward deployment' remained in place, made a visit to Armenia and Georgia in March 1995. He supervised the first Russian–Armenian joint military exercises and finalized agreements on basing of Russian troops: about 10,000 in Armenia and 20,000 in Georgia. While Armenia shows strong interest in maintaining meaningful military links with Russia, Georgia has made its position (more specifically signing and ratification of the basing agreement) conditional on restoring full control on its territory, i.e. Abkhazia and South Ossetia. Indeed, the war in Chechnya has made the sustainability of Russia's peace-keeping operation in Abkhazia rather questionable despite another prolongation of its mandate at the May CIS summit.[17] As the campaign in Chechnya has seriously weakened the support base for Abkhazia in the North Caucasus (whatever the reliability of information about Abkhazian 'battalions' fighting on Dudaev's side), for Georgia it is increasingly tempting to try for another military solution – in much the same way as Croatia conducted its *blitzkrieg* to restore control over Krajina in August 1995. Providing Russia refrained from any support to Abkhazian 'separatists', the chances for success of such a forced reunification would seem quite good, but whether Georgia would actually welcome Russian troops on its territory afterwards remains doubtful.[18]

Declining political influence in the Caucasus and Central Asia and diminishing military capabilities could go hand in hand with increasing toughness and even aggressiveness in Russian foreign policy. Only by concentrating maximum resources on internal reforms and minimizing external involvements could a recovery from the deep societal crisis come about. And yet, the political leaders who will succeed Yeltsin are already now seeking 'victories' which could compensate for inevitable retreats. As the military failure in Chechnya has undermined so deeply the credibility of the 'empire-restoring' slogans, the best possible ideology for a 'pro-active' foreign policy would seem to be nationalism – which could come in various blends but with an increasing ethnic component. Andrei Kozyrev's April statement that Russia would be ready to use 'all necessary means, including military force' for protection of the Russians in the Near Abroad, appears quite symptomatic (Pushkov, 1995). For the domestic electorate Kozyrev could hardly be convincing in this role. Others – perhaps not so much Zhirinovsky as the Congress of Russian Communities (chaired jointly by Skokov and Lebed) which has made the 'Russians Abroad' issue one of the key slogans of its electoral campaign – would certainly play it more naturally and passionately.

Serious damage to Russia's relations with its Western partners could result from such 'nationalization' of the foreign and military policies. It is not only that official rhetoric infected by nationalism (with Chechnya looming in the background) makes the whole of Russia's peace-keeping activities in the CIS – which

---

17 In June 1995, both chambers of the Russian Parliament also approved the prolongation of mandate, paying scant attention to the costs of the operation (which amounted to some 31 billion roubles) or to the deadlocked problem of the return of Georgian refugees (see Rotar, 1995b).

18 The Abkhazian side sabotaged in a remarkably undiplomatic way the August–September round of talks on settlement, disregarding pressure from Moscow and obviously foreseeing changes in Russia's political course after the December parliamentary elections. (See Eggert, 1995.)

have already caused many misgivings in the West – quite unacceptable. By taking a self-assertive nationalistic course, Russia would inevitably distance and isolate itself from Europe (Baev, 1995f). Sergei Karaganov (1995) and several other influential foreign policy experts have been trying to limit the scope of such a drift by recalling the idea of 'neo-Gaullism' which, in their expectations, would make it possible to marry the tough pursuit of Russian interests with continuing partnership with the West. But as Paul Goble (1995a) has pointed out, such a 'Gaullist' policy is actually built on sand, since Russia – unlike France – cannot take its place in the Western world for granted, and the current retreat from democracy makes this place even more questionable. Jonathan Steele (1995) has aptly invoked an hour-glass model for the present-day Russian society – with a band of rulers on the top and the people at the bottom, with very little contact between the two groups – and concluded that 'the effort to implant a citizen-friendly democracy has had very little success'.

It seems barely possible that some sort of military regime could emerge in Moscow in July 1996 as a result of the subsequent parliamentary and presidential elections – though some analysts find such a scenario quite plausible (Yakhlakova, 1995). But one final general assumption can safely be made. The weakening and degradation of Yeltsin's regime and the uncertainties of political transition to a post-Yeltsin period are bringing Russia to another cross-roads in its long and turbulent history – and the force that decides the direction could well be the unreformed, politicized and frustrated Army.

References

Adamishin, Anatoli, 1993. 'Forceful Measures Are Not Our Choice', *Moscow News*, no. 33, 13 August.

Afanasyev, Yury, 1994. 'Aggression Is an Economic Category', *Moskovskie Novosti*, no. 66, 25 December – 1 January (in Russian).

Afanasyev, Yury & Len Karpinsky, 1995. 'Again at a Russian Crossroads', *Moskovskie Novosti*, no. 32, 7–14 May (in Russian).

Akhromeev, Sergei F. & Georgi M. Kornienko, 1992. *Glazami Marshala i Diplomata* (Through the Eyes of Marshal and Diplomat). Moscow: Mezhdunarodnye Otnosheniya.

Allison, Graham, 1993. 'Defense and Military Cooperation in Denuclearization', pp. 146–162 in Graham Allison, Ashton B. Carter, Steven E. Miller & Philip Zelikov, eds, *Cooperative Denuclearization: From Pledges to Deeds*. CSIA Studies in International Security no. 2. Cambridge, MA: Harvard University Press.

Allison, Roy, 1994. *Peacekeeping in the Soviet Successor States*. Chaillot Paper no. 18, November. Paris: Institute for Security Studies WEU.

Ambartsumov, Evgeni, 1994. 'The Echo of Bombings in Bosnia', *Moskovskie Novosti*, no. 15, 10–17 April (in Russian).

Arbatov, Alexei, 1993a. 'START II, Red Ink and Boris Yeltsin', *Bulletin of the Atomic Scientists*, vol. 49, no. 3, April, pp. 16–21.

Arbatov, Alexei, 1993b. 'Russia's Foreign Policy Alternatives', *International Security*, vol. 18, no. 2, Fall, pp. 5–43.

Arbatov, Alexei, 1993c. 'Fascism Didn't Succeed, but Democracy Suffered a Defeat', *Nezavisimaya Gazeta*, 22 October (in Russian).

Arbatov, Alexei, 1994a. 'Big Policy or Petty Game?', *Moskovskie Novosti*, no. 6, 6–13 February (in Russian).

Arbatov, Alexei, 1994b. 'Russia: National Security in the 1990s', *Mirovaya Ekonomika i Mezhdunarodnye Otnosheniya*, no. 7, July, pp. 5–15; no. 8–9, August-September, pp. 5–18 (in Russian).

Arbatov, Alexei, 1995a. 'Army Reform in Midst of Disaster', *Moscow News*, no. 3, 20–26 January.

Arbatov, Alexei, 1995b. 'Duma Steps Back from Military Reform', *Moscow News*, no. 14, 14–20 April.

Arbatov, Alexei, 1995c. 'NATO and Russia', *Security Dialogue*, vol. 26, no. 2, June, pp. 135–146.

Arbatov, Alexei & Gennady Batanov, 1995. 'What Kind of Army Can We Afford?', *Moskovskie Novosti*, no. 67, 1–8 October (in Russian).

Arbatov, Alexei & Boris Makeev, 1992. 'The Kuril Barrier', *Novoe Vremya*, no. 42, November, pp. 24–26 (in Russian).

The Arms Control Reporter, 1993, 1994, 1995. Cambridge, MA: Institute for Defense and Disarmament Studies.

'Army: Everything for Sale', 1994. *Moscow News*, no. 34, 26 August – 1 September.

Aron, Leon, 1994. 'The Emergent Priorities of Russian Foreign Policy', pp. 17–34 in Leon Aron & Kenneth M. Jensen, eds, *The Emergence of Russian Foreign Policy*. Washington DC: United States Institute of Peace Press.

Asmus, Ronald D.; Richard L. Kugler & F. Stephen Larrabee, 1995. 'NATO Expansion: The Next Steps', *Survival*, vol. 37, no. 1, Spring, pp. 7–33.

Baev, Pavel, 1993. 'Russia's Rapid Reaction Forces: Politics and Pitfalls', *Bulletin of Arms Control*, no. 9, February, pp. 12–17.

Baev, Pavel, 1994a. 'Russia's Armed Forces: Spontaneous Demobilization', *Bulletin of Arms Control*, no. 13, February, pp. 8–13.

180   REFERENCES

Baev, Pavel, 1994b. 'The Impact on Relations between Western Europe and Russia', pp. 35–49 in Mathias Jopp, ed., *The Implications of the Yugoslav Crisis for Western Europe's Foreign Relations*. Chaillot Paper no. 17. Paris: Institute for Security Studies WEU.

Baev, Pavel K., 1994c. 'Russian Perspectives on the Barents Region' pp. 175–186 in Stokke & Tunander, eds, *The Barents Region*.

Baev, Pavel, 1994d. 'Russia's Conflicting Interests in the Baltic Area', pp. 427–436 in Renate Platzöder & Philonene Verlaan, eds, *The Baltic Sea: New Developments in National Policies and International Cooperation*. Ebenhausen: Stiftung Wissenschaft und Politik.

Baev, Pavel, 1994e. 'Russia's Experiments and Experience in Conflict Management and Peacemaking', *International Peacekeeping*, vol. 1, no. 3, Autumn, pp. 245–260.

Baev, Pavel, 1994f. 'Russian Military Thinking and the "Near Abroad"', *Jane's Intelligence Review*, vol. 6, no. 12, December, pp. 531–533.

Baev, Pavel, 1995a. 'Russian Minorities in the Former Soviet Union', in *Conflicts in the OSCE Area*. Oslo: PRIO.

Baev, Pavel, 1995b. 'Georgia and North Caucasus', in *Conflicts in the OSCE Area*. Oslo: PRIO.

Baev, Pavel, 1995c. *Russia's Policy in the North Caucasus and the War in Chechnya*. FSS Briefing no. 2, March. London: The Royal Institute of International Affairs.

Baev, Pavel K., 1995d. 'Old and New Border Problems in Russia's Security Policy', pp. 86–103 in Tuomas Forsberg, ed., *Contested Territory*.

Baev, Pavel, 1995e. 'Russia's Peacekeeping in the Caucasus', pp. 95–110 in Espen Barth Eide, ed., *Peacekeeping in Europe*. Peacekeeping and Multinational Operations no. 5. Oslo: Norwegian Institute of International Affairs (NUPI).

Baev, Pavel, 1995f. 'Drifting Away from Europe', *Transition*, vol. 1, no. 11, 30 June, pp. 30–33.

Baev, Pavel, 1995g. 'The Lull Yeltsin May Not Survive', *European Brief*, vol. 2, no. 7, June, pp. 73–74.

Baev, Pavel. 1995h. 'A Little Less Hostility, a Little More Olive Branch', *European Brief*, vol. 2, no. 8, July/August, pp. 42–43.

Baev, Pavel, 1995i. 'The Influence of the Balkan Crisis on Russia's Peacekeeping in its "Near Abroad"', pp. 67–81 in Jonson & Archer, eds, *Peacekeeping and the Role of Russia in Eurasia*.

Baev, Pavel; Sergei Karaganov, Victor Shein & Vitaly Zhurkin, 1990. *Tactical Nuclear Weapons in Europe*. Moscow: Novosti Press Agency Publishing House.

Balburov, Dmitry, 1995. 'Russia – for Russian Communities?', *Moskovskie Novosti*, no. 24, 9–16 April (in Russian).

Baranovsky, Vladimir, 1994. 'Conflict Developments on the Territory of the Former Soviet Union', pp. 169–203 in *SIPRI Yearbook 1994*.

Barber, Tony, 1995. 'Stakes Raised as Alliance Treads Dangerous Line', *The Independent*, 31 August.

Barry, Charles L., ed., 1994. *The Search for Peace in Europe: Perspectives from NATO and Eastern Europe*. Washington, DC: National Defense University Press.

'Basic Provisions of the Military Doctrine of the Russian Federation', 1994. *Jane's Intelligence Review*, Special Report, January.

Bathurst, Robert B., 1993. *Intelligence and the Mirror: On Creating an Enemy*. London: Sage.

Bathurst, Robert, 1996. 'The Politics of Espionage', *Dagens Næringsliv*, 19 February (in Norwegian).

Batur, Nur, 1994. 'The Secret Turkish–Russian War in NATO', *Milliyet*, 10 June (in FBIS-WEU-94–119).

Berdal, Mats R., 1993. *Whither UN Peacekeeping?* Adelphi Paper 281, London: Brassey's (UK)/IISS.

Berdal, Mats R., 1994. 'Fateful Encounter: the United States and UN Peacekeeping', *Survival*, vol. 36, no. 1, Spring, pp. 30–50.

Bertram, Christoph, 1995a. 'NATO on Track for the 21st Century?', *Security Dialogue*, vol. 26, no. 1, March, pp. 65–71.

Bertram, Christoph, 1995b. 'Multilateral Diplomacy and Conflict Resolution', *Survival*, vol. 37, no. 4, Winter, pp. 65–82.

Beyerchen, Alan, 1992/93. 'Clausewitz, Non-Linearity and the Unpredictability of War', *International Security*, vol. 17, no. 3, Winter, pp. 59–90.

Bezugly, Vladimir, 1995. 'Why Dudaev Simply Cannot Be Apprehended', Interview with *Komsomolskaya Pravda*, 23 March (in Russian).

Bildt, Carl, 1993. 'Watch Russia's Baltic "Near Abroad"', *International Herald Tribune*, 27 August.

Blackwill, Robert D. & Sergei A. Karaganov, eds, 1994. *Damage Limitation or Crisis? Russia and the Outside World*. CSIA Studies in International Security no. 5. Washington, DC: Brassey's (US).

Blagovolin, Sergei, 1993. 'Tadzhikistan: To Go or to Stay', *Moskovskie Novosti*, no. 31, 1 August (in Russian).

Boldirev, Yury, 1993. 'The Victory, but over Whom?', *Moskovskie Novosti*, no. 43, 24 October (in Russian).

Boldirev, Yury, 1994. 'What Matters Is Not Who Stole or How Much, but How This Became Possible', Interview with *Izvestia*, 4 November (in Russian).

Bonnart, Frederic, 1994. 'Bosnia: An Emerging Russian View Might Want War to Go On', *International Herald Tribune*, 20 April.

Borodulin, Vladislav, 1994. 'The Government Has Promised to Foot 70 Percent of the Military Bill', *Kommersant-Daily*, 24 November.

Borovik, Artem, 1989. 'Afghanistan: Drawing the Conclusion', Interview with General Valentin Varennikov, *Ogonyek*, no. 12, March, pp. 6–8, 30–31 (in Russian).

Brodie, Bernard, 1984. 'A Guide to the Reading of *On War*', pp. 641–711 in Carl von Clausewitz, *On War*, edited and translated by Michael Howard & Peter Paret. Princeton, NJ: Princeton University Press.

Brusstar, James H. & Ellen Jones, 1995. *The Russian Military's Role in Politics*. McNair Paper 34. Washington, DC: National Defense University.

Brzezinski, Zbigniew, 1995. 'A Plan for Europe', *Foreign Affairs*, vol. 74, no. 1, January/February, pp. 26–42.

Bungs, Dzintra, 1994a. 'Tensions in Latvia over Detention of Two Russian Generals', *RFE/RL News Brief*, 10 January.

Bungs, Dzintra, 1994b. 'Baltic Premiers Say Kozyrev's Statement a Threat', *RFE/RL News Brief*, 20 January.

Bungs, Dzintra, 1994c. 'Seeking Solutions to Baltic-Russian Border Issues', *RFE/RL Research Report*, vol. 3, no. 13, 1 April, pp. 25–32.

Burbyga, Nikolai, 1992. 'The Point of View of Army General Konstantin Kobets', *Izvestia*, 12 February (in Russian).

Burlatski, Fedor, 1990. *Vozhdi i Sovetniki* (Leaders and Advisers). Moscow: Progress Publishing.

Bush, Keith, 1994. 'Budget Maneuvers Continue', *RFE/RL News Brief*, no. 10, 4 March.

Callaghan, Jean, 1993. 'History and Current State of US Defense and Military-to-Military Contacts with the Former Soviet Union' pp. 163–175 in Graham Allison, Ashton B. Carter, Steven E. Miller & Philip Zelikov, eds, *Cooperative Denuclearization: From Pledges to Deeds*. CSIA Studies in International Security no. 2. Cambridge, MA: Harvard University Press.

'CFE Treaty: Consequences for Russia', Report of the Centre for National Security and International Relations, 1992. *Nezavisimaya Gazeta*, 29 July (in Russian).

Chernyak, Igor, 1993. 'The Influence of the Big Caliber', 'The Generals Continue the Fight', *Komsomolskaya Pravda*, 7 October, 8 October (in Russian).

Churkin, Vitaly, 1994. 'Russian "Blue Helmets" May Leave Former Yugoslavia', Interview with *Komsomolskaya Pravda*, 24 November (in Russian).

Clark, Bruce, 1995. 'Elite Troops Refusing to Fight in Chechnya', *Financial Times*, 6 January.

Clark, Susan L., 1994. 'The Russian Military in the Former Soviet Union – Actions and Motivations', *Jane's Intelligence Review*, vol. 6, no. 12, December, pp. 538–543.

Clarke, Douglas L., 1992. 'Former Soviet Armed Forces in the Baltic States', *RFE/RL Research Report*, vol. 1, no. 16, 17 April, pp. 43–49.

Clarke, Douglas L., 1993a. 'Rusting Fleet Renews Debate on Navy's Mission', *RFE/RL Research Report*, vol. 2, no. 25, 18 June, pp. 25–32.

Clarke, Douglas L., 1993b. 'The Russian Military and the CFE Treaty', *RFE/RL Research Report*, vol. 2, no. 42, 22 October, pp. 38–43.

Clarke, Douglas L., 1995a. 'Uncomfortable Partners', *Transition*, 1994 in Review: Part II, February, pp. 27–31.

Clarke, Doug, 1995b. 'Russia May Suspend CFE Cuts if NATO Expands', *OMRI Daily Digest*, no. 67, 4 April [e-mail].

Clarke, Douglas L. & Alfred Reisch, 1992. 'Grachev Fights Politicization of Army', *RFE/RL Research Report*, vol. 1, no. 36, 11 September, pp. 71–72.

Cohen, Richard, 1995. 'The Marshall Center – An Experiment in East–West Cooperation', *NATO Review*, vol. 43, no. 4, July, pp. 27–31.

Colton, Timothy, 1979. *Commissars, Commanders and Civilian Authority.* Cambridge, MA: Harvard University Press.

Colton, Timothy, 1990. 'Perspectives on Civil–Military Relations in the Soviet Union' in Timothy Colton & Thane Gustafson, eds, *Soldiers and the Soviet State.* Princeton, NJ: Princeton University Press.

'The Concept of the Foreign Policy of the Russian Federation', 1993. *Diplomatichesky Vestnik*, January (in Russian).

Corley, Felix, 1994. 'The Ingush–Ossetian Conflict', *Jane's Intelligence Review*, vol. 6, no. 9, September, pp. 401–403.

Crow, Suzanne, 1992a. 'The Theory and Practice of Peacekeeping in the Former USSR', *RFE/RL Research Report*, vol. 1, no. 37, 18 September, pp. 31–36.

Crow, Suzanne, 1992b. 'Russian Peacekeeping: Defense, Diplomacy, or Imperialism?', *RFE/RL Research Report*, vol. 1, no. 37, 18 September, pp. 37–40.

Crow, Suzanne, 1992c. 'Competing Blueprints for Russian Foreign Policy'. *RFE/RL Research Report*, vol. 1, no. 50, 18 December, pp. 45–50.

Crow, Suzanne, 1993a. 'Russia Seeks Leadership in Regional Peacekeeping', *RFE/RL Research Report*, vol. 2, no. 15, 9 April, pp. 28–32.

Crow, Suzanne, 1993b. 'Russian Views on an Eastward Expansion of NATO', *RFE/RL Research Report*, vol. 2, no. 41, 15 October, pp. 21–24.

Crow, Suzanne, 1993c. 'Russia Asserts Its Strategic Agenda', *RFE/RL Research Report*, vol. 2, no. 50, 17 December, pp. 1–8.

Crow, Suzanne, 1994. 'Why Has Russian Foreign Policy Changed?', *RFE/RL Research Report*, vol. 3, no. 18, 6 May.

Dale, Catherine, 1993. 'Turmoil in Abkhazia: Russian Responses', *RFE/RL Research Report*, vol. 2, no. 34, 27 August, pp. 48–57.

Dale, Catherine, 1995. 'The Case of Abkhazia (Georgia),' pp. 121–138 in Jonson & Archer, eds, *Peacekeeping and the Role of Russia in Eurasia.*

Danilovich, A.A., 1992. 'On New Military Doctrines of the CIS and Russia', *The Journal of Soviet Military Studies*, vol. 5, no. 4, December, pp. 517–538.

Dean, Jonathan, 1994. *Ending Europe's Wars: The Continuing Search for Peace and Security.* New York: Twentieth Century Fund Press.

Desch, Michael C., 1993. 'Why the Soviet Military Supported Gorbachev and Why the Russian Military Might Only Support Yeltsin for a Price', *The Journal of Strategic Studies*, vol. 16, no. 4, December, pp. 455–489.

Devyanin, Nikolai, 1995. 'The "Nuclear Suitcase" Was Unavoidable', *Moscow News*, no. 5, 3–8 February.

Dick, Charles J., 1992. 'Initial Thoughts on Russia's Draft Military Doctrine', *The Journal of Soviet Military Studies*, vol. 5, no. 4, December, pp. 552–566.

Dick, Charles, 1994. 'The Military Doctrine of the Russian Federation', *Jane's Intelligence Review*, Special Report, January.

Dobbie, Charles, 1994. 'A Concept for Post-Cold War Peacekeeping', *Survival*, vol. 36, no. 3, Autumn, pp. 121–148.

Donnelly, Christopher, 1989. 'Development of Military Policy under Gorbachev', pp. 121–148 in Christopher Donnelly, ed., *Gorbachev's Revolution.* London: Jane's Information Group.

Donnelly, Christopher, 1992. 'Evolutionary Problems in the Former Soviet Armed Forces', *Survival*, vol. 34, no. 3, Autumn, pp. 28–42.

Donnelly, Christopher, 1995. 'Armies and Society in the New Democracies', *Jane's Intelligence Review*, vol. 7, no. 1, January, pp. 3–5.

Downing, John, 1995. 'The Status of the Russian Navy', *Jane's Intelligence Review*, vol. 7, no. 6, June, pp. 243–245.

'Draft Military Doctrine of the Russian Federation', 1992. *Voennaya Misl*, Special Issue, May (in Russian).

'Draft Soviet Military Doctrine', 1991. *Voennaya Misl*, Special Issue, December (in Russian).

Dudaev, Dzhokhar, 1994. 'This Is Intervention, Pure and Simple', Interview with *Moscow News*, no. 48, 2–8 December.

Dunay, Pál, 1991. *The CFE Treaty: History, Achievements and Shortcomings*. PRIF Report No. 24. Frankfurt am Main: Peace Research Institute Frankfurt.

Eggert, Konstantin, 1995. 'The Idea of Federalism Finds Scant Support in Georgia and Abkhazia', *Izvestia*, 31 August (in Russian).

Eggert, Konstantin & Maxim Yusin, 1995. 'Boris Yeltsin Has Corrected His Balkan Initiative', *Izvestia*, 11 August (in Russian).

Erlanger, Steven, 1993. 'In the "Near Abroad", Unfamiliar Roles for the Russian Army', *International Herald Tribune*, 30 November.

Ermolin, Vladimir, 1993. 'The Government Raises Alarm: There Is No One to Draft into the Army', *Krasnaya Zvezda*, 17 September (in Russian).

'Ethnic Cleansings Come to Russia', 1992. *The Economist*, 28 November, p. 38.

Evangelista, Matthew A., 1982/1983. 'Stalin's Postwar Army Reappraised', pp. 283–311 in Sean M. Lynn-Jones, Steven E. Miller & Stephen Van Evera, eds, *Soviet Military Policy*. Cambridge, MA: MIT Press.

Eyal, Jonathan, 1994. 'Letting Russia Draw the Line', *The Independent*, 21 February.

Fadin, Andrey, 1995. 'Time of Feudal Lords', *Obshchaya Gazeta*, 11–17 May (in Russian).

Falichev, Oleg, 1993. 'The Draft of Autumn 1993 – One of the Most Difficult in the Whole History of Our Army', *Krasnaya Zvezda*, 20 October (in Russian).

Falkenrath, Richard A., 1995. 'The CFE Flank Dispute: Waiting in the Wings', *International Security*, vol. 19, no. 4, Spring, pp. 118–144.

Feinstein, Lee, 1992. '25 Nations Sign CFE Follow-Up', *Arms Control Today*, July/August, p. 29.

Feinstein, Lee, 1993. 'Russia Asks CFE Partners to Allow Increase in Arms on Southern Border', *Arms Control Today*, November, p. 25.

Felgengauer, Pavel, 1993a. 'The Army Voted No Worse and No Better than the People', *Segodnya*, 15 December (in Russian).

Felgengauer, Pavel, 1993b. 'Mikhail Kolesnikov: Real Reduction of the Army Goes Ahead of Plans', *Segodnya*, 29 December (in Russian).

Felgengauer, Pavel, 1995a. 'Russian-American Relations on the Threshold of New Tests', *Segodnya*, 4 April (in Russian).

Felgengauer, Pavel, 1995b. 'The Taking of Samashki Is MVD Troops' First Independent Operation', *Segodnya*, 12 April (in Russian).

Fetherston, A.B., 1994. *Towards a Theory of United Nations Peacekeeping*. New York: St Martin's Press.

'Financial Injections into the Defence Sector Are a Myth', 1994. *Krasnaya Zvezda*, 14 October (in Russian).

Fitchett, Joseph, 1993. 'Armed Forces Win a Bigger Say in Russia's Destiny', *International Herald Tribune*, 5 October.

FitzGerald, Mary C., 1992. 'A Russian View of Russian Interests', *Air Force Magazine*, October, pp. 42–44.

Florinsky, Michael T., 1969. *Russia: A Short History*. London: Macmillan.

Forsberg, Tuomas, ed., 1995. *Contested Territory: Border Disputes at the Edge of the Former Soviet Empire*. Brookfield, VT & Aldershot, England: Edward Elgar Publishing.

Foye, Stephen, 1990. 'Gorbachev, the Army, and the Union', *Report on the USSR*, RFE/RL, vol. 2, no. 49.

Foye, Stephen, 1993a. 'Russia's Fragmented Army Drawn into the Political Fray', *RFE/RL Research Report*, vol. 2, no. 15, 9 April, pp. 1–7.

Foye, Stephen, 1993b. 'End of CIS Command Heralds New Russian Defense Policy?', *RFE/RL Research Report*, vol. 2, no. 27, 2 July, pp. 45–49.

Foye, Stephen, 1993c. 'Rebuilding the Russian Armed Forces: Rhetoric and Realities', *RFE/RL Research Report*, vol. 2, no. 30, 23 July, pp. 49–57.

Foye, Stephen, 1993d. 'Russia's Defense Establishment in Disarray', *RFE/RL Research Report*, vol. 2, no. 36, 10 September, pp. 49–54.

Foye, Stephen, 1993e. 'Kokoshin: Army Leadership Behind Yeltsin', *RFE/RL Daily Report*, 29 September [e-mail].

Foye, Stephen, 1993f. 'Confrontation in Moscow: The Army Backs Yeltsin, for Now', *RFE/RL Research Report*, vol. 2, no. 42, 22 October, pp. 10–15.

Foye, Stephen, 1993g. 'Updating Russian Civil–Military Relations', *RFE/RL Research Report*, vol. 2, no. 46, 19 November, pp. 44–50.

Foye, Stephen, 1994a. 'Armed Forces Under 1.5 Million?', *RFE/RL News Brief*, 2 March.

Foye, Stephen, 1994b. 'Manning the Russian Army: An Update', *RFE/RL News Brief*, 9 March.

Foye, Stephen, 1994c. 'Deputy Defense Minister on Peacekeeping Plans', *RFE/RL News Brief*, 23 March.

Foye, Stephen, 1994d. 'Manning the Russian Army: Is Contract Service a Success?', *RFE/RL Research Report*, vol. 3, no. 13, 1 April, pp. 36–45.

Foye, Stephen, 1994e. 'Confusion in Moscow on Military Base Directive', *RFE/RL News Brief*, 8 April.

Foye, Stephen, 1994f. 'Civilian and Military Leaders in Russia's 'New' Political Arena', *RFE/RL Research Report*, vol. 3, no. 15, 15 April, pp. 1–6.

Foye, Stephen, 1994g. 'Russia Reconsiders Joint Military Exercises with US', *RFE/RL News Brief*, 27 April.

Foye, Stephen, 1994h. 'Grachev Threatens Estonia with Reinforcements', 'Grachev on Joint Exercise with US, NATO Partnership', *RFE/RL News Brief*, 9 May.

Foye, Stephen, 1994i. 'Grachev: Armed Forces To Be Cut', *RFE/RL News Brief*, 14 June.

Foye, Stephen, 1994j. 'Huge Military District in North Caucasus Planned', *RFE/RL News Brief*, 30 June.

Foye, Stephen, 1994k. 'Grachev on Mobile Forces, Defense Budget', *RFE/RL News Brief*, 5 July.

Foye, Stephen, 1994l. 'Jostling for Control of Border Forces', *RFE/RL News Brief*, 14 July.

Freeland, Chrystia, 1995. 'Top Guns Swell the Ranks of Private Forces', *Financial Times*, 17 January.

Freeland, Chrystia & Bruce Clark, 1995. 'Summit Fails to Narrow Gap Over NATO', *Financial Times*, 11 May.

Fuller, Elizabeth, 1993. 'Paramilitary Forces Dominate Fighting in Transcaucasus', *RFE/RL Research Report*, vol. 2, no. 25, 18 June, pp. 74–82.

Fuller, Elizabeth, 1994a. 'The Transcaucasus: War, Turmoil, Economic Collapse', *RFE/RL Research Report*, vol. 3, no. 1, 7 January, pp. 51–58.

Fuller, Elizabeth, 1994b. 'The Karabakh Mediation Process: Grachev Versus the CSCE?', *RFE/RL Research Report*, vol. 3, no. 23, 10 June, pp. 13–17.

Gajdar, Yegor, 1994. 'The New Course', *Izvestia*, 10 February (in Russian).

Gajdar, Yegor, 1995a. 'We Can't Go Away or Hide from the Elections. We Must Win Them', *Izvestia*, 7 April (in Russian).

Gajdar, Yegor, 1995b. 'The Election Test', *Izvestia*, 28 June (in Russian).

Galeotti, Mark, 1993a. 'Baltic Military Structures', *Jane's Intelligence Review*, vol. 5, no. 8, August, pp. 352–354.

Galeotti, Mark, 1993b. 'Another *Shtorm* – Forces of the 1993 Moscow Coup', *Jane's Intelligence Review*, vol. 5, no. 12, December, pp. 539–540.

Galeotti, Mark, 1994a. 'Russia's Internal Security Forces – Does More Mean Better?', *Jane's Intelligence Review*, vol. 6, no. 6, June, pp. 271–272.

Galeotti, Mark, 1994b. 'Decline and Fall – the Russian Defence Budget', *Jane's Intelligence Review*, vol. 6, no. 9, September, p. 386.

Galeotti, Mark, 1994c. 'Decline and Fall – Who Needs Another Coup?', *Jane's Intelligence Review*, vol. 6, no. 11, November, p. 482.

Galeotti, Mark, 1994d. 'Russia and Eurasia – Out-of-Area Operations and Peacekeeping', pp. 30–35 in *The World in Conflict 1994/95*, Jane's Intelligence Review Yearbook.

Galeotti, Mark, 1995. 'Decline and Fall – Moscow's Chechen War', *Jane's Intelligence Review*, vol. 7, no. 2, February, pp. 50–52.

Gareev, M.A., 1992. 'On Military Doctrine and Military Reform in Russia', *The Journal of Soviet Military Studies*, vol. 5, no. 4, December, pp. 539–551.

Garthoff, Raymond L., 1983. 'The Soviet SS-20 Decision', *Survival*, vol. 25, no. 3, May-June, pp. 110–119.

Garthoff, Raymond L., 1994. *The Great Transition: American–Soviet Relations and the End of the Cold War*. Washington, DC: The Brookings Institution.

Gevorkyan, Natalya & Alexander Zhilin, 1993. 'A President's Trap? A Trap for the President?', *Moscow News*, no. 42, 15 October.

Glantz, Mary E., 1994. 'The Origins and Development of Soviet and Russian Military Doctrine', *The Journal of Slavic Military Studies*, vol. 7, no. 3, September, pp. 443–480.

Glenny, Misha, 1994. 'Hope for Bosnia', *The New York Review of Books*, 7 April, p. 7.

Goble, Paul A., 1993. 'Russia and Its Neighbors', *Foreign Policy*, no. 90, Spring, pp. 79–88.

Goble, Paul A., 1995a. 'Moscow's New Policies Built on Sand', *Broadcast: The Prism*, 14 July [e-mail].

Goble, Paul A., 1995b. 'Between Poverty and Power. The Current State of the Russian Army', *Broadcast: The Prism*, 25 August [e-mail].

Golovnev, Anatoly, 1995. 'Fighting in Chechnya: Lessons and Conclusions', Interview with *Krasnaya Zvezda*, 16 February (in Russian).

Goncharov, Aleksei, 1995. 'Zigzag as the General Line', *Moskovskie Novosti*, no. 54, 13–20 August (in Russian).

Gorbachev, Mikhail, 1991. *The August Coup: The Truth and the Lessons.* London: Harper Collins.

Gorbachev, Mikhail, 1994. 'NATO's Ultimatum Was the Worst Possible Solution for the Bosnian Crisis', *Nezavisimaya Gazeta*, 22 February (in Russian).

Gordon, Michael R., 1993. 'Russian Military Turns to Regional Peacekeeping', *International Herald Tribune*, 30 November.

Gorodetskaya, Natalia, 1994. 'South Ossetia Dreams about Joining Russia', *Segodnya*, 20 October (in Russian).

Gostev, Sergei, 1995. 'General Lebed as a Mirror of Russian Evolution', *Izvestia*, 8 August (in Russian).

Gow, James, 1995. 'Strategic Peacekeeping: Unprofor and International Diplomatic Assertion', pp. 75–94 in Espen Barth Eide, ed., *Peacekeeping in Europe*. Peacekeeping and Multinational Operations no. 5. Oslo: Norsk Utenrikspolitisk Institutt.

Grachev, Pavel. 1993. 'Russian Army: A New Time', Interview with *Nezavisimaya Gazeta*, 8 June (in Russian).

Grachev, Pavel. 1994a. 'Guidelines of Military Doctrine of Russian Federation'. Remarks by Minister of Defence of the Russian Federation, General of the Army Pavel Grachev, addressed to Defence Ministers of NATO Member-Countries. *Military News Bulletin*, June, pp. 1–12.

Grachev, Pavel, 1994b. 'Military Doctrine and Russia's Security', *Nezavisimaya Gazeta*, 9 June (in Russian).

Grachev, Pavel, 1995. 'We Must Proceed from the Fact that This Was a Special Operation', Speech delivered at the Assembly of Military Leadership on 28 February, *Krasnaya Zvezda*, 2 March (in Russian).

'Grachev Saved by Good Connections', 1995. *Moscow News*, no. 26, 7–13 July.

Grau, Lester W., 1994. 'The Bear Went Over the Mountain: Soviet Tactics and Tactical Lessons During the War in Afghanistan', *The Journal of Slavic Military Studies*, vol. 7, no. 3, September, pp. 587–665.

Grau, Lester W., 1995. 'Russian Urban Tactics: Lessons from the Battle for Grozny', *Strategic Forum*, no. 38, July. Institute for National Strategic Studies, National Defense University.

Greene, James M., 1993. 'The Peacekeeping Doctrines of the CIS', *Jane's Intelligence Review*, vol. 5, no. 4, April, pp. 156–159.

Grigoryev, Sergei, 1993. 'What Can Ukraine Do with the USSR's Nuclear Heritage?', *Nezavisimaya Gazeta*, 3 June (in Russian).

Gromov, Boris, 1993a. 'Nowhere Do Russian Forces Wage Combat Operations', Interview with *Moscow News*, no. 30, 23 July.

Gromov, Boris, 1993b. 'Peace-keeping Is a Concern Not Only for the Military', Interview with *Krasnaya Zvezda*, 27 November (in Russian).

Gromov, Boris V. 1994. *Ogranichenny Kontingent* (The Limited Contingent). Moscow: Voenizdat.

Gromov, Boris, 1995a. 'Chechnya Plans Kept from Deputy Defense Minister', Interview with *Moscow News*, no. 2, 13–19 January.

Gromov, Boris, 1995b. 'Reform Is Harmful for the Army', interview with *Izvestia*, 10 December (in Russian).

Gukasov, Grant, 1995. 'Estonia Allays the Law on Foreigners', *Moscow News*, no. 27, 14–20 July.

Gustafson, Thane, 1990. 'Conclusions: Toward a Crisis in Civil–Military Relations?' in Timothy Colton & Thane Gustafson, eds, *Soldiers and the Soviet State*. Princeton, NJ: Princeton University Press.

Hall, Robert, 1993. 'Russia's Mobile Forces – Rationale and Structure', *Jane's Intelligence Review*, vol. 5, no. 4, April, pp. 154–155.

Hanson, Philip, 1993. 'Estonia's Narva Problem, Narva's Estonian Problem', *RFE/RL Research Report*, vol. 2, no. 18, 30 April, pp. 17–23.

Harmonizing the Evolution of US and Russian Defense Policies. 1993. Center for Strategic and International Studies, Washington, DC and Council on Foreign and Defense Policy, Moscow.

Heuser, Beatrice, 1993. 'Warsaw Pact Military Doctrine in the 1970s and 1980s: Findings in the East German Archives', *Comparative Strategy*, vol. 12, no. 4, October–December, pp. 437–457.

van Heuven, Marten, 1994. 'Rehabilitating Serbia', *Foreign Policy*, no. 96, Fall, pp. 38–48.

Higgins, Andrew, 1993. 'Army Tells Yeltsin to End Power Struggle', *The Independent*, 4 March.

Hoagland, Jim, 1992. 'With the Baltics, Yeltsin Heads Down that Same Unfortunate Path', *International Herald Tribune*, 5 November.

Holloway, David, 1989/1990. 'State, Society, and the Military under Gorbachev', *International Security*, vol. 14, no. 3, Winter, pp. 5–24.

Holoboff, Elaine, 1995. 'Oil and the Burning of Grozny', *Jane's Intelligence Review*, vol. 7, no. 6, June, pp. 253–257.

Huntington, Samuel P., 1957. *The Soldier and the State: The Theory and Politics of Civil–Military Relations.* Cambridge, MA: Harvard University Press.

Hurd, Douglas & Andrei Kozyrev, 1993. 'Challenge of Peacekeeping', *Financial Times*, 14 December.

Iivonen, Jyrki. 1995. 'Expansionism and the Russian Imperial Tradition', pp. 62–85 in Tuomas Forsberg, ed., *Contested Territory*.

'Imperfect Peace', 1992. *The Economist*, 14 November, pp. 39–40.

Jonson, Lena & Clive Archer, eds, 1995. *Peacekeeping and the Role of Russia in Eurasia.* Boulder, CO: Westview Press.

Kalashnikov, Victor, 1993. 'Who Can Build the New Model of Russia's Foreign Policy', *Nezavisimaya Gazeta*, 25 November (in Russian).

Kandel, Pavel, 1993. 'Derzhavnost Is Harmless for the Interests of Derzhava', *Moskovskie Novosti*, no. 35, 29 August (in Russian).

Karaganov, Sergei, 1992a. 'Russia and Nuclear Weapons', *Nezavisimaya Gazeta*, 9 June (in Russian).

Karaganov, Sergei, 1992b. 'Presentiment of Imperialism', *Moscow News*, no. 44, 6 November.

Karaganov, Sergei, 1993. 'NATO's Expansion Leads to Russia's Isolation', *Moscow News*, no. 38, 17 September.

Karaganov, Sergei, 1994a. 'We Should Arrive First at NATO's Doors', *Izvestia*, 24 February (in Russian).

Karaganov, Sergei, 1994b. 'Russia's Elites', pp. 41–54 in Blackwill & Karaganov, eds, *Damage Limitation or Crisis?*

Karaganov, Sergei, 1994c. *Where Is Russia Going? Foreign and Defence Policies in a New Era.* PRIF Reports No. 34. Frankfurt am Main: Peace Research Institute Frankfurt.

Karaganov, Sergei, 1994d. 'European Security System Is Undergoing the Deepest Crisis', *Segodnya*, 26 August (in Russian).

Karaganov, Sergei, 1995. 'Remember "Neo-Gaullism"', *Moskovskie Novosti*, no. 47, 9–16 July (in Russian).

Karpov, Mikhail, 1993. 'Russia's Military Doctrine', Interview with First Deputy Defence Minister Andrei Kokoshin. *Nezavisimaya Gazeta*, 3 June (in Russian).

Kaufman, Stuart J., 1994. 'Organizational Politics and Change in Soviet Military Policy', *World Politics*, vol. 46, no. 3, April, pp. 355–382.

Keegan, John, 1992. 'Peace by Other Means?', *The Times Literary Supplement*, 11 December.

Keeny, Spurgeon M., 1994. 'The Theater Missile Defense Threat to US Security', *Arms Control Today*, vol. 24, no. 7, September, pp. 3–7.

Kennan, George F., 1992. 'Building Stability in Russia and the Baltics', *International Herald Tribune*, 10 November.

Kennedy, Paul, 1989. *The Rise and Fall of the Great Powers.* New York: Vintage Books.

Kincade, William, 1993. 'Nuclear Weapons in Ukraine: Hollow Threat, Wasted Asset', *Arms Control Today*, vol. 23, no. 6, July/August, pp. 13–18.

Kirch, Aksel & Marika Kirch, 1995. 'Search for Security in Estonia: New Identity Architecture', *Security Dialogue*, vol. 26, no. 4, December, pp. 439–448.

Kirchner, Walter, 1950. *A History of Russia.* New York: Barnes & Noble.

Kjølberg, Anders, 1994. 'The Barents Region as a European Security-Building Concept' pp. 187–199 in Stokke & Tunander, eds, *The Barents Region.*

Klepikova, Elena & Vladimir Solovyov, 1995. *Zhirinovsky: The Paradoxes of Russian Fascism.* London: Viking.

Kobets, Konstantin, 1992. 'Priorities of Russia's Military Policy', *Nezavisimaya Gazeta*, 5 February (in Russian).

Kokoshin, Andrei, 1988. 'A. Svechin About War and Politics', *Mezhdunarodnaya Zhizn*, no. 10, October, pp. 133–142 (in Russian).

Kokoshin, Andrei, 1993. 'Russia's Military Doctrine', Interview with *Nezavisimaya Gazeta*, 3 June (in Russian).

Kokoshin, Andrei, 1994. 'Defense Industry Conversion in the Russian Federation', pp. 43–74 in Teresa P. Johnson & Steven E. Miller, eds, *Russian Security After the Cold War.* Washington, DC: Brassey's (US).

Kokoshin, Andrei, 1995. 'We Must Return to Basic Ideas of the Formation of the Russian State', Interview with *Moscow News*, no. 9, March 3–9.

Kolesnikov, Andrei, 1994. 'Tankodrom', *Moskovskie Novosti*, no. 38, 11–18 September (in Russian).

Kolesnikov, Mikhail, 1994. 'Problems of Flanks and Future of the Treaty on Conventional Armed Forces', *Krasnaya Zvezda*, 19 April (in Russian).

Kolkowicz, Roman, 1967. *The Soviet Military and the Communist Party.* Princeton, NJ: Princeton University Press.

Kolkowicz, Roman, 1984. 'The Political Role of the Soviet Military' pp. 74–83 in Joseph L. Nogee, ed., *Soviet Politics: Russia after Brezhnev.* New York: Praeger.

Kolpakov, Alexandr, 1995. 'Generals Request Fire', *Moskovsky Komsomolets*, 10 December (in Russian).

Kolstoe, Paul, 1995. *Russians in the Former Soviet Republics.* London: Hurst & Co.

Kondrashev, Stanislav, 1996. 'Loyal Andrei Goes: Why and What Next?', *Izvestia*, 10 January (in Russian).

Kondratyev, Georgi, 1993. 'Russia's Blue Helmets', *Krasnaya Zvezda*, 16 February (in Russian).

Konovalov, Alexandr, 1994. 'Towards a New Division of Europe? Russia and the North Atlantic Alliance', *Nezavisimaya Gazeta*, 7 December (in Russian).

Korotchenko, Igor, 1994. 'Boris Yeltsin Was Rather Critical About the Situation in the Army', *Nezavisimaya Gazeta*, 15 November (in Russian).

Koulik, Sergei & Richard Kokoski, 1994. *Conventional Arms Control: Perspectives on Verification.* Oxford: Oxford University Press.

Kovalev, Sergei, 1995a. 'The Militarization of Russia', *War Report*, no. 34, June, pp. 20–23.

Kovalev, Sergei, 1995b. 'How the West Should Not React to Events in Russia', *Transition*, vol. 1, no. 9, 9 June, pp. 42–43.

Kozyrev, Andrei, 1992a. 'The Party of War Is Attacking in Moldova, Georgia and Russia', *Izvestia*, 30 June (in Russian).

Kozyrev, Andrei, 1992b. 'Transfiguration or Kafkaesque Metamorphosis', *Nezavisimaya Gazeta*, 20 August (in Russian).

Kozyrev, Andrei, 1993a. 'Partnership in Creating Peace', *Segodnya*, 6 July (in Russian).

Kozyrev, Andrei, 1993b. 'Heed a Russian "Cry of Despair" in Estonia', *International Herald Tribune*, 14–15 August.

Kozyrev, Andrei, 1993c. 'UN: Concerns and Hopes of the World', *Rossiiskaya Gazeta*, 30 October (in Russian).

Kozyrev, Andrei, 1994a. 'Russia and NATO: A Partnership for a United and Peaceful Europe', *NATO Review*, no. 4, August, pp. 3–6.

Kozyrev, Andrei, 1994b. 'Peace with a Sword', *Moscow News*, no. 36, 9–15 September.

Kreikemeyer, Anna & Andrei Zagorski, 1995. 'The Commonwealth of Independent States (CIS)', pp. 157–172 in Jonson & Archer, eds, *Peacekeeping and the Role of Russia in Eurasia.*

Krotov, Yakov, 1993. 'Great Russia Means Great Upheavals', *Moskovskie Novosti*, no. 52, 31 December (in Russian).

Kryuchek, Oleg, 1994. 'Gen. Grachev: Army Will Not Take Orders from Civilians', *Segodnya*, 26 October (in Russian).

Kupchan, Charles, 1994. *The Vulnerability of Empire*. Ithaca, NY: Cornell University Press.

Kuvaldin, Viktor, 1992. 'Caucasian Options for Russia and Georgia', *Moscow News*, no. 43, 25 October – 1 November.

Kvashnin, Anatoly, 1995. 'Troops Acquired Combat Maturity in Grave Ordeals', Speech delivered at the Assembly of Military Leadership on 28 February, *Krasnaya Zvezda*, 2 March (in Russian).

Lachowski, Zdzislaw, 1994. 'Conventional Arms Control and Security Co-operation in Europe', pp. 565–600 in *SIPRI Yearbook 1994*.

Lambeth, Benjamin S., 1995. 'Russia's Wounded Military', *Foreign Affairs*, vol. 74, no 2, March/April, pp. 86–98.

Latsis, Otto, 1993a. The Dragon Has Many Heads: On the Nature of the Conspiracy Tormenting Russia', *Izvestia*, 13 October (in Russian).

Latsis, Otto, 1993b. 'What Has Happened and What Will Happen with Us', *Izvestia*, 25 December (in Russian).

Latsis, Otto, 1995. 'Duma Has Abandoned Military Reform', *Izvestia*, 11 April (in Russian).

Lavrov, Sergei, 1994. 'Russia Reserved about New Peacekeeping Operations', Interview with *Moscow News*, no. 34, 26 August – 1 September.

Lebed, Alexandr, 1994a. 'Russia Has the Army, But Is It Indeed Army?', *Nezavisimaya Gazeta*, 16 November (in Russian).

Lebed, Alexandr, 1994b. 'I Will Remain a General', interview with *Novaya Ezhednevnaya Gazeta*, 22 November (in Russian).

Lebed, Alexandr, 1995a. 'Regiments of Boy-Soldiers Suffer a Defeat', *Moscow News*, no. 1, 6–12 January.

Lebed, Alexandr, 1995b. 'General Lebed Has Passed the Test', Interview with *Moscow News*, no. 5, 3–9 February.

Lebow, Richard Ned, 1985. 'The Soviet Offensive in Europe: The Schlieffen Plan Revisited?', pp. 312–346 in Sean M. Lynn-Jones, Steven E. Miller & Stephen Van Evera, eds, *Soviet Military Policy*. Cambridge, MA: MIT Press.

Lenin, V.I., 1974 [1915]. 'Socialism and War', pp. 295–338 in *Collected Works*, vol. 21. Moscow: Progress Publishers.

Lenin, V.I., 1974 [1918]. 'Left-Wing Childishness and the Petty-Bourgeois Mentality', pp. 323–354 in *Collected Works*, vol. 27. Moscow: Progress Publishers.

Lenin, V.I., 1974 [1919]. 'All Out for the Fight against Denikin', pp. 436–455 in *Collected Works*, vol. 29. Moscow: Progress Publishers.

Lepingwell, John W.R., 1992. 'Soviet Civil–Military Relations and the August Coup', *World Politics*, no. 44, July, pp. 539–572.

Lepingwell, John, 1993a. 'Grachev on Reorganization of Far East Forces', *RFE/RL News Brief*, no. 18, 22 April.

Lepingwell, John W.R., 1993b. 'Is the Military Disintegrating from Within?', *RFE/RL Research Report*, no. 25, 18 June, pp. 9–16.

Lepingwell, John W.R., 1993c. 'Restructuring the Russian Military', *RFE/RL Research Report*, vol. 2, no. 25, 18 June, pp. 17–24.

Lepingwell, John W.R., 1994a. 'The Trilateral Agreement on Nuclear Weapons', *RFE/RL Research Report*, vol. 3, no. 4, 28 January, pp. 12–20.

Lepingwell, John, 1994b. 'Yeltsin on Military Reform', *RFE/RL News Brief*, 13 June.

Lepingwell, John W.R., 1994c. 'The Russian Military and Security Policy in the "Near Abroad"', *Survival*, vol. 36, no. 3, Autumn, pp. 70–92.

Litovkin, Viktor, 1995a. 'Decay. The Crime Trial of Three Officers of the Northern Fleet', *Izvestia*, 12 May (in Russian).

Litovkin, Viktor, 1995b. '*Admiral Kuznetsov* Goes to the Mediterranean', *Izvestia*, 27 December (in Russian).

Litvin, Volodimir, 1994. *Politichna Arena Ukrainy* (Ukraine's Political Arena). Kiev: Abris.

Lobov, Vladimir, 1993. 'Not to Reform but to Build Anew', *Moscow News*, no. 4, 31 January.

Lobov, V.N., 1994. 'Military Reform: The New Army', pp. 75–102 in Teresa P. Johnson & Steven E. Miller, eds, *Russian Security After the Cold War*. Washington, DC: Brassey's (US).

Lobov, Vladimir, 1995. 'How to Reform the Russian Army', *Rossiiskaya Gazeta*, 25 January (in Russian).

Lopatin, Vladimir, 1992. 'Will the Red Army Defend the White House?', *Izvestia*, 13 February (in Russian).

Lopatin, Vladimir, 1993. 'An Army for the State, Not a State for the Army', *Izvestia*, 26 May (in Russian).

Lopatin, Vladimir, 1994. 'A Professional Army Instead of An Armed Nation', *Novaya Ezhednevnaya Gazeta*, 26 May (in Russian).

Lough, John, 1993a. 'The Place of the "Near Abroad" in Russian Foreign Policy', *RFE/RL Research Report*, vol. 2, no. 11, 12 March, pp. 21–29.

Lough, John, 1993b. 'Defining Russia's Relations with Neighboring States', *RFE/RL Research Report*, vol. 2, no. 20, 14 May, pp. 53–60.

Lough, John, 1993c. 'Constraints on Russian Responses to the Yugoslav Crisis', *Jane's Intelligence Review*, vol. 5, no. 8, August, pp. 365–366.

Luboshits, Efim & Vitaly Tsimbal, 1992. 'How to Frame Russia's Military Budget', *Nezavisimaya Gazeta*, 9 July (in Russian).

Lukin, Vladimir, 1992. 'Russia and Its Interests', *Diplomatichesky Vestnik*, no. 21–2, November (in Russian).

Lukin, Vladimir, 1995. 'The Medicine for Geopolitical Psychosis', *Obozrevatel*, no. 6, June, pp. 10–14 (in Russian).

Lundestad, Geir, 1993. 'The Fall of Great Powers, Peace, Stability and Legitimacy', Unpublished paper presented at a seminar at the Nobel Institute, Oslo, 10 June.

Lundestad, Geir, ed., 1994. *The Fall of Great Powers: Peace, Stability and Legitimacy*. Oslo & Oxford: Scandinavian University Press & Oxford University Press.

Lynch, Allen & Reneo Lukic, 1993. 'Russian Foreign Policy and the Wars in the Former Yugoslavia', *RFE/RL Research Report*, vol. 2, no. 41, 15 October, pp. 25–32.

Mackintosh, Malcolm, 1994. 'Reform in the Russian Armed Forces', *Jane's Intelligence Review*, vol. 6, no. 12, December, pp. 534–537.

McCausland, Jeffrey D., 1995. 'The CFE Treaty – a Cold War Anachronism?', Paper presented at an International Institute for Strategic Studies seminar, London, 24 March.

Menon, Rajan, 1995. 'In the Shadow of the Bear: Security in the Post-Soviet Central Asia', *International Security*, vol. 20, no. 1, Summer, pp. 149–181.

Meri, Lennart, 1994. 'Estonia, NATO and Peacekeeping', *NATO Review*, no. 4, April, pp. 7–9.

Meyer, Stephen M., 1991/1992. 'How the Threat (and the Coup) Collapsed', *International Security*, vol. 16, no. 3, Winter, pp. 5–38.

Miasnikov, Vladimir S., 1994. 'Russia and China', pp. 227–240 in Blackwill & Karaganov, eds, *Damage Limitation or Crisis?*

Migranyan, Andranik, 1994a. 'Russia and the Near Abroad', *Nezavisimaya Gazeta*, 12 January (in Russian).

Migranyan, Andranik, 1994b. 'Russia's Foreign Policy: Disastrous Results of Three Years. Time to Pause and Change Both Policy and Minister', *Nezavisimaya Gazeta*, 10 December (in Russian).

Mihalka, Michael, 1994a. 'Squaring the Circle: NATO's Offer to the East', *RFE/RL Research Report*, vol. 3, no. 12, 25 March, pp. 1–9.

Mihalka, Michael, 1994b. 'European-Russian Security and NATO's Partnership for Peace', *RFE/RL Research Report*, vol. 3, no. 33, 26 August, pp. 34–45.

Mikadze, Akaki, 1993. 'Big Changes on the Western Front', *Moskovskie Novosti*, no. 44, 31 October (in Russian).

Mikadze, Akaki, 1994. 'Georgia–Abkhazia: Between Unitarism and Independence', *Moskovskie Novosti*, no. 40, 18–25 September (in Russian).

The Military Balance (annually). International Institute for Strategic Studies. London: IISS/Brassey's (UK), from 1995/96 Oxford University Press.

The Military Balance in Northern Europe, 1993–1994; 1994–1995. Oslo: The Norwegian Atlantic Committee.

'The Military Mess in Russia', 1994, *The Economist*, 17 December, p. 28.

Miliukov, Paul, 1967. *Political Memoirs 1905–1917*, edited by Arthur P. Mendel. Ann Arbor, MI: University of Michigan Press.

Miliukov, Paul, 1968. 'Peter the Great: The Reign Continued', pp. 280–334 in Paul Miliukov, Charles Seignobos & L. Eisenmann, eds, *History of Russia*, vol. 1. New York: Funk & Wagnalls.

Milstein, Ilya, 1994. 'How We Feel about October, 1993', *Moscow News*, no. 40, 7–13 October.

Minasyan, Liana & Igor Rotar, 1994. 'We Do Not Want to Scare the World', Interview with General Ivashov and General Pyankov, *Nezavisimaya Gazeta*, 3 June (in Russian).

Mironov, Valeri, 1995. 'Dictatorship of Common Sense Is Needed', interview with *Moskovskie Novosti*, no. 13, 13–26 February (in Russian).

Mlechin, Leonid, 1995. 'The Balts Continue to Fight the Non-Existing Enemies', *Izvestia*, 9 August (in Russian).

Moskva. Osen-93: Khronika Protivostoyania, 1994. (Moscow. Autumn-93: The Chronicle of Confrontation). Moscow: Respublika.

Myakotin, V. 1968. 'The Union of Little Russia with the Muscovite State', pp. 159–173 in Paul Miliukov, Charles Seignobos & L. Eisenmann, eds, *History of Russia*, vol. 1. New York: Funk & Wagnalls.

Nagorski, Andrew, 1992. 'A Tug of War in the Baltics', *Newsweek*, 9 November, p. 14.

Naumkin, Vitaly V., 1994. 'Russia and the States of Central Asia and the Transcaucasus', pp. 199–216 in Blackwill & Karaganov, eds, *Damage Limitation or Crisis?*

Nazarbaev, Nursultan, 1995a. 'The Difficult Topic of the Chechen Crisis', *Moskovskie Novosti*, no. 3, 15–22 January (in Russian).

Nazarbaev, Nursultan, 1995b. 'Politicians Lag Behind Their People', *Moscow News*, no. 7, February 17–23.

Nedimoglu, Necil, 1994. 'NATO and Partner Countries Cooperate in Implementing the CFE Treaty', *NATO Review*, vol. 42, no. 3, June, pp. 18–20.

Nelan, Bruce W., 1995. 'Why It All Went So Very Wrong', *Time*, 16 January, pp. 21–22.

Nesvizhsky, Vadim, 1995. 'The Constitutions Block the Solution of the Border Problem between Russia and Estonia', *Segodnya*, 1 September (in Russian).

Neumann, Iver B., 1993a. 'The Russian Debate about Europe, 1800–1991', Thesis submitted for the degree of D.Phil. in Politics at Oxford University.

Neumann, Iver B., 1993b. *The Caucasus between Russia, Turkey and Iran*. NUPI Working Paper no. 495, June. Oslo: Norwegian Institute of International Affairs.

Neumann, Iver B. 1994. *Tadzhikistan and the Near Abroad*. Security Policy Library no. 11. Oslo: Norwegian North Atlantic Committee (in Norwegian).

Neumann, Iver B. & Sergei Solodovnik, 1995. 'The Case of Tajikistan', pp. 83–102 in Jonson & Archer, eds, *Peacekeeping and the Role of Russia in Eurasia*.

de Nevers, Renée, 1994. *Russia's Strategic Renovation*. Adelphi Paper 289. London: IISS/Brassey's (UK).

Nguyen, Hung P., 1993. 'A Russian Bonaparte?', *US Naval Institute Proceedings*, vol. 119, no. 2, February, pp. 68–72.

Nikitinsky, Leonid, 1995. 'Lessons of the "Chechen Case"', *Moscow News*, no. 30, 4–10 August.

Nikonov, Viacheslav, 1994. *The Democratic Transformation of Russia: Challenges from Without*. Special Report. Political Committee, North Atlantic Assembly, Brussels.

Nilsen, Thomas & Nils Bøhmer, 1994. *Sources to Radioactive Contamination in Murmansk and Arkhangelsk Counties*. Bellona Report vol. 1. Oslo: The Bellona Foundation.

Nitze, Paul H., 1994. 'Replace Nuclear Umbrella', *International Herald Tribune*, 19 January.

Nodia, Ghia, 1995. 'Waiting for the Russian Bear', *War Report*, no. 34, June, pp. 39–40.

Odom, William, 1993. 'Yeltsin's Faustian Bargain', *Moscow Times*, 27 October.

'On the Effectiveness of State Power in Russia', 1995. President Yeltsin's Annual Message to the Federal Assembly. *Rossiiskaya Gazeta*, 17 February (in Russian).

'On the Implementation of the Treaty on Conventional Armed Forces in Europe', 1993. *Military News Bulletin*, November.

'On the Military Doctrine of the Warsaw Pact Member States', 1987. *Pravda*, 30 May (in Russian).

Orlov, Vladimir, 1993a. 'Head of Security Council Forced to Resign', *Moscow News*, no. 20, 14 May.

Orlov, Vladimir, 1993b. 'Nuclear Ukraine: Big Bluff or Big Threat?', *Moscow News*, no. 45, 7 November.

Orr, Michael, 1994a. 'Peacekeeping – a New Task for Russian Military Doctrine', *Jane's Intelligence Review*, vol. 6, no. 8, July, pp. 307–309.

Orr, Michael, 1994b. 'Peacekeeping and Overstretch in the Russian Army', *Jane's Intelligence Review*, vol. 6, no. 9, August, pp. 363–364.

Ovsienko, Sergei, 1993. 'Rapid Reaction Forces', *Rossiiskie Vesti*, 5 March (in Russian).

Pain, Emil, 1994. 'Russia and Post-Soviet Space', *Moscow News*, no. 8, 25 February – 3 March.

Parish, Scott, 1995. 'Russian Peacekeepers Ready for Bosnia', *OMRI Daily Digest*, 21 December (e-mail).

Parkhomenko, Alexandr, 1992a. 'A Certain Skokov', *Nezavisimaya Gazeta*, 31 July (in Russian).

Parkhomenko, Alexandr, 1992b. 'Security at the Highest Level', *Nezavisimaya Gazeta*, 4 August (in Russian).

Parkhomenko, Sergei, 1994. 'Pavel Grachev Charges Duma for the Dislocation of the Army', *Segodnya*, 19 November (in Russian).

Parkhomenko, Sergei, 1995. 'Merlin's Tower', *Moscow News*, no. 16, 28 April – 4 May.

Petersen, Phillip A. & Shane C. Petersen, 1993. 'The Kaliningrad Garrison State', *Jane's Intelligence Review*, vol. 5, no. 2, February, pp. 59–62.

Pfaff, William, 1994. 'On Bosnia, It Matters That Russia and the West Stick Together', *International Herald Tribune*, 5 August.

Pipes, Richard, 1994. *Communism: The Vanished Specter.* Norwegian Nobel Institute Lecture Series. Oxford: Oxford University Press.

Pirumov, V.S., 1994. 'Methodical Aspects in the Research of Russia's National Security Problems under Contemporary Conditions', *The Journal of Slavic Military Studies*, vol. 7, no. 3, September, pp. 367–382.

Platonov, Sergei F., 1928. *History of Russia.* New York: Macmillan.

Podkolzin, Evgeni, 1995. 'The Paratroopers Are Tired of Losses', Interview with *Moskovskie Novosti*, no. 51, 30 July – 5 August (in Russian).

Pogorely, Mikhail, 1995. 'More Contacts, Fewer Suspicions', *Krasnaya Zvezda*, 4 April (in Russian).

Portnikov, Vitaly, 1991. 'The End of Geopolitical Baltia', *Nezavisimaya Gazeta*, 13 November (in Russian).

'Post-Soviet Armies', 1993. *RFE/RL Research Report*, Special Issue, vol. 2, no. 25, 18 June.

Pozdnyakov, Elgiz, 1993. 'Russia Is a Great Power', *Mezhdunarodnaya Zhizn*, January (in Russian).

Prihodko, Natalia, 1994. 'Alexander Lebed – For Freezing of the Situation', *Nezavisimaya Gazeta*, 29 November (in Russian).

'Progress Report to Ministers by the NACC Ad Hoc Group on Cooperation in Peacekeeping', 1993. *NATO Review*, vol. 41, no. 6, December, pp. 27–30.

Pushkov, Alexei, 1994a. 'Kozyrev Started a Game on Alien Field', *Moskovskie Novosti*, no. 4, 23–30 January (in Russian).

Pushkov, Alexei, 1994b. 'Tame Foreign Minister Seeks New Image', *Moscow News*, no. 50, 16–22 December.

Pushkov, Alexei, 1995. 'Kozyrev Loses Credibility Both at Home and Abroad', *Moscow News*, no. 17, 5–11 May.

Putko, Alexander, 1992. 'The Military Are Also Concerned about the Mood in the Army', *Nezavisimaya Gazeta*, 5 February (in Russian).

Putnam, Tonya L., 1994. 'The States of Central Asia and the Transcaucasus and Russia', pp. 217–226 in Blackwill & Karaganov, eds, *Damage Limitation or Crisis?*

Raevsky A. & I.N. Vorob'ev, 1994. *Russian Approaches to Peacekeeping Operations.* UNIDIR Research Paper no. 28. Geneva: UNIDIR.

Rahr, Alexander, 1994. 'Russia's Five Armies', *RFE/RL News Brief*, no. 22, 25 May.

Reznik, Boris, 1994. 'Explosion after Explosion', *Izvestia*, 27 May (in Russian).

Roberts, Adam, 1994. *The Crisis in Peacekeeping.* Forsvarsstudier no. 2. Oslo: Norwegian Institute for Defence Studies [IFS].

Rogov, Sergei, 1993a. 'Russian Defense Policy: Challenges and Developments'. Occasional Paper of the Institute of USA and Canada Studies, Moscow, and Center for Naval Analysis, Alexandria, VA, USA, February.

Rogov, Sergei, 1993b. 'Will Ukraine Cross the Nuclear Rubicon?', *Moscow News*, no. 29, 16 July.

Rogov, Sergei, 1994a. 'Will Russia's Armed Forces Continue?', *Nezavisimaya Gazeta*, 3 November (in Russian).

Rogov, Sergei, 1994b. 'The Results Are Pitiful, but There Is a Way Out: Three Years of Trial and Error in Russian Foreign Policy', *Nezavisimaya Gazeta*, 31 December (in Russian).

Rosecrance, Richard, 1995. 'Overextension, Vulnerability, and Conflict: The "Goldilocks Problem" in International Strategy', *International Security*, vol. 19, no. 4, Spring, pp. 145–163.

Rosen, Stephen P., 1991. *Winning the Next War*. Ithaca, NY: Cornell University Press.

Rotar, Igor, 1995a. 'Resort Hears the Echo of the Yesterday's War', *Izvestia*, 19 August (in Russian).

Rotar, Igor, 1995b. 'Not Wanted', *Izvestia*, 25 August (in Russian).

Royen, Christoph, 1995. 'The Concept of "Near Abroad" in Russian Foreign Policy', pp. 39–44 in *The Concept of 'Near Abroad' in Russia's Foreign Policy*. Papers of the German-Russian Forum, 23–24 May, Bonn (in Russian).

'Russian General Varennikov Frustrated the Traitors of the Motherland', 1994. *Zavtra*, no. 32, August (in Russian).

'Russians in the Near Abroad', 1993. Report of the Gorbachev Foundation, *Nezavisimaya Gazeta*, 7 September (in Russian).

Rutskoi, Alexandr, 1992. 'We Must Build an Army Worthy of Great Russia', *Krasnaya Zvezda*, 14 May (in Russian).

Rutskoi, Alexandr, 1993. 'Russia's Military Policy – Content and Direction', *Voennaya Misl*, no. 1, January (in Russian).

Sabov, Dmitri, 1995. 'Whose Napkins Are a Threat to Peace?' *Moskovskie Novosti*, no. 54, 13–20 August (in Russian).

Safire, William, 1992. 'Russian Reform: Thanks, Kozyrev, for That Slap', *International Herald Tribune*, 18 December.

Sakwa, Richard, 1993. *Russian Politics and Society*. London & New York: Routledge.

Samsonov, Viktor, 1994. 'On the CIS Collective Security System', *Nezavisimaya Gazeta*, 26 November (in Russian).

Samsonov, Viktor, 1995. 'The Security Treaty Is the Shield of the CIS Not Its Sword', Interview with *Rossiiskie Vesti*, 8 February (in Russian).

Savelyev, Alexandr, 1994. 'Joint Defence Against Ballistic Missiles', *Nezavisimaya Gazeta*, 11 March (in Russian).

Scott, Harriet F. & William F. Scott, 1981. *The Armed Forces of the USSR*. Boulder, CO: Westview.

Semena, Nikolai, 1995. 'New Brothers in Arms?', *Izvestia*, 29 July (in Russian).

Sergounin, Alexander A., 1993. *Russian Foreign Policy Thinking: Redefining Conceptions*. Working Papers no. 11. Copenhagen: Centre for Peace and Conflict Research.

Sharp, Jane M.O., 1993. 'Conventional Arms Control in Europe', pp. 591–617 in *SIPRI Yearbook 1993*.

Sharp, Jane M.O., 1994. 'Should the CFE Treaty Be Revised?', *Bulletin of Arms Control*, no. 15, August.

Sharp, Jane M.O. & Vladimir Baranovsky, 1993. 'For a NATO–Russian UN Intervention to End the War in Bosnia', *International Herald Tribune*, 26 February.

Shashenkov, Maxim, 1994. 'Russian Peacekeeping in the "Near Abroad"', *Survival*, vol. 36, no. 3, Autumn, pp. 46–69.

Shelov-Kovedyaev, Fedor, 1992a. 'In the Criticism of Russia's Foreign Policy We Confront a Dangerous Dilettantism', *Nezavisimaya Gazeta*, 30 July (in Russian).

Shelov-Kovedyaev, Fedor, 1992b. 'Strategy and Tactics of Russian Foreign Policy in the Near Abroad'. Paper circulated at a meeting of the Council on Foreign and Security Policy, Moscow, November (in Russian).

Shermatova, Sanobar, 1995a. 'New Allies in the Old War', *Moskovskie Novosti*, no. 24, 9–16 April (in Russian).

Shermatova, Sanobar, 1995b. 'Double-Edged Neighbourhood', *Moskovskie Novosti*, no. 42, 18–25 June (in Russian).

Sherr, James, 1994. 'Russia's Elections – the Military Implications', *Jane's Intelligence Review*, February, pp. 67–68.

Shevelyov, Mikhail, 1994. 'Moscow Facing Chechnya Challenge', *Moscow News*, no. 48, 2–8 December.

Shevtsova, Lilia, 1993. 'From an August of Hope to an August of Awakening', *Moscow News*, no. 34, 20 August.

Shevtsova, Lilia, 1994a. 'Is Russia Heading Towards Dictatorship?', *Moscow News*, no. 3, 24 January.

Shevtsova, Lilia, 1994b. 'Boris Yeltsin: At a New Threshold', *Moscow News*, no. 33, 19–25 August.

Shevtsova, Lilia, 1994c. 'Russia Facing New Choices: Contradictions of Post-Communist Development', *Security Dialogue*, vol. 25, no. 3, September, pp. 321–334.

Shlykov, Vitaly V., 1995. 'Economic Readjustment within the Russian Defense–Industrial Complex', *Security Dialogue*, vol. 26, no. 1, March, pp. 19–34.

Simonsen, Sven G., 1995a. 'Going His Own Way: A Profile of General Alexander Lebed', *The Journal of Slavic Military Studies*, vol. 8, no. 4, December.

Simonsen, Sven G., 1995b. 'Genosse Konsens: Porträt des russischen Duma Präsidenten Iwan P. Rybkin', *Osteuropa*, vol. 45, no. 12, December, pp. 1144–1154 (in German).

Sinaisky, A.S., 1992. 'Geopolitics and Russia's National Security', *Voennaya Misl*, no. 10, October, pp. 4–19, (in Russian).

SIPRI Yearbook (annually). Stockholm International Peace Research Institute. Oxford: Oxford University Press.

Smith, Dan, 1993. 'Real Intervention, Unreal Debate', *War Report*, February/March, pp. 20–21.

Smith, Dan, 1994. 'Just War, Clausewitz and Sarajevo', *Journal of Peace Research*, vol. 31, no. 2, May, pp. 136–142.

Smithers, Peter, 1995. 'Why the Council of Europe Should Put Conglomerate Russia on Hold', *International Herald Tribune*, 2 February.

Socor, Vladimir, 1992. 'Russia's 14th Army and the Insurgency in Eastern Moldova', *RFE/RL Research Report*, vol. 1, no. 36, 11 September, pp. 41–48.

Socor, Vladimir, 1993. 'Russia's Army in Moldova: There to Stay?', *RFE/RL Research Report*, vol. 2, no. 25, 18 June, pp. 42–49.

Socor, Vladimir, 1994. 'Lebed Affair: Political Aspect', *RFE/RL News Brief*, 9 August.

Sokolov, Mikhail, 1993. 'Even the Minister Is Under Suspicion', *Komsomolskaya Pravda*, 7 October (in Russian).

Sokolovskiy, V.D. 1975. *Soviet Military Strategy*, edited by Harriet Fast Scott. New York: Crane, Russak & Company.

Solzenitsyn, Alexandr, 1990. 'Rebuilding Russia: Reflections and Tentative Proposals'. Enclosure to *Literaturnaya Gazeta*, 19 September (in Russian).

Stalin, J.V., 1953 [1920]. 'The Policy of the Soviet Government on the National Question in Russia', pp. 363–376 in *Works*, vol. 4, Moscow: Foreign Languages Publishing House.

Stankevich, Sergei, 1992. 'A Power in Search of Itself', *Nezavisimaya Gazeta*, 28 March (in Russian).

Starostina, Yulia, 1995. 'Paying General Antonov's Bills', *Moskovskie Novosti*, no. 75, 29 October – 5 November (in Russian).

Starr, Barbara, 1993. 'Russia Still Looking to Amend CFE Treaty', *Jane's Defence Weekly*, 18 September, p. 7.

Starr, Barbara, 1994. 'Perry Wants Speedier Russian Disarmament', 'US DoD Review Charts Inventory Changes', *Jane's Defence Weekly*, 1 October.

Steele, Jonathan, 1995. 'Take the Money or Keep Your Friends', *The Guardian*, 28 August.

Stokke, Olav Schram & Ola Tunander, eds, 1994. *The Barents Region: Cooperation in Arctic Europe.* London: Sage.

Strada, Vittorio, 1991. 'Old and New Border. Soviet and Russian Borders as a Phenomenon', *Nezavisimaya Gazeta*, 6 November (in Russian).

'Strategy for Russia'. Theses for the Report of the Council on Foreign and Defence Policy, 1992. *Nezavisimaya Gazeta*, 19 August (in Russian).

'Strategy for Russia – 2'. Theses of the Council on Foreign and Defence Policy, 1994. *Nezavisimaya Gazeta*, 27 May (in Russian).

Strugovets, Vitaly, 1994. 'Shots in the Back: Russian Border Guards Are Under Fire', *Krasnaya Zvezda*, 24 December (in Russian).

'Sweden's Baltic Bulwark', 1994. *The Economist*, 9 July, p. 30.

Taylor, Brian D., 1994. 'Russian Civil–Military Relations after the October Uprising', *Survival*, vol. 36, no. 1, Spring, pp. 3–29.

Teague, Elizabeth, 1994. 'Russians Outside Russia and Russian Security Policy', pp. 81–106 in Leon Aron & Kenneth M. Jensen, eds, *The Emergence of Russian Foreign Policy.* Washington DC: United States Institute of Peace Press.

Tishkov, Valery, 1993. *The Russians as Minority: The Case of Estonia.* Working Papers in Applied and Urgent Ethnology no. 52. Moscow: Institute of Ethnology and Anthropology (in Russian).

Tishkov, V.A., E.L. Beliaeva & G.V. Marchenko, 1995. *The Chechen Crisis.* Moscow: Centre for Social Studies and Marketing (in Russian).

Tolstaya, Tatyana, 1994. 'Boris the First', *The New York Review of Books*, June 23.

'The Total in Writing. Price Is No Object?', 1995. *Obshchaya Gazeta*, 19 January (in Russian).

Trenin, Dmitry, 1993. 'Blessed Are the Peace-Makers', *Novoye Vremya*, no. 24, (in Russian).

Trenin, Dmitry, 1994. 'Collective Security and Collective Defence', *Nezavisimaya Gazeta*, 4 November (in Russian).

Tunander, Ola, 1989. *Cold Water Politics: Maritime Strategy and Geopolitics of the Northern Front.* London: Sage.

Tunander, Ola, 1994. 'Inventing the Barents Region', pp. 31–44 in Stokke & Tunander, eds, *The Barents Region.*

Tunander, Ola, ed., 1995. *Europa och Muren* (Europe and the Wall). Ålborg Øst: Nordisk Sommeruniversitet (in Swedish).

'Ukraine Near Control of ICBMs, US Fears', 1993. *International Herald Tribune*, 30 May.

Ulam, Adam B., 1974. *Expansion and Coexistence. Soviet Foreign Policy, 1917–1973.* Second Edition. New York: Praeger.

Umnov, Alexandr, 1994. 'The Shadow of Afghanistan', *Moskovskie Novosti*, no. 40, 18–25 September (in Russian).

'Unaccounted Trillions of the Chechen War', 1995. *Izvestia*, 25 August (in Russian).

Urquhart, Brian, 1990. 'Beyond the "Sheriff's Posse"', *Survival*, vol. 32, no. 3, May/June, pp. 196–205.

Vinogradov, Boris, 1994. '3000 Peace-Makers to Create Conditions for Settlement in Karabakh', *Izvestia*, 9 December (in Russian).

Vinogradov, Boris, 1995a. 'Russia's Security Council Face to Face with Chechnya', *Izvestia*, 26 August (in Russian).

Vinogradov, Boris, 1995b. 'The Chechens Refuse to Say: "Farewell to Arms"', *Izvestia*, 31 October (in Russian).

Vladykin, Oleg, 1992. 'Russia's Mobile Forces', *Krasnaya Zvezda*, 18 December (in Russian).

Vorobyev, Ivan, 1993. 'What Kind of Mobile Forces Do We Need?', *Voennaya Misl*, no. 2, February, pp. 13–20 (in Russian).

Vorobyev, Ivan, 1994. 'White Spots in the Theory or What Is Lacking for Peacekeeping', *Krasnaya Zvezda*, 22 February (in Russian).

Walking, Sarah, 1995. 'CFE Parties Reach Milestone in Conventional Force Reductions', *Arms Control Today*, vol. 25, no. 1, January/February, p. 23.

'Weapons in Europe Before and After CFE', 1992. *Arms Control Today*, vol. 22, no. 6, June, p. 32.

Westad, Odd Arne, 1993. 'The Road to Kabul: The Soviet Union and the Afghan Communists, 1978–1979'. Unpublished paper presented at a seminar at the Nobel Institute, Oslo, 25 February.

'Why the "Thunder" Did Not Crash', 1994. *Moskovskie Novosti*, no. 29, 17–24 July (in Russian).

Wilcox, Mark R., 1994. 'Colonel General Boris Vsevolodovich Gromov, Deputy Minister of Defense of the Russian Federation: A Biographical Study', *The Journal of Slavic Military Studies*, vol. 7, no. 2, June, pp. 270–291.

Woff, Richard, 1993. 'Russian Mobile Forces 1993–95', *Jane's Intelligence Review*, vol. 5, no. 3, March, pp. 118–119.

Woff, Richard, 1994a. 'Options for Change – Russia's Defence Minister', *Jane's Intelligence Review*, vol. 6, no. 8, August, pp. 339–341.

Woff, Richard, 1994b. 'Trial in Public Is Tough Test for "Hero" Pavel Grachev', *Jane's Defence Weekly*, 19 November.

Woff, Richard, 1995a. *The Armed Forces of the Former Soviet Union*, vol. I; Update 1. Portsmouth: Carmichael & Sweet.

Woff, Richard, 1995b. 'Grachev, Grozny and the Moscow Snipers', *Jane's Defence Weekly*, 21 January, p. 20.

Woff, Richard, 1995c. 'Who Is Who in the Chechen Operation', *Jane's Intelligence Review*, vol. 7, no. 4, April, pp. 158–161.

Woff, Richard. 1995d. 'The Command of Today's Russian Airborne Forces', *Jane's Intelligence Review*, vol. 7, no. 6, June, pp. 250–252.

Wæver, Ole, 1992. 'From Nordism to Baltism', pp. 26–38 in Mare Kukk, Sverre Jervell & Pertti Joenniemi, eds, *The Baltic Sea Area*. Oslo: Europa-programmet.

Yakhlakova, Tatyana, 1995. 'Military–Political Campaign', *Moskovskie Novosti*, no. 56, 20–27 August (in Russian).

Yakov, Valeri, 1995. 'President of Swiss Firm Takes Control of Chechen Oil', *Izvestia*, 26 August (in Russian).

Yakovleva, Elena, 1995. 'Budget Covers Only Soldiers' Breakfasts', *Izvestia*, 17 August (in Russian).

Yavlinsky, Grigory, 1995. 'Split of the Democrats Is No Tragedy', *Izvestia*, 12 July (in Russian).

Yeltsin, Boris, 1995. *The Struggle for Russia*. New York: Times Books.

'Yeltsin Regrets', 1993. *The Economist*, 9 October, pp. 15–16.

'Yeltsin Turns Nasty', 1992. *The Economist*, 16 October, pp. 16–17.

Yemelyanenko, Vladimir, 1994. 'Caucasian War Threatens to Blow Up Russia', *Moscow News*, no. 49, 9–15 December.

Yemelyanenko, Vladimir, 1995. 'Transdniestria Fights for Property, Independence', *Moscow News*, no. 27, 14–20 July.

'You'd Be Nervous Living Next to a Bear', 1993. *The Economist*, 15 May, pp. 19–21.

'Your Policy or Mine?', 1993. *The Economist*, 30 October, pp. 35–36.

Yushenkov, Sergei, 1994. 'We Must Increase in Order to Reduce', *Rossiiskaya Gazeta*, 24 November (in Russian).

Zagorski, Andrei, 1995. 'What Kind of the CIS Would Do?', *Aussenpolitik*, vol. 46, no. 3, English Quarterly Edition, pp. 263–270.

Zamyatina, Tamara, 1995. 'Anatoly Romanov and Aslan Maskhadov: We Won't Be Able to Shoot at One Another Again', *Izvestia*, 18 August (in Russian).

Zhilin, Alexandr, 1994a. 'If the War Comes Tomorrow', *Moskovskie Novosti*, no. 2, 9–16 January (in Russian).

Zhilin, Alexandr, 1994b. 'Nice Gesture? Or Resignation of the Chief of the General Staff?', *Moskovskie Novosti*, no. 7, 13–20 February (in Russian).

Zhilin, Alexandr, 1994c. 'Generals in Business', *Moscow News*, no. 24, 17–23 June.

Zhilin, Alexandr, 1994d. 'Controversy Surrounds Transdniestr Commander', *Moscow News*, no. 33, 19–25 August.

Zhilin, Alexandr, 1995. 'Defense Minister Waging a Battle in the Apparat', *Moscow News*, no. 7, 17–23 February.

Zhilin, Alexander & Dmitry Ukhlin, 1995. 'Contract-Soldiers in Chechnya Regret Their Pledges', *Moscow News*, no. 31, 11–17 August.

Zubkov, Radii & Mikhail Vinogradov, 1994. 'Fleet against Fleet, Not Fleet against Shore', *Nezavisimaya Gazeta*, 25 October (in Russian).

Name Index

Subject Index